The Tyne-Tees
Steam Shipping Company
and its Associates

by

Nick Robins

FOREWORD

by

W Kirby Robinson
Tyne-Tees Steam Shipping Company, 1948-1969

It is a pleasure to write these few words of introduction about the history of a company that was well respected and gave worthy service to industry and business.

My connection with the company began in 1948 as an office junior. Over the years I worked in several departments ultimately becoming Chief Accountant after gaining wide experience and passing my examinations. Having worked in these departments I was able to understand and apply myself to the many sometimes complex aspects of the shipping industry.

Tyne-Tees Steam Shipping Company had a long and respected history with many valuable associations. This portrayal of the company endeavours to inform the reader about the interesting story. I was always conscious of the traditions and ethos of the company, particularly as I experienced its strengths and weaknesses, and also as I witnessed events that had an impact upon it.

Sadly, as the shipping industry changed, embracing both containerization and roll-on/roll-off traffic, the company was unable to respond effectively and the competition from these developments gradually eroded the company until it reached a point when it ceased trading. Although I left in 1969 I still maintained contact until it finally closed down.

This publication will be a valuable record of a prominent company and a valuable addition to maritime history.

I will always remember with affection and satisfaction my years with the company. This timely history comes with my commendation.

W Kirby Robinson
Heaton, Newcastle-upon-Type
June, 2014

Published by Bernard McCall, 400 Nore Road, Portishead, Bristol, BS20 8EZ, England.
Telephone/fax: +44 (0)1275 846178 Email: bernard@coastalshipping.co.uk Web: www.coastalshipping.co.uk
All distribution enquiries should be addressed to the publisher.

Printed by Gomer Press Ltd, Llandysul Enterprise Park, Llandysul, Ceredigion, SA44 4JL.
Telephone: +44 (0)1559 362371 Fax: +44 (0)1559 363758 Web: www.gomer.co.uk

ISBN: 978-1-902953-64-9

FRONT COVER: The *Sir William Stephenson* (1906).   *(painting by A J Jansen)*

BACK COVER: The *Stormont* (1954) is seen in Middlesbrough Dock on 20 August 1976 on one of her final sailings.

(Michael Green)

FRONTISPIECE: The *Novian Coast* (1936) at Jersey.   *(Dave Hocquard)*

THE TYNE-TEES
STEAM SHIPPING COMPANY
AND ITS ASSOCIATES

CONTENTS

PREFACE

The terms for the newly created Tyne-Tees Steam Shipping Company were agreed in October 1903 by the respective Chairmen from the Tyne Steam Shipping Company, the Tees Union Shipping Company and Furness Withy & Company. The merger of the Tyne and Tees companies with Christopher Furness' Hartlepool to London coastal interests placed the Tyne-Tees Steam Shipping Company in a strong position to compete with others on its passenger and cargo services to London, and near Continental ports. The company maintained a diverse customer base with an express passenger and cargo service between Newcastle and London, and passenger and cargo liner services to Hamburg, Bremen, Rotterdam, Amsterdam, Ghent and other near Continental ports, and these were combined with bulk shipments of coal to London and Continental ports returning with grain or silver sand for glass making. In addition the company focussed on the transport of factored steel goods. Tyne-Tees withdrew from passenger carrying with the declaration of World War II in 1939.

The story of the company and antecedent companies and associate interests has never been told in full before. It is an interesting and exciting story of which Tynesiders, Teessiders, and the people of both Sunderland and Hartlepool are deservedly proud. Champion of the company history was James Layton of Acklam, Middlesbrough who prepared notes on company ships and company activities, some of which have been published in the *Tees Packet*, the World Ship Society's Teesside Branch journal, and as letters to *Sea Breezes*. Today the role of champion falls to Harold Appleyard at Wolviston and it is through Harold that I have been able to access some of James Layton's work. Other sources, of course, include Public Records offices, libraries and museums, whose staff have all been a pleasure to work with. The comment was made more than once that the company history was best written by an outsider because a Tynesider would bring his own baggage to the plot much as a Teessider would bias the story to his own ends!

I am particularly grateful to Mark Cordell at the Enquiries Team of the Tyne & Wear Archives in Newcastle for his patient and efficient help in sifting through records relating to the Tyne and Tyne-Tees companies. I am also grateful to The Local Studies library, City Library, Sunderland for access to the Alf Rodenby Collection, to Norman Kirtlan of Sunderland Antiquarian Society for information on Furness Withy and for his trouble in supplying copies of relevant material, and to Martin Routledge, Keeper of History at Sunderland Museum and Winter Gardens, for information on individual Hudson-owned ships and general advice and support. Above all I am grateful to Linda Gowans of Sunderland for greatly assisting in the research of various threads of the company ancestry, to George Nairn of Chester-le-Street for locating and allowing me to publish historic photographic postcards (many by R Gibson of Gateshead) from his extensive collection, and of course to Harold Appleyard.

I am also grateful to maritime authors, Richard Danielson and Gil Mayes, for critical review of the manuscript and for access to Richard's own collection of photographs. The very capable book production team at Coastal Shipping have once again produced a high quality product which we all hope you will enjoy.

The book is dedicated to the late James Layton.

Dr Nick Robins
Crowmarsh, Oxfordshire
June, 2014

CHAPTER 1

ANTECEDENTS

First the Dudgeon, then the Spurn,
Flamborough Head comes next in turn,
Whitby now lies in the bight,
Then Hartlepool, the dull red light.
If all goes right we'll be in
Canny auld Shields tomorrow night.

The Tyne-Tees Steam Shipping Company was created in 1903 by the merger of one shipping company from Newcastle, one from Middlesbrough, part of one from West Hartlepool and a subsidiary company of the first two based in London. Once created it was viewed with envy by both Christopher Furness and Owen Phillips, while Furness was instrumental in blocking Phillips' advances which would have put the new company into the Royal Mail group. As it was, the Tyne-Tees Steam Shipping Company retained its independence until the Second World War when Coast Lines took charge, its new parent later taking it into the ownership of P&O. The Tyne-Tees story is an exciting tale of business that served the interests of north-east England by providing passenger and cargo links to London and to a number of near-Continental ports notably in Holland and Germany.

Tyne-Tees was almost unique in that its core business was extremely diverse. It encompassed cargo and passenger liner services principally to Ghent, Antwerp, Rotterdam, Amsterdam, Hamburg and Bremen as well as between London and Newcastle and Middlesbrough, the carriage of factored steel goods (many of the cast iron tunnel rings on the London Underground travelled from Middlesbrough to London aboard ships belonging to one of the Tees or Tyne companies), and with bulk cargoes of coal, grain and glass sand. Almost without exception the people involved with the

Archway over the entrance to the yard, Hotel du Vin, at what was once the former workshops and stores in City Road, Newcastle.

(Author)

company and its antecedents, the Board members and Chairmen, sea-going officers and men as well as the many shore-based staff, were colourful yet all were determined and, above all, professional.

The background to the story goes back long before 1903. In the seventeenth century Newcastle had become an important port as a result of the growing coal trade. Its role as the transhipment port for coal extracted from the Durham and Northumberland coalfields encouraged industry to develop along the banks of the Tyne and attracted people to the area to work in the factories. In the years following the Industrial Revolution, the war with France now at an end, the port of Newcastle and the Customs ports of North and South Shields, were set to blossom. The main trade remained coal, much of it destined for London. The coal was shipped down the river in keels, open barges that were broad in the beam, for loading onto the sea-going sailing ships, the colliers, which stood in mid-river to await their cargo. The coal was brought aboard in baskets and dumped into the hold ready to be trimmed. It was a laborious and dirty business.

A " Geordie " collier

A 'Geordie' collier from a pen and ink sketch by Roger Finch, 1952.

The colliers depended on favourable winds. In adverse conditions, such as persistent and strong south-easterlies, they were holed up in port; the fires of London were regularly extinguished as a result. By 1818 the first steamboat on the river, the **Tyne Steamboat**, was used as a tug. In 1822 a strike by the keelmen was broken by one of the colliery owners who mounted one of the steam land traction engines, which normally hauled coal down to the keels, aboard one of the idle keels. He replaced the traction engine drive wheels with a makeshift paddle wheel. The improvised tug, like the land traction engine, was named **William Dilly**, Dilly being a common abbreviation of Diligent. She towed a string of deeply loaded keels downriver to deliver to the sailing colliers waiting to voyage south, catching the striking keelmen by surprise and so breaking their strike. Steam tugs were thereafter able to tow the keels and help the sailing ships head out into the south easterlies and so sustain the supply of fuel to the Thames. By December 1830 there were 30 steam tugs working on the Tyne.

The **Virginian Coast** (1930), typical of the big colliers later developed for the Tyne-Tees company fleet, seen getting up steam while at anchor.

(Harold Appleyard collection)

The first passenger carrying paddle steamer to sail between Newcastle and London was the Gateshead-built **Rapid** of just 24 tons burthen which first departed from Newcastle Quay on 11 August 1823. Bad weather forced her captain to unload the passengers at Whitby and turn back. Her owner, Joseph Shield, was undeterred and he resumed the service in May the following year. Thereafter the **Rapid** had a weekly departure throughout the summer from the Thames and the Tyne taking typically 60 hours for the journey north and south. She did not take up the service in 1825 and was sold to Algerian owners.

London-based General Steam Navigation Company (GSN) was next to run a passenger service between Newcastle and London. It deployed the **Hylton Joliffe** on the run from June 1827. She was a more robust paddle steamer than the **Rapid** and was able to carry her 50 passengers to their destination in about 40 hours, exceptionally only 35 hours. GSN retained a monopoly on the run for several decades and employed various paddlers including the **Tourist** which succeeded the **Hylton Joliffe** at Newcastle, and then the **City of Hamburg**, **London Merchant**, **Neptune** and latterly the **Dragon**. The monopoly of the London firm ended in March 1853 when the pioneering iron-hulled screw collier **John Bowes** stood down from the coal trade, working for John Bowes & Partners of Newcastle, to run a parcel service between Newcastle and London. Now owned jointly by William Laing and William Davies Stephens (always known as W D Stephens), the former collier was joined by the steamer **Chanticleer** which had accommodation for passengers. Cargo handling problems at London led the service to be abandoned in September 1853. The **John Bowes** went on to lead a charmed life until the age of 81. Then as the Spanish-owned **Villa Selgas**, loaded with iron ore, she sprang a leak off the Spanish coast and foundered in October 1933.

In January 1854 Laing and Stephens put the chartered steamer **Monarch** onto the London service until their own ship, the **Volunteer**, was ready in April. A contemporary advertisement read:

*Steam between Newcastle and London, once a week. The New Iron Screw Steamer **Volunteer** (Captain Hossack), now running, weather permitting, sails from Newcastle every Wednesday Morning, and returns from Irongate Wharf, London, every Saturday Evening, carrying Goods at moderate Rates of Freights. This vessel is registered 312 tons, and is constructed with 'tween Decks and every Appliance requisite for the careful*

Stowage and Transit of Goods between Newcastle and London, for which trade she has been expressly built by the Owners, who respectfully solicit the Support of the Community.

Alas, the new service had hardly got going when the **Volunteer** was requisitioned for service in the Crimea. Nevertheless, the partners soon had a twice weekly service running between London and Newcastle with departures from both terminals on Wednesdays and Saturdays. In 1858 the route was operated by the **Volunteer**, **Brigadier** and the **Lifeguard**. In 1862 Laing withdrew from the partnership with W D Stephens to concentrate on a new route between Newcastle and Leith. Stephens was later instrumental in establishing the Tyne Steam Shipping Company in 1864 out of the interests of W D Stephens, the Tyne and Continental Steam Navigation Company and the Newcastle, Antwerp and Dunkirk Steam Shipping Company. In 1865 the new company was advertising '*first class screw steamers leave Newcastle twice a week for Hamburg and Rotterdam and once a week for Antwerp and Dunkirk*'. The fares were 15/- single and 22/6d return Best Cabin, and 7/6d Fore Cabin single and 11/- return, the returns valid by any of the company's routes. The agent at Newcastle for Hamburg and Rotterdam was Ormston, Dobson & Company, and for Antwerp was Robert Fell; the Tyne Steam Shipping Company (see Appendix 1, Fleet Lists) being designed to co-ordinate the trade and coasting interests based at Newcastle Quay. Between 1864 and 1903 the company operated routes out of Newcastle, to Hull, Yarmouth and London, as well as to the Continent including the ports of Antwerp, Hamburg, Rotterdam, Dunkirk and Copenhagen. In the 1890s the number of passengers carried annually exceeded 20,000.

Trade burgeoned also at Middlesbrough, which until the early 19th century was farmland, the port then being up river at Stockton, and at the Hartlepools, both of which developed thriving trades with coal exports south and wheat and general goods north. Trade with the near continent grew as European partners recovered from the expense of war, enough at least to start buying Britain's exports.

Soon the coastal passenger and parcels trade from the Tees evolved from sailing smacks and schooners to wooden-hulled paddle steamers. As the paddlers' engines became more robust and more powerful so hull sizes increased and the smoky steamers were finally able to venture out onto the North Sea all year round. They were owned on the 64th share basis, many within families, and the master was often the majority shareholder although he was also beholden to brothers and cousins, uncles and aunts. The small east coast steamers were given celebratory names such as the **Lord Nelson** working out of Hull and the **Queen of Scotland** on the Aberdeen to London run, although the steam packets in north-east England had more parochial names of local people and places despite its share of military names. Many had set trading patterns, the **Lord Nelson** for example, ran regularly between Newcastle, Gainsborough, Hull and King's Lynn, while others went further afield to London and Calais or London and Amsterdam. Trade with Scotland, however, was almost exclusively by Scottish owned ships although the General Steam Navigation Company of London maintained a twice weekly service to Leith from London with the **Monarch** and **Trident**.

The **Lord Nelson** (1831), a typical East Coast wooden paddle steam packet used on the Gainsborough-Hull-Lynn (now King's Lynn) route. She was 91 feet long by 19 feet breadth with a depth of 10 feet and was 130 tons burden.

(Contemporary engraved glass by permission of Delomosne & Son Ltd)

William Lillie in his *History of Middlesbrough* tells of an early maritime initiative from the Tees:

*An important step towards better communication was taken in the year 1831 when William Fallows formed the Middlesbrough & London Steam Shipping Company which commenced running a ship of 375 tons called the [paddle] steamship **Majestic** under Captain Main. It ran a weekly service, leaving the Wilkinson and Harris Wharf at Middlesbrough and returning from the Steam Packet Wharf, St Katherine's Dock, London on Saturdays. The freight list 16 March 1831 tells us that there were separate apartments for ladies and accommodation for carriages, horses, cattle and livestock. A chief cabin cost £2-2-0d [£2 10 pence in today's money], second cabin £1-10-0d [£1 50 pence] and deck passengers 15/- [75 pence]... The boat became so famous that newspapers spread themselves by reporting feats that baffle all calculations... Unfortunately its success roused the jealousy of Stockton as they thought they were pioneers with regard ships and sea travel.*

They placed a steamship, the **James Watt**, and later a second vessel, the **Enterprise**, on the London route. This was too much for the available trade, and they all failed. The **Majestic**, however, continued to ply unprofitably until in 1837 she had to be sold.

Trade from the Tees benefitted greatly from 1879 onwards when iron ore was first brought down from the Cleveland hills to be worked into steel. In 1881 the North Eastern Steel Company was incorporated, merging with the Acklam Iron Works five years later when production, using the new Bessemer process, amounted to at least 50,000 tons of steel per year. Of course, shipbuilding was the natural secondary industry to develop on the river. The South Gare breakwater was opened in 1881 and the North Gare in 1891. The ports of Middlesbrough and Stockton were set to boom.

Family ownership of ships was a comfortable arrangement but one which was bound to alter once the capital outlay increased as larger and more sophisticated ships took up trade. The step change occurred when the screw steamer and the iron hull started to serve the coal trade, so providing a considerable reduction in freight rates due to the greatly increased deadweight capacity of the screw steamers. By 1855 there were just 18 iron-hulled screw steamers registered at Newcastle, each with an average 450 tons burthen. Few in number though they were, they took a major share of the cargoes on offer at freight rates that the old paddlers could never match. Owners of these ships were the richer merchants of the day, each keen to invest in new technology and to reap the rewards. The owners were also aware of the benefits of pooling their resources and sharing management responsibilities, and it was in this setting that both the Tyne Steam Shipping Company and the Tees Union Shipping Company were created.

Considerable records relating to the Tyne Steam Shipping Company and the Tyne-Tees Steam Shipping Company survive at the Tyne and Wear Archives in Newcastle (Ref DT.TT). They include: corporate records, financial records; shareholders records, staff records; records of vessels, freight records, property records, publicity material. There are also letters, photographs and documents relating to the subsidiary company, the Free Trade Wharf Company of London. Similar material is held at the Middlesbrough and Sunderland central libraries focussing on the Tees Union company and the Havelock Line (see Chapter 4).

The **Tynesider** (1888) on her afternoon arrival in the Tyne, seen off Wallsend with the Cunard Line's **Mauretania** (1907) fitting out alongside.

(R Gibson)

CHAPTER 2

THE TYNE AND THE TEES

Ownership of the big iron-hulled steamers on the Tyne was divided between just a handful of men by the mid-nineteenth century. William Laing and W D Stephens together owned three of the ships which they operated to London in competition with the General Steam Navigation Company's first iron-hulled screw steamers **Dragon** and **Pioneer**, built for them on the Tyne in 1853. John Ormston and J T Dobson owned a further five steamers registered at Newcastle, some jointly with W J van Haansbergen, a merchant with business contacts in Rotterdam. Other Newcastle steamers were owned by Charles M Palmer in the newly organised Newcastle, Antwerp & Dunkirk Steam Shipping Company, managed by George and W H Palmer and one further ship, the **Carbon**, was owned by Thomas Hedley. These men formed the Tyne Steam Shipping Company in 1864 by taking over the business and three steamers of William D Stephens, merging it with John Ormston's four steamers of the Tyne and Continental Steam Navigation Company (Messrs Ormston, Dobson & Company) along with the three steamers of the Newcastle, Antwerp and Dunkirk Steam Shipping Company. The Chairman of the new company was Charles Palmer, who had been instrumental in its formation, and his Directors were: John Ormston, William Stephens, Thomas Hedley, and W J van Haansbergen, and local industrialists Joseph Cowan, a firebrick manufacturer, Henry Parker of the Elswick Lead Works, William Hawthorn, ship builder, and R W Hodgson, a Tyne Commissioner (as also was Joseph Cowan). The original fleet comprised: the **Admiral**, **Brigadier**, **Earl Percy**, **Chevy Chase**, **Lord Raglan**, **Ocean Queen**, **Otter** and **Sentinel** (see Appendix 1, Fleet Lists), but was soon increased to ten ships.

William D Stephens advert, 1863.

Formed on 1 July 1864, the Tyne Steam Shipping Company was a joint stock company with limited liability. The company's stated aim was '*To amalgamate the principal steam trade of the Tyne, home as well as foreign, under one Board*'. The nominal capital was £300,000 in 12,000 shares of £25 each, a quarter of which was taken up by the former owners of the companies involved and the remainder sold locally. The company inherited established services to London, Dunkirk, Antwerp, Rotterdam, and Hamburg, and soon added Hull to its portfolio, although Dunkirk was not offered after 1868. The business of the company is described by Northway (1973):

Their vessels were general-cargo carriers, rather than bulk carriers of one or two products such as the steam colliers of Palmer. They carried a wide range of commodities both imported and exported. The imports were particularly varied, including food for the growing population of the region such as pork and dairy produce, flour and grain, but also cattle and other livestock, and fruit, wine and spirits. Certain raw materials were also brought in such as pig-iron, clay, copper, pig-lead, and manure and manufactured products such as drapery goods and furniture. They carried from the Tyne the products of most of the region's most important industries, mention having been made in their prospectus of the region's increasing iron production and of the Tyne's growing chemical trade, but they also exported lead, machinery, bricks and some coal.

Archway over the company HQ at 25 King Street which later also became the offices of the Tyne-Tees Steam Shipping Company. Frontage of the building to Newcastle Quay is just one window width!

(Author)

Passenger traffic was also a key revenue earner and some 14,000 passengers travelled each year by the company's steamers in the 1870s. It was essential for company ships to adhere to set timetables for departure and arrival times and such punctuality coupled with careful advertising attracted passengers for services to London and the Continent, some as holiday packages run in conjunction with the railway companies. In 1867 great play was made of the attractions of the Paris Exhibition and in 1873 attention switched to Vienna for the Great Exhibition. The staple passenger service, however, was that between Newcastle Quay and Free Trade Wharf, Stepney, a route which offered deck passenger fares that undercut the railway, as well as berths in second class and state rooms in first class for the well-to-do. Public rooms were furnished in attractive wood panelling; there was a piano and even a small library. The entire fleet, normally ten ships, was so adorned except for one small cargo-only steamer, the **Busy Bee**, which was bought secondhand in 1883. Her role was to supplement the London services when there was more cargo on offer than the two regular passenger and cargo steamers could cope with.

Life was not all plain sailing and serious competition had arisen on a number of fronts. The London-based General Steam Navigation Company tended to offer to share routes rather than go head-to-head in a price war and a sharing agreement was put in place between it and the Tyne company as early as 1865. The Shields Steam Shipping Company set up in competition with the combined strength of the Tyne Steam Shipping Company and General Steam Navigation Company but was forced to withdraw in 1867 for fear of going bankrupt. Ten years later there was also an extremely dangerous freight rate war on the Hamburg route but the Newcastle company won after losing money on the service for nearly two years. One war the Tyne Steam Shipping Company did lose was on its service to Copenhagen which commenced from Newcastle in 1874. A purpose-built passenger and cargo steamer, the **Royal Dane**, was delivered from Wigham Richardson's yard at Low Walker in June 1875. She was paid for by issuing 1,900 new shares so that in 1876 the total capital stood at £228,000. The contract for the new ship was £36,000. Almost at the same time the Kjobenhaven & Newcastle Steam Shipping Company was formed and shortly afterwards the North Jutland Shipping Company joined the fray. Tyne Steam Shipping Company ceded the route in 1877 and sold its interests to the Danes. Nevertheless, the **Royal Dane** received plenty of praise from her passengers as described in 1884 in the *Newcastle Examiner*:

*The saloons and cabins are placed near the deck level, and as a consequence the air is always fresh and plentiful. The **Royal Dane** has been recently fitted with the electric light and this has tended to the further sweetening of the atmosphere on board. When we crossed the bar on Saturday afternoon about 1 o'clock there was a considerable breeze blowing from the east, but only one of the passengers was affected by sea sickness in a serious form… Nothing can exceed the cleanliness of the saloons and cabins of the **Royal Dane**, and that passenger must be very exacting who can find fault with the attention paid to his comfort and convenience by Mr George Isbister and Mrs Milburn, the chief steward and stewardess of the **Royal Dane**.*

TYNE STEAM SHIPPING COMPANY, LIMITED.

KING STREET,

NEWCASTLE-ON-TYNE,

MARCH 15th, 1883.

SIR,

I am directed to inform you that an EXTRAORDINARY GENERAL MEETING of the Members of the TYNE STEAM SHIPPING COMPANY, LIMITED, will be held at the Company's Offices, King Street, Newcastle-on-Tyne, on Thursday, the 29th day of March, now next ensuing, at Two o'clock in the Afternoon, for the purpose of confirming as special resolutions the following resolutions, which were unanimously passed at the Extraordinary General Meeting of Members held on the 12th inst.:—

1.—That out of the sum of undivided profits accumulated by the Company, up to the 31st day of December last, the sum of £1 per share be returned to the Shareholders in reduction of the paid-up capital of the Company, the unpaid capital of the Company being increased by the amount of £1 per share, and the paid-up capital being thereby reduced from 12,000 shares of £16 each to 12,000 shares of £15.

2.—That the capital of the Company be reduced from 12,000 shares of £25 each to 12,000 shares of £20 each by extinguishing £5 per share of the unpaid capital of the Company.

I am, yours obediently,

RICHARD WELFORD,

SECRETARY.

Notice of Extraordinary General Meeting of the Members of the Tyne Steam Shipping Company to be held on 29 March 1883.

(Harold Appleyard collection)

It appears that on the Saturday evening the electric light failed because the '*Siemen's engine is driven at great speed and is liable to get heated*'.

In 1875 the Yarmouth Line was acquired along with its two ships the **Miaca** and **Zingari**. However, Yarmouth was found to be poorly profitable and calls at Yarmouth ceased five years later.

For the most part the Tyne company fleet did not greatly increase nor did the number of routes greatly expand. Northway again:

Throughout the company's history there was little growth in the number of vessels in their fleet. They began in 1864 with ten ships and had the same number in 1885, although they did own thirteen for a short time in the 1870s. Nevertheless it was the company's continued policy to improve and increase the size of their vessels. Their older ships were lengthened and as these were either wrecked or sold they were replaced by larger ones, usually specially built to the company's order and adapted to their trade. The ten ships of 1864 had averaged just over 450 tons, but those of 1885 had an average of over 800 tons.

Ownership of the company was focussed essentially on the businessmen of north-east England as Milne described in his book *North East England 1850-1914 – the dynamics of a maritime industrial region*:

The Tyne Steam Shipping Company deliberately sought local investors when it was established in the 1860s, and by the 1890s just under two thirds of the company's shares were still owned in the North East. This was above average for Newcastle joint stock shipping, but the diaspora effect was nevertheless conspiring to gradually scatter the firm's shareholders. Its largest single investor in 1895, James Crossley Eno, had founded his health salts business in Newcastle in the 1850s and was exactly the sort of figure – thoroughly engaged in North East commerce – sought by the company in 1864. By the 1880s, though, he was working from a larger factory in London and was well on the way to establishing the multi-national operation that would make him a millionaire by the time of his death... Eno's widening horizons were hardly a problem for the Tyne company, but his career symbolises the vulnerability of individualistic ship owners to the still more individual decisions of the investors.

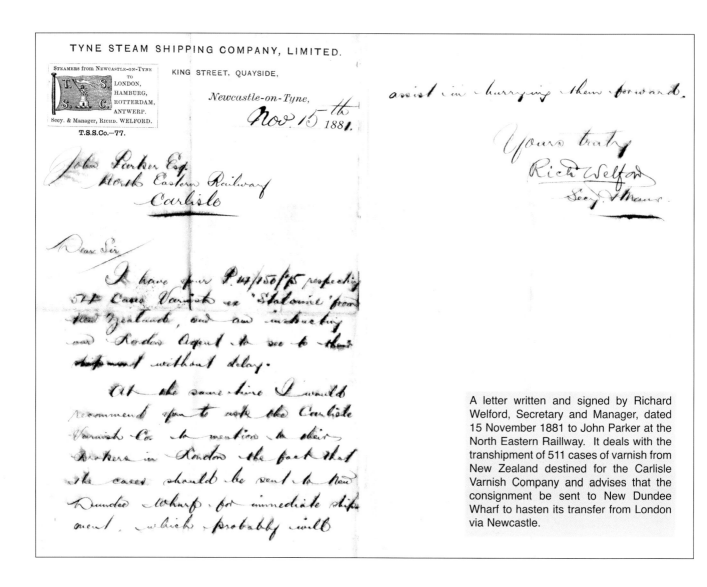

A letter written and signed by Richard Welford, Secretary and Manager, dated 15 November 1881 to John Parker at the North Eastern Raillway. It deals with the transhipment of 511 cases of varnish from New Zealand destined for the Carlisle Varnish Company and advises that the consignment be sent to New Dundee Wharf to hasten its transfer from London via Newcastle.

The first ship losses occurred as soon as 1865 when the **Earl Percy** and **Ocean Queen** were wrecked. In that same year the annual profit was declared to be £21,679 while the net profit was just £11,696. From this inauspicious start the safety record of the company was greatly improved until the **Otter** foundered off Great Yarmouth in 1873 and four years later the **Brigadier** was wrecked in the Kattegat. September 1888 was a seriously bad month for the company when the **Dragoon** stranded in the Scheldt on 3 September and became a total wreck and the second **Earl Percy** sank following collision in the North Sea on 15 September. Thomas Wilson's steamer **Juno** had to be sourced rapidly in order to maintain services. She was purchased for £28,400 and a further £3,400 was spent on refurbishing her for her new duties although in 1898 more money was required for a new boiler. Ambrose Greenway described her:

She was a three-masted [single deck iron] ship with engines aft and her hull was built on the well deck principle. Her first class accommodation amidships included a dining saloon, smoking room and promenade deck whilst sleeping arrangements were provided for 20 persons with provision for an increase to 40 if required. A small cabin aft could accommodate about eight second class passengers and temporary fittings were placed in the 'tween decks for some 200 emigrants, though this number could be increased if needed to a maximum of 400.

She was one of the last ships in the already numerous Wilson fleet to be built with an uneconomical compound engine and her deck machinery included a single steam crane in addition to derricks and winches.

Transfer of shares notice issued by Tyne Steam Shipping Company on 8 September 1886.

(Harold Appleyard collection)

David Moffat, Chief Superintendent, wryly reported in the shareholder's 25th Annual Report that year '*No new boilers shall be needed this current year,*' and '*The new steamer the **Tynesider** started in the London trade in May 1888, has not missed her weekly voyage since, and is improving as we go along*'. Finally he conceded that '*The loss of the **Dragoon** and **Earl Percy** both in September 1888 made a gap with us…*'. By then Thomas Hedley had become Chairman and his Board comprised Vice Chairman William Stephens and Ordinary Board members William Stephenson, James Leathart, William Pattinson and John Dobson. Richard Welford was Company Secretary. The **Tynesider** was built for £28,400 and quickly became the pride of the fleet, regularly completing the Newcastle to London voyage in just 22 hours. However, a consort was not ordered as the price had risen by £6,000 when enquiries were made, and this was considered by the Board to be excessive.

The passing of the **Earl Percy** was marked by a correspondent in the *Weekly Courant*:

There used to be fun on board during the summer months when the old vessel ran between Newcastle and London… so many people preferring the sea voyage to a dismal ride in the train, to say nothing of the lower rates.

TYNE STEAM SHIPPING CO., LIMITED.

DIRECTORS.

MR. THOMAS HEDLEY ... ... CHAIRMAN.

MR. WM. DAVIES STEPHENS, VICE-CHAIRMAN.

MR. WILLIAM HASWELL STEPHENSON. | MR. JAMES LEATHART.

MR. WILLIAM WATSON PATTINSON. | MR. JOHN TWEDDEL DOBSON.

TWENTY-FIFTH ANNUAL REPORT.

(To be presented to the Shareholders at the Ordinary General Meeting on Saturday, the 23rd day of February, 1889.)

The Directors beg to submit to the Shareholders a statement of the Company's operations during the year 1888.

The gross profit accruing from the Company's business amounts to £26,381. 7s. 2d., and after deducting the ordinary working expenses, a sum of £21,271. 4s. 3d. remains available for distribution. The Directors recommend that the profit be appropriated as follows :—

	£ s. d.	£ s. d.
In meeting the Interim Dividend of 7s. per share, paid on the 1st August last	4,200 0 0	
In payment of a further Dividend of 11s. per share on the 1st March next...	6,600 0 0	
In payment of a bonus of 3s. per share on the 1st March next to celebrate the 25th year of the Company's trading	1,800 0 0	
Equal to a Dividend for the year of 7½ per cent.... ...		12,600 0 0
The Balance of profit, amounting to £8,671. 4s. 3d., the Directors propose to carry to Depreciation Account...		8,671 4 3
		£21,271 4 3

For the first time in seven years the Directors have to report the loss of a portion of the Company's Fleet. The "Dragoon" stranded in the Scheldt on the 3rd of September, and became a total wreck; the "Earl Percy" sank in the North Sea, after collision, on the 15th of the same month. To replace the "Earl Percy" the Directors purchased one of the fast passenger steamers belonging to Messrs. Thomas Wilson, Sons & Co., and this vessel—the "Juno," 1311 tons—running in the London trade in conjunction with the new steamer "Tynesider," will, it is hoped, maintain the character of the Company's ships for speed, comfort and convenience.

The retiring Director is Mr. WM. DAVIES STEPHENS, who is eligible for re-election.

The Auditors, Messrs. HOLMES, SPENCE & Co., retire, and offer themselves for re-election.

The Company's Fleet consists of the following Steamers :—

Name.	Tonnage.	Horse-power.	Name.	Tonnage.	Horse-power.
ADMIRAL	608 ...	120	JUNO	1311 ...	200
BUSY BEE...	945 ...	150	ROYAL DANE	1291 ...	220
GRENADIER	926 ...	125	TYNESIDER	1290 ...	350
JOHN ORMSTON... ...	933 ...	160	WARKWORTH	676 ...	85

TUG BOATS, &c.

IONA ...	67 tons	...	27 H.P.	MINX (Barge) ...	51 tons ...	20 H.P.

By Order of the Board,

RICHARD WELFORD, SECRETARY.

Newcastle-on-Tyne, 7th February, 1889.

25th Annual Report to the shareholders of the Tyne Steam Shipping Company [sheet 1 of 3].

REPORT OF THE MARINE SUPERINTENDENT.

To the Directors of the Tyne Steam Shipping Company, Limited.

GENTLEMEN,

Again it is my duty and privilege to certify that the Company's property in Ships has been well kept up another year, and at the present time is in good condition.

The new Steamer "Tynesider" started in the London trade in May, 1888, has not once missed her weekly voyage since, and is improving as we go along.

The loss of "Dragoon" and "Earl Percy," both in September, 1888, made a gap with us, but the speedy purchase of the "Juno" soon met the demand to a large extent.

No new boilers should be needed this current year.

I remain, Gentlemen,

Yours obediently,

DAVID MOFFAT.

Workshops, Quayside, Newcastle-on-Tyne,

January 29th, 1889.

AUDITORS' REPORT.

GENTLEMEN,

We have to report that we have Audited the Accounts of your Company for the year ending 31st December last, and have found all in order. The Balance Sheet and Profit and Loss Account herewith, bearing our Certificate of Audit, is in our opinion a full and fair Balance Sheet, containing the particulars required by your Articles of Association and the Joint Stock Companies' Act, and gives a true and correct view of the position of your Company.

Soliciting the honour of re-election as your Auditors,

We remain, Gentlemen,

Your obedient Servants,

HOLMES, SPENCE & Co.,

CHARTERED ACCOUNTANTS.

10, Royal Arcade, Newcastle-on-Tyne,

7th February, 1889.

25th Annual Report to the shareholders of the Tyne Steam Shipping Company [sheet 2 of 3].

THE BALANCE SHEET

OF THE

TYNE STEAM SHIPPING COMPANY, LIMITED,

From 1st January to 31st December, 1888.

LIABILITIES.	£ s. d.	£ s. d.	1887. £
CAPITAL:—			
12,000 Shares, £14 paid	......	168,000 0 0	168,000
DEBTS OWING BY THE COMPANY		8,152 13 4	6,050
COMPANY'S INSURANCE FUND:—			
Amount from last Balance Sheet ... 17,689 16 8			
Less—Carried to Depreciation from			
last Balance Sheet..£3,000 0 0			
Loss of "Dragoon" &			
"Earl Percy" ...10,000 0 0			
————— 13,000 0 0			
4,689 16 8			
Credit Balance of Company's			
Underwriting Account, 1888 ... 4,787 1 1			
—————	9,476 17 9	17,689
BOILER FUND:—			
Amount from last Balance Sheet ... 4,082 0 0			
From Profit & Loss do. ... 1,000 0 0			
—————	5,082 0 0	4,082
BILLS PAYABLE		1,500 0 0	
PROFIT AND LOSS 21,271 4 3			18,030
Less—Interim Dividend 4,200 0 0			
—————	17,071 4 3	13,830
		£209,282 15 4	

ASSETS.	£ s. d.	£ s. d.	1887. £
PROPERTY:—			
Steamers, Buildings, &c., from			
last Balance Sheet 176,119 13 7			
Add—"Tynesider" and "Juno" 46,118 13 10			
222,238 7 5			
Depreciation from			
last Balance Sheet £6,230 14 6			
From Insurance			
Fund per last			
Balance Sheet ... 3,000 0 0			
Loss of "Dragoon"			
& "Earl Percy" 28,000 0 0			
————— 37,230 14 6			
		185,007 12 11	176,119
STORES IN HAND, at cost		1,689 15 11	1,559
DEBTS OWING TO THE COMPANY		16,199 9 7	13,959
CLAIMS ON UNDERWRITERS		221 18 5	937
BANKERS' ACCOUNTS:—			
Woods & Co. 2,628 9 6			
North-Eastern Banking Co. ... 2,516 13 8			
—————	5,145 3 2	16,757
CASH IN HAND		10 4 11	12
INSURANCE REBATE		1,008 10 5	306
		£209,282 15 4	

PROFIT AND LOSS ACCOUNT.

TO EXPENSES:—	£ s. d.	£ s. d.	£
Head Office Salaries, Directors' and			
Auditors' Fees 2,021 0 0			1,995
Rents, Rates, Taxes, &c. 1,537 16 5			1,749
Postages, Telegrams and Petties ... 558 12 4			561
Stationery, Printing & Advertising 508 3 0			487
Interest and Discount 167 11 7			Law Chgs. 2
Travelling Expenses 158 8 9			57
—————	4,951 12 1	4,851
Bad Debts		158 10 10	
Balance		21,271 4 3	18,030
		£26,381 7 2	

	£ s. d.	£	
BY PROFITS on Navigation, &c.	26,381 7 2	22,882	
	£26,381 7 2		

	£ s. d.	£ s. d.	£
To Interim Dividend at 7s. per Share... 4,200 0 0			
,, Proposed do. 11s. 6,600 0 0			
,, Proposed Bonus 3s. 1,800 0 0			
————— 8,400 0 0			
		12,600 0 0	10,800
			Boiler Fnd 1,000
,, Balance to Depreciation Account...		8,671 4 3	6,230
		£21,271 4 3	

	£ s. d.	£
By Balance brought down	21,271 4 3	18,030
	£21,271 4 3	

Audited and Certified,

HOLMES, SPENCE & Co.,

Newcastle-on-Tyne, 7th February, 1889.

CHARTERED ACCOUNTANTS,

AUDITORS.

25th Annual Report to the shareholders of the Tyne Steam Shipping Company [sheet 3 of 3].

The *Tynesider* (1888) with passengers lining the foredeck. Note that the Tyne Steam Shipping Company colours of black hull and boot topping, black funnel with white over red band were retained for the whole of the fleet of the Tyne-Tees Steam Shipping Company when it was formed in 1903.

(Harold Appleyard collection)

There were numerous other incidents, reflecting the difficult conditions in the North Sea and the busy waterways that needed to be navigated. For example, General Steam Navigation Company's veteran iron-hulled cargo and passenger paddle steamer *Hollandia* collided with the Tyne Company's big passenger steamer *John Ormston* on 12 November 1883. Although both vessels were damaged and the paddle steamer started making water, both ships were able to complete their voyages.

The *John Ormston* (1873) served the Tyne Steam and Tyne-Tees Steam companies for a total of 37 years.

(R Gibson, George Nairn collection)

By the end of 1888 the key Newcastle to London twice-weekly service was in the hands of the *Tynesider* and *Juno*. Accidents, great and small, continued to happen which reflected the hazardous business of the company. On 28 February 1889 it was reported that while loading coal for London at the Hamburg Wharf, Newcastle Quay, a crewman was killed aboard the *Juno* when a brake slipped on a crane causing a bucket to smash against the plank where he was standing and he fell to his death. Later in the year on 17 October the *Busy Bee* was in collision in the Tyne with the *Confride Whinfrido*, newly completed by Joseph Thomson shipbuilders. The *Busy Bee* was later held responsible for the accident.

By 1889 the fleet comprised: the *Admiral*, *Busy Bee*, *Grenadier*, *John Ormston*, *Juno*, *Royal Dane*, *Tynesider* and *Warkworth*. The London service during the summer of 1889 was extended to three departures a week with '*the Tynesider and Royal Dane, both with electric lighting, supported by the Juno*'.

Company Chairman Alderman Thomas Hedley, MP along with his Company Secretary and Manager Richard Welford declared an annual company profit of £26,381 against a net profit of £21,271 at the Annual General Meeting on 23 February 1889. It was suggested that a better matched consort than the *Juno* to run alongside the *Tynesider* on the London run had finally become a possibility. Thomas Hedley died in 1890 and was succeeded by W D Stephenson, earlier described in the *Stock Exchange*, 11 May 1889:

The most prominent man on the board is Mr W D Stephenson, the Vice-Chairman, who was Mayor of Newcastle last year. He is a jolly rubicund person, with a flower always blooming in his button hole, and is exceedingly fond of a joke. Mr Stephenson is the merriest of public speakers and is almost always on the platform...

The key services from Newcastle in 1889 were:

London:	**Tynesider** and **Royal Dane**, departures on Saturday and Wednesday
Antwerp:	**Juno**, departure on Saturday
Hamburg:	**John Ormston**, departure on Saturday
Rotterdam:	**Busy Bee**, departure on Tuesday
Terneuzen and Ghent:	**Warkworth**, departure on Tuesday.

In April 1891 the **Tynesider** left Newcastle Quay at 3.00 pm for London with 57 passengers. Abreast of Wallsend it was noticed that smoke was rising from beneath the hatch covers over the forward hold. Attempts to enter the hold and extinguish the fire were assisted by the port's fire barge which pumped water into the hold. The ship was turned and put back to the London Wharf where the fire was finally extinguished by 9.00 pm with the help of the Newcastle Fire Brigade. The vessel was largely undamaged and was soon back in service although there were smoke stains in the main lounge which became a talking point for several years. The cargo, which included chemicals in barrels, was a complete write-off.

The consort for the **Tynesider** was finally delivered from the Schlesinger Davis shipyard at Wallsend in June 1891, having been launched two months earlier as **Londoner**. On 4 June during her trials she was worked up to a speed above her design requirement that was slightly in excess of 15 knots. She was unique in the fleets of both the Tyne and Tees companies as she was the only ship to have two funnels, very much befitting her role as flagship of the Tyne Steam Shipping Company fleet. Her contract price, £38,000, was higher than that of the **Tynesider** partly due to inflation and partly because she had more powerful engines. Both the **Londoner** and **Tynesider** could accommodate about 200 berthed passengers and more unberthed. The arrival on the London service of the new flagship allowed the **Royal Dane** to be displaced to the Hamburg service so allowing the **John Ormston** to replace the **Busy Bee** at Rotterdam.

Despite the occasional accidents, life aboard ship was a jolly affair as Dick Keys and Ken Smith describe in their book *Tales from the Tyne*:

Concerts were often held aboard the Newcastle-London boats, with passengers and sometimes stewards or stewardesses taking part… Recitals of poems and excerpts from plays seem also to have been popular. An observer writing in the Northern Weekly Leader in the late 1880s tells us of the aftermath of one such concert, aboard the **Tynesider** *with Captain John Cracknell in command. 'The official programme was exhausted at 10 o'clock. There was an adjournment up on deck and on the lee-side an impromptu sing-song of glees and solos proceeded for a couple of hours.'*

Excursions were offered from Newcastle to Rotterdam in 1891 with one night ashore at the Grand Hotel at The Hague for £3-12-00 all inclusive. A more adventurous 12 day excursion to the Ardennes and the Rhine Valley was also operated using the regular service to Antwerp operated by the **Juno** for £13. By this time through bookings could be made to Antwerp, Rotterdam and Hamburg from a variety of destinations in north-east England with the North Eastern Railway.

The **Londoner** and **Tynesider** duo was a great success on the London service. In May 1892 a man was seen to fall overboard from the **Londoner**. The ship was off Lowestoft, the sea was moderate and the visibility good. The **Londoner** turned and slowed to a position marked by lifebelts that had been thrown into the sea. One very lucky but exhausted gentleman was recovered from the water to continue his journey. It was estimated that he was in the sea for just 11 minutes before he was brought safely back aboard ship.

Britain awoke to the shocking news report under the banner headline *'The* **Londoner** *sunk'* in the *Daily Chronicle* dated 15 May 1893:

The steamship **Londoner** *of Newcastle foundered in the North Sea off Palling, on Sunday morning after collision with another large steamer. A dense mist, which had hung over the sea all night, was lifting, when she struck a north-bound steamer the name of which has not transpired [***Sheffield***] and was so seriously damaged that she foundered shortly afterwards. Her crew took to the boats, and were picked up by Her*

*Majesty's ship **Bullfrog**, which conveyed them to Cromer. The **Londoner** was a fine double-funnelled steamer of upwards of a thousand passengers.*

The **Londoner** was lost in collision with the Manchester, Sheffield & Lincolnshire Railway's steamer **Sheffield** on the morning of 14 May 1893, off North Haisborough whilst on passage to Newcastle. The **Sheffield** was also badly damaged in the collision but was beached and later repaired. The **Londoner** under Captain Coy, had on board a crew of 36 as well as 90 passengers. Amazingly, only one person lost his life in the incident, a passenger who was injured in the collision and later died shortly after arriving at hospital. He was an Italian on his way to Tyneside for the first time to take over the management of a pub. Press reports also suggested that a second passenger had '*gone insane*' but this was later retracted when the passenger in question was reported the next day to have been sent home. Passenger reports in the press described how the crew calmly gathered the passengers together in the main lounge preparatory to dispatching them into the lifeboats and liferafts. There was no panic and the whole procedure was organised and efficient. The crew and passengers arrived at Cromer with only the clothes they wore but they were quickly dispatched by train to Newcastle, the passengers to register claims for loss and damages at the King Street offices of Tyne Steam Shipping Company. Tyneside eventually reconciled itself to its loss and the press carried various laments to the former flagship of the fleet '*no longer can we hear the familiar sound of the **Londoner**'s claxon as she leaves the London Wharf to begin her journey south...*'.

At the subsequent Inquiry Captain Coy was found to be blameless subject to his not hearing the whistle of the **Sheffield** as the two ships approached each other in the fog and all blame was laid against the **Sheffield**. Various stores were recovered from the **Londoner** including two life boats towed into Cromer by the **Bullfrog**, numerous life rafts and life belts, hatches, lanterns, spas, oars and other stores. These were all sold by auction at Cromer on 26 May. Details of the incident, correspondence dealing with the Board of Trade and the insurers, as well as with the Inquiry and even of the expenses of personnel involved are all recorded in folder DT/TT.27 at the Tyne and Wear Archive in Newcastle.

The **Royal Dane** was drafted back onto the London route to replace the two year-old steamer **Londoner**. Her successor was the **New Londoner**, delivered in April the following year by Wigham Richardson at a price of £34,000, reflecting less powerful engines than had been installed in the **Londoner**. It had been found an expensive option to operate the **Londoner** at full speed when the **Tynesider** could not keep up. The **New Londoner** was lavishly furnished with a saloon completed in polished mahogany with olive-green tapestries, gold curtains and furnished with couches, swing chairs, tables and mirrors. The smoking room also had gold curtains with the furniture upholstered in green morocco leather. The dining saloon was equally plush, complete with sideboards and the all-essential piano. The dining saloon could seat 52. The ship had electric lighting and steam heating.

Both the **Tynesider** and **New Londoner** were three-masted steamers with a short well-deck and a long raised quarter deck. The engines were placed threequarters aft. So successful were they that a third similar ship, the **Grenadier**, was built for the Rotterdam route. The **Grenadier** was a direct replacement for her older namesake which had been lost in collision on 1 August 1894.

The Tyne Steam company's **New Londoner** (1894) featured on a pre-1902 plain back postcard. Note the different bridge configuration with later photographs, e.g. page 30 and the same funnel colours as Tyne-Tees Steam company.

(R Gibson, George Nairn collection)

The old **Grenadier** was in collision with the steamer **August Korft** in the North Sea while on passage to Newcastle from Rotterdam and sank at 31° 03' latitude and 30° 25' east. The new **Grenadier** was built by Wigham Richardson at a cost of £22,000 and was ready for service in summer 1895. Lord Ambrose Greenway described the new ship in his book on North Sea passenger steamers:

She could accommodate 56 passengers in first class on the main and saloon decks, with comfortable state rooms, a large oak panelled saloon and separate ladies and smoking rooms. In addition, two rooms were provided under the foc'sle for sixteen second class passengers, and for general comfort steam heating and electric lighting were fitted throughout.

The **Grenadier** (1895), in Tyne-Tees grey livery, was a replacement for her namesake lost in collision in the North Sea.

(R Gibson, George Nairn collection)

Autumn of 1892 brought with it the usual problems of operating in congested waters. On 4 October the **Busy Bee** struck the Spanish vessel **Daviz** lying at Hamburg. The **Daviz** was split in two and immediately sank. The impact killed the master, mate and pilot on the bridge of the stricken vessel. The **Busy Bee** received only superficial damage to her bows. A month later on 7 November the **Royal Dane** hit and sank the collier **Edgar** in the Tyne. The **Edgar** was beached at Whitehall Point while the **Royal Dane** was able to continue her voyage to Hamburg.

Services from Newcastle were interrupted in February 1896 when the Tyne partly froze over and shipping was menaced by ice floes! The ports of Hamburg and Antwerp were also closed for a while although the Dutch ports and the Thames remained navigable. The last ship to enter the Tyne company fleet was the cargo only **Faraday**, completed by T & W Smith for G Reid & Company of Newcastle in 1873. The Tyne Steam Shipping Company acquired her in 1896 as a replacement for the **Busy Bee** which sank off the Belgian Wielingen Light following a collision with the German-owned cargo ship **Lindenfels** earlier in the year. The **Busy Bee** was on passage from Newcastle to Antwerp with general cargo.

On 3 November 1899, when the **Royal Dane** was inbound on the Tyne, light loaded, she struck the **Refulgent** and this time it was the **Royal Dane** that had to run to shore and be beached. At the subsequent Inquiry it was concluded that the **Royal Dane** was to be blamed as she had been on the wrong side of the channel. It was also concluded from this spate of accidents that the Tyne company's captains seemed to believe that maintaining schedules was more important than safe navigation.

The **Faraday** (1873) replaced the **Busy Bee** in 1896 on cargo only duties after the **Busy Bee** was sunk in collision off the Belgian coast.

The company owned its own tug. The first was the wooden-hulled paddle tug **Hussar** which was sold to John Ormston Junior in 1869. The second paddlel tug **Iona**, also had a wooden hull, built in 1866. She was replaced by the screw tug **WDS** in 1892. The **WDS** was named after W D Stephenson and was built by Schlesinger, Davis & Company at Wallsend. They took the **Iona** in part exchange for the new vessel. The new screw tug was built of steel and had a compound steam engine that provided 240 indicated horse power.

On the Tees a weekly service for passengers and cargo commenced in 1857 when the Stockton & London Steamship Company commissioned the **Stockton**, a small steamer of 288 tons burthen. A second steamer, the **Thames**, was added in 1866 to allow twice weekly departures. The **Thames** was an altogether more suitable ship for the route offering handsome passenger accommodation in a ship that measured approximately 400 tons gross. Meanwhile James Taylor set up first the Middlesbrough & London Steam Shipping Company and later merged it with other key Middlesbrough interests, the London & Middlesbrough Steamship Company. Taylor also set up the foundations of what was to become the Tyne-Tees Wharf, although financial difficulties forced him to sell it to Sir Joseph Pease in 1875 so that it eventually became the property of the Tees Union Company. The merged forces of Middlesbrough were more than adequate to take on the competition from the Stockton company, while both companies increasingly also vied for trade against the Tyne Steam Shipping Company at its base further north at Newcastle Quay. James Layton in William Lillie's *The History of Middlesbrough* describes the Middlesbrough interests:

*James Taylor commenced business as a wharfinger on the site occupied by Tyne-Tees Wharf, in 1853. The next year he took delivery of his first boat the screw steamer **Advance**, built by South Stockton Iron Shipbuilding Company (later Richardson Duck), being the first iron ship built on the Tees. She was sold in December 1869, and lost in the North Sea 23 March 1872. In May 1861 the **Onward** [the first passenger ship on the London service] joined the **Advance**. She was built by Richardson Duck, but was lost in 1862. The **Lady Havelock** [built in 1861 for John Smurthwaite of Sunderland] was leased until a new ship **Gladstone** was completed in March 1863, built by Richardson Duck. She was wrecked on 12 March 1875. The **Cobden** built by Richardson Duck 1866 joined the Tees–London trade in 1875, to 1898 when she was sold to Germany.*

A local newspaper advert for October 1862 read:

Lady Havelock sails from London every Saturday at 4.00 pm, and from Middlesbrough every Wednesday. The Advance sails from London on Wednesdays and from Middlesbrough every Saturday. They are fitted with a lounge. Passengers: saloon 10/- (50p) single, 15/- (75p) return; second class 5/-. Signed Jas Taylor, Wharfinger and Manager for Middlesbrough & London Steam Shipping Company.

The various Middlesbrough-based interests were merged in the 1870s to form a new company somewhat confusingly called the London & Middlesbrough Steam Shipping Company. The obvious consequence of competition between the Stockton Steam Shipping Company and the London & Middlesbrough Steamship Company was a merger to form the Tees Union Shipping Company in 1880. The new company was formed by Joseph Pease in association with Joseph Richardson of the London & Middlesbrough Steam Shipping Company and Joseph Cradock, Chairman of the Stockton & London Steam Shipping Company. The Managing Director of the merged companies was James Taylor who had earlier been declared bankrupt as owner of the **Cobden** in 1875. The smaller Stockton ships, the **Thames** and **Stockton**, were sold and the service placed in the hands of the **Cobden** and **Dione** acquired in 1879 by Joseph Richardson's Middlesbrough company.

The merger was precipitated partly by competition from the Tees & Thames Screw Steam Shipping Company which operated the cargo-only steamer **James Shaw** on a weekly circuit between London and Stockton. The Tees Union Shipping Company was made a limited liability company in 1887 and in the same year Joseph Cradock was elected Chairman, a post he held until the formation of the Tyne-Tees Steam Shipping Company in 1903. In 1893 the Tees Union company purchased the Scarborough Shipping Company and its one ship, the **Andalusia**, and the goodwill of its service to London. At the time the **Andalusia** maintained a weekly round trip to London under the command of Captain Hestrip.

The complex succession of modernisation and change in ownership is illustrated by notes prepared by Gil Mayes on the history of the **Andalusia**:

*13.10.1863: Launched by J & R Swan, Kelvin Dock, Maryhill for Mories, Monro & Co Ltd, Glasgow as **Andalusia**. 11.1863: Completed. 24.11.1863: Registered at Glasgow. 1866: Sold to Gifford & Co Ltd, Leith (William Gifford, manager). 1867: Glasgow registry closed; registered at Leith (5.1867). 1874: Sold to Thomas W Sweet, Exmouth, Devon. 3.12.1875: Sold to William John Armstrong, Glasgow (managing owner).*

1875: Leith registry closed; registered at Glasgow. 1879: Re-registered at Glasgow following alterations and re-engining. 1882: Sold to William McLeod, Middlesbrough (managing owner). 1886: Sold to The Scarborough Steam Shipping Co Ltd, Scarborough (John Stephenson, manager). 1886: Glasgow registry closed; registered at Scarborough. 1893: Sold to The Tees Union Shipping Co Ltd, Middlesbrough (James Taylor, manager). 1893: Scarborough registry closed, registered at Stockton. 1898: Sold to Boye Joachim Flood, London (managing owner). Stockton registry closed; registered at London. By 1903: Sold to John McDowell, London (managing owner). 1906: Sold to George H. Young, Leith (managing owner). 1909: Sold to William Jackson, Edinburgh (Andrew Buchan Jnr & John M. Hogg, Grangemouth, managers). 1910: Sold to William Hopkin, Grangemouth (managing owner). By 1912: Sold to Matthew Kirton & Sons Ltd, Newburn-on-Tyne (Mathew Kirton, manager). 1915: Sold to Matthew Worth, Newcastle-on-Tyne (managing owner). 1924: Broken up at Cardiff. Registry closed.

Even the engineering history of the ship was complex:

1863: Iron-built hull, 274 gross 210 net tons, 137.2 x 19.8 x 11.7 feet, with 2-cylinder compound engine (50 nhp) by Forrest & Barr, Port Dundas, Glasgow.
1875: Re-measured 266 gross 181 net tons.
1876: Re-measured 268 gross 167 net tons.
1879: Lengthened to 147.7 feet, 289 gross 160 net tons, re-engined compound 2-cylinder (60 nhp) by Hutson & Corbett, Kelvinhaugh, Glasgow
1916: Re-measured 298 gross 181 net tons.

The **Andalusia** was found to be too big to maintain a weekly Scarborough service and from 1894 onwards was used also on the Continental routes. A new passenger and cargo steamer for the London service, the **Tees** was delivered by Richardson, Duck & Company of Thornaby in May 1893. She was the first in the fleet to be equipped with a triple steam expansion engine.

The Union company was not without accident and its passenger ship the **Dione** acquired particular notoriety in 1884. On 3 August, the **Dione** was involved in a tragic incident in the Thames in which ten crew and thirteen passengers, many of them from Teesside, lost their lives. The ship was under the command of Captain Frederick Hood, not a Teessider but a resident of Dover. She had a crew of 20 and was carrying 20 passengers and a cargo of 300 tons of wheat and about 150 tons of general goods.

The **Dione** was reportedly running fast on the ebb tide down the Thames when just after midnight she was confronted by the inbound steamer **Camden**. The **Camden** was a much bigger vessel, and was coming up the Thames with a cargo of Mexican mahogany, under tow, having lost her propeller at sea. In the collision the **Dione** suffered considerable damage and sank very quickly. Ten crew and thirteen passengers drowned that night in the dark waters, the luckier ones were picked up by boat. The subsequent enquiry found that the collision was caused by neglect solely on the part of Captain Hood. The **Dione** was later raised refurbished and reinstated on the Middlesbrough to London run.

A new passenger and cargo steamer **Claudia**, like the **Tees** before her, was equipped with a single triple expansion steam engine and was launched by her sponsor and namesake. I illie again:

*The darling of the Tees-Thames run was the **Claudia** built in 1897 and launched 17 February of that year by Miss Claudia Pease. She could accommodate 48 first class, 48 second class and 36 deck passengers. Fares first class return 17/6d, or 12/- single in 1897 were only sixpence more in 1914. Her maiden voyage was from Tees Union Wharf 20 May 1897. She passed to the ownership of Tyne-Tees Steam Shipping Company in 1903 and Captain Jordan replaced Captain Battrum.*

Captain Jordan had been first mate on the bridge of the **Dione** on her fateful run down the Thames on 3 August 1884.

A typical Bill of Lading, this one issued for the **Dione** in 1896 for 46 tons of iron, concludes:

*Shipped by the Grace of God, in good order and well-conditioned, by the Weardale Iron and Coal Company, in and upon the good steam ship called the **Dione**, whereof is Master, under God, for the present voyage, Captain Jordan, and now riding at anchor in the River Tees and by God's Grace, bound for London. And so God send the good ship to her port in safety. Amen.*

The **Dione** (1868) in the colours of the Tees Union Shipping Company from a contemporary painting.

The **Claudia** (1897), evening departure from the Tees. *(From an oil painting by the author)*

A staple cargo on the London run at this time was the cast iron arc segments which when bolted together formed the tunnel lining for the burgeoning London Underground rail network. Many thousands were produced on Wearside and many thousands were shipped to London by the Tees Union company.

Both the Tyne Steam Shipping Company and the Tees Union company had for many years used the Free Trade Wharf on the north bank of the River Thames, just over one mile downstream from the Tower of London, in preference to other wharves. The wharf was originally owned by the East India Company when it could accommodate two of the John Company's big old wooden walled sailing ships. On 1 January 1884 Joseph Cradock, James Taylor and William Davies Stephenson representing the Tyne and the Tees interests formed a joint interest in the London terminal in order that the 'wharf lessees, wharfingers, carriers, warehousemen become the Free Trade Wharf Company'. On 29 January 1885 the two companies conspired to create a shared subsidiary, the Free Trade Wharf Company, an independently managed company wholly owned by the Tyne and the Tees Union companies in which the Tees Union company held the majority interest of £21,000 in 4,200 shares. The agreement was signed by many well-known businessmen for and on behalf of the companies involved:

Joseph Richardson of Stockton, Shipbuilder
Joseph Cradock of Stockton, Merchant
James Taylor of Middlesbrough, Wharfinger
James Greig of London, Wharfinger
Thomas Hedley of Newcastle, Shipowner
William Davies Stephenson of Newcastle, Shipowner
William Haswell Stephenson of Newcastle, Coalowner
John Sweddell Dobson of Newcastle, Shipowner
Richard Welford of Newcastle, Shipowner
Thomas Jefferson of London, Wharfinger.

The new subsidiary company was managed at London by James Greig on a salary of £250 a year plus 5% of the profits and Thomas Jefferson who was without a salary but given 3% of the annual profits. Part of the deal was that the Tyne Steam Shipping Company was to withdraw from its contract to use the Dundee, Perth & London Shipping Company wharf on the Thames and to transfer allegiance wholly to the new Free Trade Wharf Company facilities. In return the Tyne steamers would receive no wharfage charges for passengers and their baggage.

The new Free Trade Wharf Company was commissioned to continue to provide wharfage and to act as the London agents for both parent shipping companies. The agreement was made with a 21-year commitment from both the Tyne and the Tees Union shipping companies. The Free Trade Wharf company also serviced several other coastal cargo liner companies including the Little Western Steamship Company of George Bazeley based at Penzance.

The final thread of antecedents to the Tyne-Tees Steam Shipping Company came from West Hartlepool. Thomas Furness commenced running sailing ships from West Hartlepool across the Atlantic to Boston in 1876. Christopher Furness, his younger brother became the shipowner in 1882 when Thomas reverted to the grocery and merchanting side of the family business. Christopher then had five modern steamers and capital of £100,000. Christopher Furness soon expanded his services to include Halifax and in summer also Quebec. In 1888 Furness announced yet another new venture, a passenger and cargo service from West Hartlepool to London designed to service the transhipment needs of his deep sea fleet as well as to provide for local businesses. At first it ran to a sporadic timetable and was operated by tonnage that happened to be available,

but it soon developed into a weekly departure from both Hartlepool and London and, in due course, calls were also made at French & Company's Wylam Wharf at Sunderland. Furness' vessels were transferred to Furness Withy in 1892 when shipbuilding and ship owning interests were merged.

Wylam Wharf on the south bank of the Wear at Sunderland was managed by French & Company.

(Linda Gowans collection)

Furness Withy acquired a number of elderly ships as part exchange for ship sales. Many only lasted in the fleet for a short time before being sold or scrapped. Some of the small ships, however, provided useful support on the Hartlepool and Sunderland to London route, cargo services from the Tyne and on the occasional trip to Continental ports. The **Scandinavia** and **Chanticleer** were two such ships both employed principally in the North Sea. The **Zebra** and **Albert** came on service in the mid-1890s, there having been no dedicated ship serving London since 1891 when the **Scandinavia** had been sold. The service was, however, consolidated in 1896 when the **Oporto** was acquired and set to work on a weekly passenger and cargo service from Hartlepool and Sunderland to London. The **Oporto** was in collision in the Thames near Northfleet in August 1902. She was beached with no loss of life but the damage was considered too great to warrant repair of a 32 year-old ship. Her loss put a temporary end to the passenger service although the **Buccaneer** was bought from Tatham Bromage of London in 1902, but she did not offer many passenger berths. The **Buccaneer** started on the London run on 21 January 1902. Not content with terminating at Hartlepool with a call at Sunderland, this ship with slightly more speed than the **Oporto**, was able to include a departure south from Newcastle on Saturdays at 11.00 am, leaving London on Wednesday for the return trip. The Newcastle call was in direct competition with the Tyne Steam Shipping Company's direct London to Newcastle service.

The replacement for the **Oporto**, the **New Oporto**, was the only purpose-built coastal liner in the Furness Withy fleet and was delivered from Irvine's Shipbuilding & Dry Docks Company, which was wholly owned by Furness Withy, in July 1903. She was a magnificent steamer with accommodation for passengers in two classes and certificated to carry also deck passengers. She had a reliable service speed of 12 knots and provided a new standard for the North Sea coastal services. A sistership was planned but events were to overtake the need for a second passenger ship (see Chapter 3).

The **New Oporto** (1903) was built for Furness Withy but was commissioned just before the formation of the Tyne-Tees company whose colours she is seen wearing here.

(Harold Appleyard collection)

All the east coast companies were subject to the vagaries of trade. Particularly depressed years included 1866, when incidence of cattle plague coincided with an exceptionally good local fruit harvest, the labour disputes of 1871 and between 1892 and 1893, the exceptional bad winters of 1881 and 1896, and the depressed years of 1885 and 1894. One consequence of these fluctuations in trade was that the Tyne Steam Shipping Company had to reduce its passenger rates in 1874, but it took a good two years before the new rates had any impact on the number of passengers carried in the company's ships. Northway reports on the finances of the Tyne company:

There were, of course, a multitude of expenses to be faced in operating ten or twelve large steamships, but the main items were wages, coal for bunkering, harbour dues, repairs and insurance. Taken together the operating costs remained very high, as is indicated by the fact that, on an income of more than £150,000 in 1873 the gross profits were only £27,000. Similarly in 1883, when revenue was still nearly £130,000 after the payment of operating costs and before the deduction of overheads, they were only left with a gross profit of £8,000.

Insurance was reduced by turning away from Lloyds to the East Coast Insurance Association, typical of the many insurance clubs that had arisen at that time. The East Coast Insurance Association offered an attractive rebate when a ship was inactive for just fifteen days whereas Lloyds would not reduce the premium for any lay-up of less than 30 days duration. Another key expense was the constant lengthening and upgrading of ships and above all there was the ever present drain on funds for boiler replacements in the days when boilers were still unreliable. The first *Grenadier*, for example, received new boilers in 1869, again in 1874 and again in 1883, the latter a stronger steel fabricated boiler rather than the earlier iron structures.

Shortly after the Tees Union company had been incorporated, Christopher Furness slowly and stealthily became a significant shareholder so that he had a controlling interest by 1902. Negotiations for the purchase of the Tees Union Shipping Company by Furness Withy & Company took place at the House of Commons when MP Joseph Pease of the Tees Union Shipping Company was asked to make his case to MP Christopher Furness 'when he sees him in the House'. From then on the destiny of the Tees company was in the hands of Furness Withy & Company. So too it seems was the destiny of the Tyne Steam Shipping Company. On 2 April 1903 it was speculated in the press that Chistopher Furness was on the point of a take-over of the Tyne Steam Shipping Company which, had he also acquired the Tees company, would collectively would have given him a daily departure to London from any one of the three north-east ports, Newcastle, Sunderland or Hartlepool.

As the drab years of the reign of The Widow Victoria came to a close, a groundswell of optimism and new beginning spread throughout England. Now, with King Edward on the throne, the ship owners serving the London and near continental routes were slowly brought together to discuss the merits of pooling their resources. Christopher Furness had a second reason for promoting such a merger of interests as he was keen to see the management of his own coastal services from Hartlepool transferred to a third party so that he could concentrate on expanding his deep sea prospects. And so it was that Furness brought to the table the Tyne Steam Shipping Company, the Tees Union Shipping Company and their jointly-owned subsidiary the Free Trade Wharf Company of London and, of course, Furness Withy's own interests. A new era was indeed about to commence.

The Tyne-Tees Steam Shipping Company cap badge.

The *Tees* (1893)

By James Layton from the *Tees Packet*

Many ships have carried the name ***Tees*** across the oceans of the world but I doubt if any have had a more varied career than the Tees Union Shipping Company's vessel of that name.

She was launched from the yard of Messrs Richardson Duck & Company on 18 March 1893 and entered service early in May of that year. A steel ship of 569 gross tons with dimensions 172.6ft x 26ft x 10.7ft, she had accommodation for 30 first class, 22 second class and 23 deck passengers. Her triple expansion engine built by Blair & Company gave her a speed of about 10 knots. Electric lighting was installed and this no doubt added to her appeal as a passenger ship.

She traded regularly along the east coast until April 1896 when she was sold to the Hudson Bay Company. She steamed out to Victoria BC where she hoisted the flag of the Canadian Pacific Navigation Company, who placed her on the mail and passenger service along the west coast of Vancouver Island. Hardly had she settled on this run when she was diverted to transport the gold hungry masses to the Alaskan gold fields. She returned to her normal service in 1899 and remained so until 1917 when she was relegated to the role of reserve ship.

In August 1918 she was chartered by the British Columbia Salvage Company for 12 months and then reverted to her role of reserve ship. A further charter to the Pacific Salvage Company in 1923 was followed by a period of laying up, prior to being sold to that company in September 1925.

During the refit which preceded her entry into service as a salvage tug her after deck house was removed and a towing winch installed. Her name was also changed to the ***Salvage Queen***. She remained in the salvage business until about 1934 when she changed hands for the last time. Her new owners were the Island Tug & Barge Company and they used her for towing barges in the waters around British Columbia. These barges were converted sailing ships and it was whilst towing one of these that the ***Salvage Queen*** met her end.

In December 1936 with the barge ***Island Gatherer*** (ex-***Walkure***) in tow she was crossing Queen Charlotte Sound when she was caught in a heavy storm. The towing spring parted and due to the mountainous sea running it could not be reconnected, but her crew of four were rescued. Soon after, the barge disappeared and was not seen again. The ***Salvage Queen***, her superstructure wrecked and her hull pierced, set course for Victoria which she reached under her own power. She was surveyed by her owners and underwriters and written off as a constructive total loss. She was broken up soon afterwards.

SAFETY IN NUMBERS

The Tyne Steam Shipping Company became the focus of some remarkable attention from 1901 onwards. The Philipps Brothers had started in shipping with a one-ship company and quickly developed it into a thriving tramp steamer fleet called the King Line. On 11 November 1901 it was prematurely announced in the press that it was proposed that the King Line was to merge with the Tyne Steam Shipping Company. King Line's owner Owen Philipps, later, of course, Lord Kylsant, was set to become one of the key figures in British ship-owning as head of the Royal Mail Group. Green and Moss describe the tussle between Philipps and Christopher Furness over the ownership of the Tyne Steam Shipping Company, following Philipps' acquisition of Northern Transport, in their history of the Royal Mail Shipping Group:

This acquisition [by the Philipps brothers], Northern Transport (Stanhope) of Newcastle, against the background of large amalgamations throughout the business world in the late Victorian period, encouraged the King Line directors to attempt a more ambitious takeover. Early in 1901 a formal approach was made to the Tyne Steam Shipping Company of Newcastle. This company owned a fleet of coastal vessels which traded from the Tyne and Northumbrian coast, London and the Continent. It was experiencing temporary difficulties and Armores Hedley, a Director of the Tyne Steam Shipping Company as well as a shareholder in the King Line, was anxious to promote a fusion between the two companies. On 26 April a formal offer of £10 cash and one paid-up share in King Line or £15 in cash was made by King Line for all the 12,000 £20 shares (£14 subscribed value) of Tyne Steam Shipping Company. Negotiations continued throughout the year. In October, when it seemed likely that agreement would be reached, finance for the deal was made possible by increasing the authorised capital of King Line to £500,000. At the same time Owen Philipps joined the Board of Tyne Steam Shipping Company. Discussion dragged on into the early months of 1902, but in May, as a result of opposition from Christopher Furness, King Line withdrew its offer and Owen Philipps and Armores Hedley left the Board. Furness owned the Tees Union Shipping Company with which Tyne Steam Shipping Company had various trading agreements. The abandonment of the King Line offer allowed Furness to bring about an amalgamation of Tyne Steam Shipping Company, Tees Union Shipping Company, Furness Withy & Company's coastal services and the Free Trade Wharf Company to form the Tyne-Tees Steam Shipping Company.

The withdrawal of the bid for Tyne Steam Shipping Company was not quite the defeat which it seemed. The bid was not dropped until the Philipps brothers, in an informal agreement with Furness, had glimpsed a new and more spectacular prize. Furness had agreed to break off negotiations for the purchase of the Royal Mail Steam Packet Company and so allow a proposal from the Philipps brothers to go forward.

The rest is history. Owen Philipps, later Lord Kylsant, did indeed acquire and lead the Royal Mail Group until his untimely downfall, the result of alleged false bookkeeping; his shipping empire collapsed but that is altogether another story.

There were several key events leading up to the eventual 'amalgamation' of the Tyne and the Tees companies. On 26 June 1903 a meeting was held in London to discuss terms of amalgamation between the Tyne Company, the Tees company and the Free Trade Wharf Company along with the coasting interests of Furness Withy & Company. It had been assessed on behalf of these parties that their respective participating amounts based on the previous financial year accounts came to a total of £270,000:

Tees Union Shipping Company	£67,706
Free Trade Wharf Company	£28,707
Tyne Steam Shipping Company	£137,338
Furness Withy & Company	£36,249

The Tees Union company complained that they had had a disastrous year in 1902 caused both by the mini recession of the early 1900s and by severe competition brought about when P&O entered the Thames to Middlesbrough cargo trade. The company demanded they be better represented. The Tyne company played the same card with the competition they were suffering at Newcastle from the Furness Line at which point Christopher Furness, having brought everybody to the table, left for another appointment. Agreement was finally reached and the Tees company grudgingly acceded the revised participating amounts:

Tees Union Shipping Company	£63,952
Free Trade Wharf Company	£25,200
Tyne Steam Shipping Company	£144,000
Furness Withy & Company	£36,848

This meant that Tees Union had a 24% share in the new company, Free Trade Wharf 9%, Tyne Steam Shipping a majority 53% and Furness Withy a 14% share, or nearly 30% with its majority ownership in the Tees Union Company.

It was proposed on 1 July 1903 that the amalgamation also take possession of the assets of the coasting interests of Furness Withy & Company. The senior management and local agents that took this decision were:

Chairman – William D Stephenson
Vice Chairman – Stephen W Furness
Managing Directors – Richard Welford and James Greig
Directors – Joseph Cradock, W R Van Haansbergen, Thomas Jefferson and Claud E Pease
Tyne Department Manager – Richard Welford
Tees Department Managers – Joseph Cradock and Claud E Pease
London Department Managers – James Greig and Thomas Jefferson
Agents at West Hartlepool – Furness Withy & Company
Agents at Sunderland – Thomas Shields & Company.

On 11 August 1903 Christopher Furness announced the withdrawal of the Furness Line from serving Newcastle and ceded the Newcastle to London route to the new Tyne-Tees Steam Shipping Company. Soon afterwards, on 24 August, a letter was issued by the Tyne Steam Shipping Company Board to its shareholders that stated:

In furtherance of this object, agreements have been provisionally entered into for the amalgamation of the undertakings of:-

1. *This Company*
2. *The Tees Union Shipping Company*
3. *The Free Trade Wharf Company, owners of the extensive premises in London at which the steamers load and discharge their cargoes*
4. *A provisional agreement has also been entered into with Furness Withy & Company, for the acquisition of two steamers used by them exclusively on their coasting trade.*

The terms for the formation of the newly created Tyne-Tees Steam Shipping Company were agreed and the amalgamation of assets completed on 6 October 1903 when the Furness Withy and Tees Union services were combined. Christopher Furness even went as far as saying to the new directors that if he was running ships down the coast to London neither he nor his shippers could afford the rates charged by the Free Trade Wharf Company and that they had better look for alternative wharfage on the Thames! Nevertheless the Tyne-Tees Steam Shipping Company was finally incorporated on 19 October 1903 when its Memorandum and Articles of Association were published. The Chairman was to be Stephen Furness, nephew of Christopher Furness, rather than W D Stephenson, a reflection of the share that Furness Withy & Company held in the new company and the important role that the Furness family had held in the creation of the Tyne-Tees combine. Stephen Furness, was well equipped for the job according to *Durham at the opening of the twentieth Century*, 1906:

Stephen W Furness, J P – Tunstall Grange, West Hartlepool; son of Stephen Furness of Berwick St James, Salisbury; born 1872; educated at Harrogate. Justice of the Peace for the County of Durham; steamship owner and Director of Furness Withy & Company, Irvine's Shipbuilding & Dry Docks Company, Weardale Steel, Coke and Coal Company, and Richardson's Westgarth & Company; has been five years Member of the West Hartlepool Corporation; Ex-Chairman of Finance Committee; was for three years Member of Durham County Council; one of the Representatives of the North Eastern Railway; on the port and harbour Commissioners. Married in 1899.

The new company's main office was at 25 Westgate. Bizarrely the company's operations were not combined and the Tyne Committee in charge of vessels and routes that served Newcastle and a separate Tees Committee, directed by Joseph Cradock, in charge of vessels and routes that served Middlesbrough, Stockton and Hartlepool were retained long after their formation at the initial amalgamation process in July. There was little if any interchange of ships between the two Committees, reflecting the dissatisfaction still held in Teesside for the merger.

Principal ship deployment was:

Tyne Committee

Tyne to London:	**Tynesider**, **New Londoner**
Tyne to Rotterdam:	**Grenadier**
Tyne to Hamburg:	**John Ormston**, **Royal Dane**

Tyne and Hartlepool to Bremen, Dordrecht, Antwerp, Amsterdam, Ghent and Calais/Dunkirk:
Admiral, **Faraday**, **Warkworth**, assisted by **Juno** (also available for reliefs).

Tees Committee

Tees to London:	**Claudia**, **Buccaneer**
Tees to Hamburg and Bremen:	**Dione**, **New Oporto**.

The adopted colours of the new company were those of the old Tyne Steam Shipping Company: black funnel with a white over red band, black hull and boot topping. The broad red band on a black funnel of the Tees Union ships and the all black Furness Line funnel colours disappeared from the new fleet adding salt to the wounds of the Tees-men. Little wonder that the shareholders of the former Tees Union company referred to the so called amalgamation as a Tyne company takeover! The Tees Union company was only finally wound up in 1906 with the sale of its remaining unwanted assets, although its wharf at Middlesbrough had been transferred to the new company and was now designated the Tyne-Tees Wharf and was being increasingly developed for the deep sea liner trades as well as the company's own arrivals and departures.

The first problem the new company faced was the sinking of the sailing fishing boat **Magge Flett** after being rammed by the **New Londoner** on her departure from the Tyne on 25 November 1903. Three of the crew of the **Maggie Flett** died in the sinking. The Inquiry ruled:

*The Court, having carefully inquired into the circumstances attending the above-mentioned shipping casualty, finds, for the reasons stated in the Annex hereto, that the collision, whereby loss of life ensued, was caused by Captain J W N Searle, the master of the **New Londoner**, failing to take proper and sufficient measures to keep out of the way of the **Maggie Flett**, by porting his helm in time and slackening his speed.*

The **New Londoner** (1894) arriving in the Tyne, decks crowded with passengers.

Fear spread through the Tyne-Tees shareholder's camp in August 1905 when the press reported a rumour that the North Eastern Railway was about to take over the Tyne-Tees company. The rumour, apparently unfounded, was denied in October when the Tyne-Tees Company was quoted as saying '*there is absolutely nothing to the report*', and indeed nothing was heard of the issue again.

Early advert for the Tyne-Tees company's Sunderland to London passenger and cargo service.

(Linda Gowans collection)

In 1898 Andrew Weir (Bank Line) had initiated an east coast feeder service for its deep sea fleet with the purchase of **Ruby** from Robertson's of Glasgow. She was joined the following year by **Burnock** which was purchased from the Garnock Steamship Company of Ayr. The two ships also maintained a service from north-east England via London to ports in northern France. The two steamers, respectively 481 and 425 tons gross, served their new owners well until October 1905 when **Ruby** sank after a collision near the Forth Bridge inbound to Grangemouth from Middlesbrough with a cargo of pig iron. Shortly afterwards Andrew Weir sold **Burnock** to Brown Jenkinson's London Transport Company and at the same time entered into a service level agreement with Tyne-Tees. The agreement gave Tyne-Tees the goodwill and business generated by the two steamers on Andrew Weir's service to northern French ports and it vested Tyne-Tees as the preferred carrier for Weir's transhipments to and from its long haul Bank Line ships to east coast ports.

Accidents still occurred. On 27 January 1906 a fatal accident was recorded aboard the **Tynesider**. An 8 cwt (400 kg) electric motor was being brought up from the motor house to the bridge deck by block and tackle for inspection, when a jack and beam failed. Later in the year the **Tynesider** hit the steamer **Tregona** in the Thames causing the latter to be beached although the **Tynesider** was later able to resume her voyage north.

The Tyne-Tees Steam Shipping Company was owner of a diverse fleet. The Continental services were maintained by several barely economical vessels such as the **John Ormston** dating from 1873 and the **Royal Dane** from 1875 and there was an obvious need for larger and newer ships to service a growing market. Ambrose Greenway describes Tyne-Tees Steam Shipping Company's first purpose-built steamer:

Towards the end of 1905 Tyne-Tees Steam Shipping ordered a new steamer for their Continental services. Launched at Yarrow by Palmers Shipbuilding Company on 6 April 1906 [by Kate Stephenson, daughter of Sir William] she was named **Sir William Stephenson**. *Trials were run just over two months later on 8 June after which she proceeded to Newcastle to load for her maiden voyage.*

She differed from previous Tyne-Tees passenger ships in having her engines amidships. …her three holds could carry about 1,300 tons of cargo handled by a mix of derricks and four steam cranes. Her [triple steam expansion] propelling machinery was supplied by Richardson Westgarth and her boilers employed forced draught.

By all accounts her public rooms were finely appointed and she brought a new degree of luxury to the Continental services. There was also space for up to 440 deck passengers. She wore a new livery with the black hull replaced by an attractive shade of grey, a scheme taken up by the other passenger units in the Tyne Committee as they were refitted, but not by the Tees committee ships.

A report in *The Syren and Shipping* dated 27 June 1906 described the ship:

*Rigged as two-masted fore and aft schooner. There is a long full poop and bridge houses of a combined length of 168 feet and a topgallant forecastle 43 feet long which is left free for cargoes. Over the fore end of the bridge house is a shade deck extending the full width of the vessel and for about 96 feet fore and aft covering the machinery openings and containing accommodation for about 60 first class passengers, a dining saloon, baths and lavatories. At the fore end of the shade deck is a steel house containing a smoke room and a ladies room. The saloon entrance is also here with a staircase leading to the first class accommodation. At the fore end are the Captain's room and the chart room, and the top of the deckhouse is extended to the sides of the vessel in order to form a promenade for the passengers. Portable accommodation is provided in the after end of the poop in two separate compartments for about 50 passengers in second class. The sea speed was nearly 14 knots with two thirds of the coal consumption of the **Royal Dane** whose place she takes on the Hamburg service.*

Typically the **Sir William Stephenson** arrived on the Tyne from Hamburg before 6.00 am on Mondays and Thursdays ready to discharge farm produce for market before loading manufactured goods for her return trips to Germany. The **Royal Dane** was sold shortly after the new ship was commissioned.

On 1 August 1906, Sir William D Stephenson reported a company profit of £38,918 and a dividend was declared at 7%. Until early in the 1905 accounting year the company was still paying expenses due to the amalgamation, but these had now ceased.

The counterpart for the **Sir William Stephenson** was ordered from Palmers Shipbuilding & Engineering in 1907. She was designed for the Hamburg passenger and cargo service as a direct replacement for the **John Ormston**. The new ship was the **Richard Welford**, a quasi-sister of the **Sir William Stephenson**. She was launched on 8 November 1907 by Mrs George Shirlaw, Richard Welford's goddaughter. The **Richard Welford** was an attractive steamer with accommodation for 94 first class and 90 second class passengers in the now accustomed luxury expected on the Hamburg service. She was also licensed to carry up to 260 deck passengers. In the pre-**Titanic** days she carried lifeboats that were designed only to carry 178 people. The **Sir William Stephenson** was even worse off, with a lifeboat capacity of only 196 against a passenger certificate for 550!

The **Sir William Stephenson** (1906), a near sister to the **Richard Welford**, was lost in World War I.

(R Gibson, George Nairn collection)

The **Richard Welford** (1908) was designed for the Continental services but initially used on the London route.

(R Gibson, George Nairn collection)

Delivery of the new Hamburg ship coincided with the sale of the elderly **Tynesider**. The **Tynesider** and **New Londoner** had provided a good matched pair on the Newcastle to London service for some years, but the economics of putting the **Tynesider** through her next survey were prohibitive. The **Tynesider** did see four further years of service under the Greek flag but was scrapped in 1912. Her departure left a gap in the London roster and, best laid plans, this was filled by the brand new **Richard Welford** and providing a reprieve for the

John Ormston. The **Richard Welford** had an operational speed of 15 knots giving her ample scope to maintain schedule in what became a wholly unbalanced partnership with the elderly **New Londoner**. The **Richard Welford** was commanded by the Commodore of the fleet, Captain John Bruce. It was not uncommon for passengers to delay sailing until the Commodore's ship took the next scheduled departure.

The **Tynesider** (1888) setting off from Newcaste.

(R Gibson, Harold Appleyard collection)

The **New Londoner** grounded at Northfleet Hope on the Thames on 8 January 1908 as reported in the *North Mail* on 21 January:

*The **New Londoner** which grounded at Northfleet Hope in the Thames above Gravesend, during a dense fog a fortnight ago, when on a voyage to Newcastle, has been successfully refloated. It was necessary, however, to wait for the high Spring Tide before it could be accomplished. There were ten passengers aboard the **New Londoner** when she grounded and they were taken ashore.*

The *Newcastle Chronicle* reported another incident on 24 February 1908, this time involving the **Dione**:

*As the SS **Dione**, owned by the Tyne-Tees Steam Shipping Company, was proceeding down the Tees on Saturday, with a general cargo for London, she came into collision with the SS **Royal Standard**, owned by the Welford Shipping Company of Sunderland. The **Royal Standard**, laden with a cargo of iron, had dropped anchor at Eston Jetty, when she swung round and collided with the **Dione**. The **Dione** was little the worse for the mishap, and was able to proceed on her voyage, but the **Royal Standard** received such damage as will necessitate her being overhauled as soon as she has discharged.*

The **Grenadier** served mainly the Rotterdam service, sometimes also Hamburg. Outward bound from Cuxhaven on 21 July 1908 she stranded between the islands of Langeoog and Spiekeroog. The crew and twelve passengers were safely taken off the ship which remained fast in increasingly heavy weather. The *Newcastle Chronicle* reported the grave news received that morning from Lloyds:

*The British steamer **Grenadier** (Captain Howe), Newcastle-upon-Tyne for Hamburg with a cargo of general goods, has gone ashore at Spiekeroog Island, Hanover, and will probably be a total wreck. Assistance is with her. A surveyor has gone to the vessel.*

Damage sustained from the battering of the 'heavy weather' included both her propeller and rudder being carried away. A passenger described the sharp crack when the poop housing was washed away and the difficulties that followed getting into the lifeboat alongside the ship in the rough seas in the *North Mail* on 25 July 1908:

Waves were breaking over the ship with a noise like thunder, and on attempting to reach the saloon I was met by a huge stream of water rushing upon me down the stairs. We found the ladies naturally excited and some of them in hysterics.

A week after her stranding, and with some cargo removed to lighten ship, she was successfully refloated and on 1 August was towed into Hamburg. The **Grenadier** left for dry docking and repairs at West Hartlepool on 5 August in charge of the tug **Atlas**.

In 1908 Tyne-Tees Steam Shipping Company had new premises built to house stores and works on City Road at the site of Millers Hill. The building was designed by Newcastle architect J Watson Taylor and was constructed to provide support and maintenance for vessels moored at the company's wharfs on the quayside and at Gateshead. The building commanded views over the company's wharves, including Hillgate Quay at Gateshead, as it was situated at the bend in the river. The original sign with the shipping company name is still visible above what was the carriage arch, now the entrance to a hotel.

Former company workshops and stores in City Road, Newcastle, now the Hotel du Vin. The company name is still visible over the hotel entrance, one time the carriage arch into the yard.

(Author)

The company's steam wherry **Minx**, which had been built for the Tyne Steam Shipping Company in 1875, was sold for further trading in March 1909. She was acquired in 1910 by the River Wear Commissioners and served at Sunderland until she was broken up there in 1929. Her sale was in anticipation of the new steam wherry **Poodle** which was delivered by Hepple & Company of South Shields four months later. The main visual difference between the two wherries was that the funnel was placed abaft the bridge on the new **Poodle**, whereas it was forward of the bridge on the **Minx**. Both the **Minx** and the **Poodle** were based on the Tyne but were used to tranship goods between various north east coast ports.

In April 1909 two of the companies vessels were involved in a collision with another ship in the Tyne. The **Sir William Stephenson** was being escorted downriver by the company tug **WDS** when the pair managed to strike the collier **Collingwood** in mid-channel. The **WDS** was badly damaged but remained afloat while the starboard bridge wing on the **Sir William Stephenson** was carried away by the impact and two of the ship's boats were smashed.

The company tug **WDS** (1892) busy on the Tyne.   *(From an oil painting by the author)*

Conscious of the mismatch on the London service, the company determined to replace the **New Londoner** with a third ship of the **Sir William Stephenson** mould. The design evolved considerably and the outcome was an altogether different and more modern design. Late in 1909 an order was placed with Irvines Shipbuilding & Drydock Company at West Hartlepool for a steamer at a contract price of £43,500. She was named after the company chairman, Stephen Furness, and launched on 10 May 1910 by his wife. The launch ceremony was a subdued affair as it followed just four days after the death of King Edward VII.

The **Stephen Furness** was a shelter deck vessel. Her registered length was 290 feet, breadth 37 feet; her bridge deck was 130 feet long and her gross tonnage was 1,712. The hull was divided by four watertight bulkheads. There were two holds, one forward of the engine compartment with two hatches and one aft with just one hatch. The **Stephen Furness** had accommodation for 250 first class and 120 second class passengers on the shelter deck and main deck plus a certificate for several hundred more deck passengers. The dining saloon was at the forward end of the bridge deck, with seating arranged in tables for four in discrete bays around the saloon. There was a smoke room and bar at the aft end of the bridge deck. Electric fans and natural draught provided ventilation to the accommodation.

The first class fare on the London service at that time was 12/- single, 18/- return first class and 8/- and 12/- second class. Meals for the voyage were arranged through the steward at 6/- first and 3/- second class per passenger.

LEFT: The **Stephen Furness** (1910) started life on the Hamburg route.

BELOW: The **New Londoner** (1894) manoeuvring off the passenger terminal at Newcastle with assistance from the company tug **WDS** (1892).

(both R Gibson, George Nairn collection)

For a second time the design plan for a new steamer was frustrated by the need to replace another steamer deployed elsewhere. The **John Ormston** had finally come to the end of her useful life with the company and so the new London steamer **Stephen Furness** sailed initially to Hamburg and the **John Ormston** stood down. The **Stephen Furness** was finally able to replace the **New Londoner** on the London service in January 1911 when she started running in partnership with the **Sir William Stephenson**. At the end of the 1911 summer season, after running as third ship as required, the **New Londoner** was finally put on the 'For Sale' list.

For the Middlesbrough to London service a new ship was ordered from Irvines Shipbuilding & Dry Dock Company in October 1908 which was to be named **Joseph Cradock**, after the Tees Committee Director. James Layton wrote in the *Tees Packet*:

*For some time the Tyne Committee had wanted the **Claudia** for the Rotterdam service but the Tees Committee would not agree to the transfer, so the provision of a new ship to replace the **Dione**, which was sold in October 1908, may have been part of a plan to obtain the release of the **Claudia**. If it was, the outcome was quite different from what the Newcastle Committee expected.*

The **Dione** was sold to owners in Spain and survived until her 95th birthday as **Aurora**, when she was eventually sold for demolition in 1964. She retained her original engines, which had been built by Blair & Company at Stockton in 1879, throughout her career.

Building of the new Tees ship progressed well, but Director Joseph Cradock fell ill and died just three weeks before the launch date. The name of the new ship was hastily changed to **Teessider** and as a mark of respect to the Cradock family the ship was registered at Stockton rather than at Middlesbrough. The **Teessider** was sponsored and launched by Mrs Claude Pease on 22 February 1909. Layton again:

*The **Teessider** was a single deck steamship with a raised forecastle and a long poop, her bridge being at the forward end of the poop and engine room just aft of the bridge. Her principal dimensions were, length overall 265 feet, breadth 35 feet, depth of hold 14 feet, moulded depth amidships 16 feet 6 inches, forecastle length 44 feet, poop 144 feet… The cargo space was divided into two holds with a total grain capacity of 74,513 cubic feet, Number 1 hold being on the well deck and Number 2 aft of the engine room. The forward hold, which was fitted with a 'tween deck, was 107 feet long and had a hatchway measuring 51 feet 9 inches by 18 feet, ideal for the iron and steel trade. Number 2 hold was 44 feet long with a hatchway of 23 feet by 18 feet. Cargo handling gear consisted of two derricks rigged on the foremast at the forward end of Number 1 hold with two steam cranes at the after end and two derricks rigged on the mainmast at the forward end of number 2 hold. Each derrick had its own steam winch and the maximum lift available was 10 tons.*

The **Teessider** (1909), seen on trials, was originally designed for the Middlesbrough to London route.

The **Teessider** also had accommodation for ten first class passengers in five staterooms in the midships house forward on the poop. Another 38 first class berths were available on the upper deck in 2 and 4 berth cabins. The first class dining saloon and pantry were located adjacent to the staterooms. In addition up to 40 second class berths were available on the main deck forward and with a few additional deck passengers her total passenger compliment was 114. Her operational speed was 13 knots sustained by 28 tons of coal a day, her bunkers carried 153 tons allowing two round trips from the north-east without taking on coal. The **Teessider** arrived at Tyne-Tees Wharf, Middlesbrough on 5 April 1909 ready for her maiden voyage to London three days later under Captain Jordan, until then in charge of the **Claudia** on the London run. The **Claudia** finally acceded to the Tyne Committee's wishes and sailed for Newcastle to load for Hamburg. On return to the Tyne she was deemed unsuitable for the Continental trade and was back alongside at Middlesbrough on 20 April. After only four London trips the new **Teessider** swapped Captains with the **Claudia** and sailed for Newcastle to become the new Hamburg and Rotterdam steamer, displacing the **Grenadier** whose passenger compliment was reduced thereafter to just twelve berths.

In May 1909 the London service was upgraded for the summer season to three departures each way with sailings on Tuesday, Thursday and Saturday. The **New Londoner** and the **Richard Welford** were supported in this by the **Teessider** or the **New Oporto**. Between the 17 and 24 July the service was advertised '*to view the Grand Naval Pageant in the Thames whereby the **New Londoner** and the **Richard Welford** will pass through lines of battleships in daylight*'.

There was considerable debate by the Board in 1911 over the design of the next new ship. She was to be able to run either to the Continent or on the London service and the Vice Chairman was strongly in favour of a repeat order of the **Stephen Furness**. Other Board members, however, were equally adamant that a **Teessider**-type ship was what was needed. In the end, and led by the Chairman, Sir William Stephenson, the vote went in favour of another **Teessider**. Stephenson had succeeded Stephen Furness as Chairman once the Furness shareholding began to diminish.

The new ship was intended to be named **Londoner**, but was launched at Irvine's West Hartlepool yard on 16 May 1912 by Mrs Jefferson, wife of the Tyne-Tees General Manager, as the **New Londoner**. The preferred name, the Board of Trade advised, was already on the register. The design was similar to that of the earlier **Teessider** although the new ship was built with a few more passenger berths with 40 first class and 28 second class berths on the bridge and main decks, although many more could be carried unberthed. First and second class had access to a dining saloon with a piano forward. Meals could be bought by arrangement with the steward before departure or from a refreshment tariff. Clearly her design allowed for use both on the London service and on any of the continental routes.

Unlike the **Teessider**, the **New Londoner** had three holds, two forward and one aft, the **Teessider** having only one forward and one aft. Some of the new ship's steam cranes came from the old **New Londoner** which had been sold minus her cargo handling gear. Like her near sister, the **New Londoner** had triple expansion engines which enabled her to steam at 13 knots on 29 tons of coal per day.

The **New Londoner** (1912), a quasi-sister to the **Teessider**, seen in the Tyne.

(R Gibson, George Nairn collection)

Both the **Teessider** and the **New Londoner** were principally employed on the Continental services. The basic schedule comprised the **New Londoner** sailing from Newcastle to Hamburg every Saturday, the **Teessider** sailing midweek to Rotterdam and the big continental steamer **Sir William Stephenson** on the Saturday departure to Antwerp. Meanwhile, the **Richard Welford** took the Saturday departure for London and the **Stephen Furness** the Wednesday sailing.

During 1912 negotiations were completed by Furness Withy for Tyne-Tees to acquire Ralph Hudson's one-ship Havelock Line (Chapter 4). The Havelock Line was thus acquired by Tyne-Tees with effect from 1 January 1913. Ralph Hudson was welcomed to the Board of Tyne-Tees Steam Shipping, and only later formerly elected a member of the Board. For the moment the **General Havelock** was maintained on her twice weekly Sunderland to London service with seasonal calls at Scarborough. There she was tendered by the Harbour Commissioners' tug **Cambria**, built in 1879, and first brought to Scarborough in 1899 where she remained in service until she stranded near Gristhorpe in 1912. Although the Havelock Line identity was retained, one significant merging of interests did take place within the Tyne-Tees Steam Shipping Company when the Tees Committee and the Tyne Committee were finally abandoned and the company was at last run as a single and coherent corporate entity.

Occasionally, for operational reasons, both the Newcastle and Middlesbrough arrivals and departures at London required passengers to be taken by tender to the ship lying off the berth. This duty normally fell to the steam tug/tender **Ich Dien**, owned by the Aberdeen Steam Navigation Company and built in 1877 to attend that company's steamers in the Thames. **Ich Dien** (German for 'I serve') was sold in 1942 when passenger arrivals and departures were suspended during World War II. Had she remained in the fleet another three years she would finally have come under the ownership of the Tyne-Tees Steam Shipping Company (see Chapter 10).

The Aberdeen Steam Navigation Company's tug/tender *Ich Dien* (1877) occasionally tendered the Tyne-Tees company's passenger ships when Free Trade Wharf was busy. Note the hinged funnel to enable her to pass under London Bridge.

The **New Londoner**, operating the important Newcastle to Hamburg service, was the first ship in the fleet to receive Marconi wireless telegraphy equipment and a radio officer. The economic benefits of such communication quickly persuaded the company to equip its other key passenger units with similar equipment and operators; safety it seems played only a small part in this decision!

During the winter refits at the end of the 1913 season the attractive grey hulls of the former Tyne Committee passenger fleet were painted over black. This was a move driven by economics as the paint preparations then available were such that rust streaks appeared with such regularity that frequent touching up became expensive in both materials and labour.

Concern over the productivity of passenger carrying was first voiced by Company Chairman William Stephenson at the 1913 Annual General Meeting. Stephenson reported that high-class passenger steamers were not as remunerative as the cargo ships and cargo ships with limited passenger accommodation because the bigger ships passenger berths remained largely empty for all but the two months of the high summer season. He stated that he did not believe the passenger traffic could be increased and that the company should concentrate on maintaining the numbers they already had. A half yearly dividend of 7$\frac{1}{2}$ % was paid to shareholders for the six months to the end of June.

The company acquired an additional cargo unit during the year when Furness Withy's coastal steamer **Howden** was ceded to Tyne-Tees. Furness Withy at this time had begun to shed its shares in Tyne-Tees although it still retained a significant interest. The problem for Furness Withy was that from the formation of the company in 1903 it had never had a controlling interest and this was not to its liking.

The company handbook for summer 1914 happily described the Middlesbrough to London service, deprived of its new purpose-built steamer the **Teessider**, as if its elderly ships were state of the art:

*Unless prevented by reasonable causes the steamers sail from London to Stockton, Middlesbrough and Scarborough every Tuesday and Saturday. These ports are served by the steamers **Claudia** and **Buccaneer**.*

*The **Claudia**, 1,144 tons gross and 1,878 ihp, specially built for the trade, contains a handsome saloon and smoke room, piano, etc, and is lighted throughout by electricity. During the summer months this steamer calls off Scarborough both ways to land and embark passengers. Passengers should book berths in advance... The **Buccaneer**, or other vessel, leaves London every Tuesday for Scarborough, Hartlepool, Middlesbrough and Stockton carrying a limited number of saloon passengers only. The **Buccaneer** does not stop at Scarborough on her passage to London, but calls there on the return journey to discharge goods.*

Stockton passengers embark and disembark at Middlesbrough. The passage between Middlesbrough and Scarborough occupies about three hours, between Middlesbrough and London about 24 hours. When sailings of the steamers take place early in the morning passengers may sleep on board the previous night.

A third ship of the **Teessider**-class was ordered from S P Austin & Sons at Sunderland in May 1914. Britain declared war on Germany before construction had progressed much beyond assembly of the basic hull; overnight the whole economics of merchant shipping were changed. The **Juno** was alongside loading at Hamburg while the **New Londoner** was due to sail from Newcastle to the German port on 1 August. Not only was the key cargo and passenger service of the company bound for suspension but its ships were immediately at risk from enemy action (Chapter 5).

The new company had come a long way in its first decade. Clearly the power and financial capacity of the merged companies behind Tyne-Tees was strong, as also was the new company's management. These factors, plus the buoyant commercial environment that prevailed in much of the Edwardian era, enabled Tyne-Tees to build five new major passenger and cargo ships with a fifth one on order. Additionally it had strengthened its hold on the Hamburg service and increased its cargo services to the Dutch ports. It had also bought the Havelock Line bringing a new route into the company. Importantly, Chairman Stephenson had already identified that passenger carrying was at its peak and that it should focus on maintaining what traffic it had while developing its cargo-carrying capacity. But the declaration of war was to put an end to those aspirations while the trading conditions that would prevail four years later would be very different indeed.

The Tyne-Tees Steam Shipping Company flag: the crest of Newcastle-upon-Tyne '*A tower argent, therefrom issuent a demi-lion rampant guardant or, holding a flagstaff sable, therefrom flowing a split banner of St George*' on a red ground. The flag is based on that of the Tyne Steam Shipping Company in which the yellow letters TSS Co were distributed in the four corners of the flag.

(DP World P&O Heritage collection)

GRENADIER Report of the enquiry into stranding

In the matter of a formal investigation held at the Moot Hall, Newcastle-upon-Tyne, on the 18th, 19th, and 21st days of September, 1908, before William Cowell and Richard Oliver Heslop, Esquires, two of His Majesty's Justices of the Peace acting in and for the City and County of Newcastle-upon-Tyne, assisted by Captains A Wood and Owen R Mitchell (Nautical Assessors), into the circumstances attending the stranding of the British steamship *Grenadier*, of Newcastle-upon-Tyne, on a reef off Langeoog Island, on the 20th day of July, 1908.

Report of Court

The Court, having carefully inquired into the circumstances attending the above-mentioned shipping casualty, finds, for the reasons stated in the Annex hereto, that the stranding of the vessel, whereby she sustained serious and material damage, was due to her making a southerly course and the Master mistaking the Norderney light vessel light for the Heligoland light, and neglecting to use the lead to ascertain and verify the vessel's position. The Court finds the Master, Thomas Ridley Howe, in default, and hereby suspends his certificate, No. 103554, for the period of six months from the date hereof.

Dated this 21st day of September, 1908.
W M Cowell,
R Oliver Heslop,
Judges.

We concur in the above report.
A Wood,
Owen R. Mitchell,
Assessors.

Annex to the Report

This was an inquiry into the circumstances attending the stranding of the British steamship *Grenadier*, of Newcastle, and was held at the Moot Hall, Newcastle-upon-Tyne, on 18th, 19th and 21st days of September, 1908, before W Cowell and R O Heslop, Esquires, assisted by Captains A Wood and O R Mitchell (nautical assessors).

Mr Burton appeared for the Board of Trade, Mr Dixon Jacks represented the Master, and Mr Middleton watched the case on behalf of the owners, but did not take part in the proceedings.

The *Grenadier* (Official Number 104282) was a steel screw steamship, built at Newcastle-upon-Tyne in the year 1895 by Messrs Wigham, Richardson, & Company. She was schooner-rigged and of the following dimensions: length 240 feet; breadth 30.2 feet; and depth in hold 14.75 feet; and was of 1004.25 gross and 591.31 net registered tonnage. She was fitted with triple-expansion engines of 165 nhp, constructed by Messrs Wigham, Richardson, & Company, at Newcastle-upon-Tyne in the year 1895. She was owned by the Tyne-Tees Steam Shipping Company, Limited, Mr Richard Welford, of 25, King Street, Newcastle-upon-Tyne, having been appointed manager on the 18 March, 1904. She was, on the voyage in question, in good condition and well found, and carried the lifeboats and other life-saving appliances in accordance with the Act. A passenger certificate, dated 13 May, 1908, was issued by the Board of Trade, under which she was certified to carry 133 passengers.

She was supplied with a blue-back chart for the North Sea, published by Messrs Imray, Laurie, Norie, and Wilson in 1908, and sailing directions for the North Sea for 1904. There was also a list of lights on board, and the Master was familiar both with Heligoland light and with the light on Norderney light vessel, having seen these lights on previous voyages.

The vessel had three compasses, which were adjusted on 30 May last, and are particularly described in the answers to the questions.

The **Grenadier** left the Tyne on 18 July last, bound for Hamburg, with a crew of 22 hands all told, under the command of Mr T R Howe, who held a Master's certificate for home trade passenger ships, numbered 103554.

The Chief Officer had a Master's certificate, but the seaman, Edward Hutchinson, who was doing second officer's duty, was uncertificated. There were twelve passengers on board and 285 tons of general cargo, the vessel's draught being 11 feet forward and 17 feet 9 inches aft.

At 5.10 pm on 18 July last the **Grenadier** passed the Tyne pier-heads, a course SE by E ³/4 E being then set for Heligoland by the standard compass, which stood on the upper bridge in front of the wheel. The deviation-card, which was produced and stated by the Master to have been always found correct, showed that there was practically no deviation on this compass on any course. The patent log (a harpoon-log) was streamed as the vessel passed out of the river, and the engines were put at full-speed, the vessel making from 11 to 12 knots through the water. The wind was strong from the northwards, and there was a considerable amount of sea on the port beam.

At 3.40 am on the 19th the fan engine eccentric rod broke and the slide rod got bent and, while these defects were being made good, the speed of the vessel was somewhat reduced till 8.00 am, when the engines were again going full-speed.

At noon on the 19th the patent log registered 196 miles, and the Master stated that the latitude he obtained from a meridian altitude of the sun was 54° 27' N. At 2.00 pm the course was altered from SE by E ³/4 E to ESE (magnetic), the wind then being NNE, with slightly hazy weather and beam sea.

About 10.45 pm a light was sighted, bearing E¹/2 S, being 1¹/2 points on the port bow. This light came suddenly in sight and was seen independently about the same time by the Master on deck and the Chief Officer, man on look-out and helmsman, who were all on the upper-bridge.

The Master stated he made this light out to be Heligoland light and that the Chief Officer confirmed him in this opinion. On the other hand, the Chief Officer stated that, though when he first saw it he might have admitted that it was Heligoland, nevertheless when he counted the flashes he could see it was Norderney light ship, and that he repeatedly expressed this opinion to the Master, who answered him 'brusquely' that it was Heligoland. The Master denied this, and said that the Chief Officer never made the slightest suggestion to him that the light was any other than Heligoland. The man on the look-out and the helmsman, who stated that they could generally hear the conversation between the Master and officer of the watch, both said that on this occasion they heard no dispute about the lights. The Court accepts the Master's version, and is of opinion that had the Chief Officer strongly represented to the Master that he was mistaken in the light and had been answered as suggested, these men would have heard the conversation.

The man at the wheel, who was a very intelligent witness, stated that the light he saw was a '*three flash light*'. Why the Master and Chief Officer should have mistaken this light for Heligoland the Court is at a loss to know. As described in the *Admiralty List of Lights, Part II*, the light on Norderney Light Vessel '*shows groups of three flashes every fifteen seconds, thus:*

Flash, a quarter of a second; eclipse 3 ¹/2 seconds;
flash, a quarter of a second; eclipse 3 ¹/2 seconds;
flash, a quarter of a second; eclipse 7 ¹/4 seconds.'

This light is exhibited 52 feet above sea level and is visible in clear weather 13 miles. The light on Heligoland is placed 269 feet above high water mark, is visible in clear weather to a distance of 23 miles and shows a bright flash one tenth-of-a-second in duration every five seconds.

The Chief Officer's subsequent conduct is not in accordance with his statement that he was aware of the dangerous course the vessel was on and had pressed this fact on the Master's notice. When relieved by the Second Officer, he does not appear to have said anything to him about the Master mistaking the lights, and after he left the bridge he went below, took off his clothes, and retired to rest. If he really believed the vessel was running into danger this was a most reprehensible part for the Chief Officer of a vessel to play, and was aggravated in this case by the circumstance that there were passengers on board.

The course ESE was continued till 11.40 pm when, the vessel being abreast of Norderney light vessel, it was altered to SE by E and continued till midnight, being then changed to SE. The weather is described as being hazy with light rain, but it could not have been very thick as the light on Norderney light vessel had been sighted at about its full range. The course SE was continued and the engines kept at full speed till about 1.00 am on the 20th, when the vessel ran aground. The engines were reversed but without effect, and they were subsequently worked ahead and astern. The vessel was striking the ground heavily, and, shortly after stranding, the fan engine broke down, the water service pipes got choked up with sand, and the main bearings became hot. At about 2.00 am, the rudder and propeller were carried away, thus rendering the engines useless. The port anchor was let go and all the cable veered out when it parted at the hawse-pipe. The starboard anchor was then let go with like result. Signals of distress were made, in response to which three lifeboats arrived from the shore. The passengers all left the vessel and were landed at Spikeroog Island. The crew remained by the *Grenadier* till 7.00 pm, when the engineers and firemen landed from the vessel, but returned on board on the 22nd. Lighters were brought out and part of the cargo was discharged into them. On the 29th the vessel floated and was towed by two salvage boats to Spiekeroog Roads, where the remainder of the cargo was discharged. The *Grenadier* was then towed to Hamburg where temporary repairs were affected, after which she was brought to Hartlepool and fully repaired. The vessel had received very serious and material damage, but no lives were lost.

It has to be noted that when the light which the Master mistook for Heligoland was sighted at 10.45 pm on the 19th, a single cast of the lead would have clearly shown the mistake that was being made.

Even had the light passed by the *Grenadier* been that on Heligoland, the distance run from 11.40 pm to 1 am and the course steered would have put the vessel ashore at the mouth of the Elbe. Although no light corresponding to that on the Elbe light ship was sighted, the *Grenadier* was kept going at full-speed after passing the position in which the Master in his error should have expected to have found it had he properly considered the matter.

A most unsatisfactory feature in this case is a false entry made by the Master's orders both in the Chief Officer's and Engineer's log books under date 20 July, 1908. In the Chief Officer's the entry is as follows: 0.50 am, stopped engines and took a cast of the lead, $4^{1}/_{2}$ fathoms water was reported. In the Engineer's log is entered: 12.50 am, stopped for soundings.

The Chief Officer and the Chief Engineer were off duty at the time this sounding was said to have been taken and made the entries in question on information supplied by the Master. These entries are declared to be false by the Second Officer, who was on the bridge at the time, and by the donkeyman, Thomas Davidson, who was in charge of the engine-room. They both stated that the engines were not stopped, but continued at full-speed till after the vessel stranded. The Master, however, swore that he was on the bridge and that he stopped the engines, and ordered the second officer to take a cast of the lead, that he did so, and reported to him (the Master) that there was $4^{1}/_{2}$ fathoms. The Second Officer stated in evidence that this was not done. He admitted that he had agreed to a statement, which was read over to him by the authorities in Hamburg, that this sounding was taken before the vessel grounded. He had been led to agree to this as it was only part of a general statement that had been made up from the log books, the greater part of which was correct, and that when he arrived in this country he made his statement to the authorities agree with what he had deposed to in Hamburg, but it was not true that the engines were stopped and $4^{1}/_{2}$ fathoms got before the vessel stranded.

The Court from all the evidence on the subject came to the conclusion that the Master did not speak the truth with regard to stopping the engines, and getting a sounding of $4^{1}/_{2}$ fathoms before the vessel stranded. The conduct of all concerned in this transaction is most reprehensible and deserving of the severest condemnation, and altogether there appears to have been an entire lack of discipline and esprit-de-corps among the officers of the vessel.

CHAPTER 4

HUDSON'S HAVELOCK LINE

The Havelock Line brand was inaugurated by Ralph R Hudson in 1867 when he bought the six year old screw steamer *Italia* from Sunderland shipbuilder James Laing. Hudson renamed his ship the *General Havelock* in memory of the Sunderland born military hero, Sir Henry Havelock, son of Sunderland shipbuilder William Havelock. General Havelock, Sir Henry Havelock, died in 1857 at Lucknow during the Indian Revolution. The ship, the *General Havelock*, spent a brief and uneventful period under Hudson's ownership and established a reliable year round service between Sunderland and London. *General Havelock* was an iron-hulled single-deck screw steamer with 90 horse power engines built by Laing. She had three masts. She was some 185 feet long with a beam of 24 feet, typical dimensions for the early coastal steamers of that era. She carried passengers as well as cargo on her twice weekly foray to the Thames. Significantly, the company and its owners already had sufficient funds to go back to Laing to ask for a purpose built steamer to be designed and built for the new service. This was the second steamer to carry the name *General Havelock*, for which part payment was made by return of the first steamer to James Laing who renamed her the *Teesdale*.

The new *General Havelock* was delivered in October 1868 following her launch on 6 September. She was marginally bigger than the earlier steamer and had an iron hull 190 feet long with a beam of 26 feet. She was a single-deck ship with an elliptical stern and two masts and had a significantly larger deadweight than the first *General Havelock*. Her public rooms were luxuriously fitted out and she was equipped to carry over 200 passengers in first and second class, with many more in deck class. She was fitted with a compound surface-condensing engine which provided a total 99 horse power. The diameter of the cylinders was 28 and 53 inches respectively, and the stroke was 36 inches. The vessel was rigged as a schooner and had an altogether pleasing, if business-like, appearance.

Calls were made at Scarborough. Described as 'a pleasant watering hole' in company advertisements, the stop was intended both as an extension for passengers using the ship as a summer cruise venue but more importantly on the southbound journey to uplift barrels of fish destined for market in London. The *General Havelock* anchored in Scarborough Bay and one of the local paddle steamers acted as tender. For many years this duty was carried out by the *Comet*, built in 1876 and of 132 tons gross and owned by the Star Tug Company of Great Yarmouth. Hudson's Managing Owner W H Thompson bought the steamer in 1882 and maintained her at Scarborough until 1896 when she was sold to the Lawson Tug Company on the Tyne. The *Comet* was also used throughout the warmer summer months to provide excursions and otherwise undertook salvage and towage duties as required. A tall basket was used to transfer passengers when the sea was rough, much akin to the Union-Castle tendering system off Port Elizabeth at that time. The basket was slung off the ship's derrick to lower two or perhaps three passengers to the deck of the tender.

The *General Havelock* developed an enviable reputation for reliability and comfort. She had a set pattern: departure from Sunderland and London at 8.00 pm with arrival at her destination at 2.30 pm the next afternoon, following a brief stop at Scarborough. But her safety record was permanently dented when she ran down and sank the fishing coble *Peace* with the loss of her crew of two, off Runswick on the Yorkshire coast on 24 April 1884. The subsequent Court of Enquiry ruled:

The Court, having carefully inquired into the circumstances of the above-mentioned shipping casualty, finds, for the reasons annexed, that the said collision and the consequent loss of life was due to the negligent navigation of the said steam vessel General Havelock, and for which the master and chief officer thereof are responsible. The Court accordingly orders the certificates of Coulson Douglas, the master, and of Christopher Hastie, the chief officer of the General Havelock, to be suspended for six and three months respectively, but recommends that during the periods of such suspension they be allowed first mate's certificates. The Court makes no order as to costs. Dated this 29th day of May 1884.

The Annex to the Inquiry described the incident as follows:

The General Havelock is an iron screw steamship belonging to the port of Sunderland, of 673 tons gross, and 439 tons net register, and is fitted with engines of 99 horse power. She was built at Sunderland in the year 1868, and at the time of the casualty which forms the subject of this inquiry she was the property of Mr Ralph Milbanke Hudson and others, Mr William Hopper Thompson, of No. 52, John Street, Sunderland, being the manager. She left London at about 10.00 am of the 23rd of April last for Sunderland, with six passengers, and about 100 to 150 tons of general merchandise.

Her crew consisted of a master, a chief officer, a carpenter who was an AB, and three other ABs, besides the usual hands in the engine room and steward's department. It seems that the vessel had two wheels on the upper bridge, one worked by hand, the other by steam; but she was generally steered by the latter, one of the officers being always at the wheel. Accordingly on leaving London the master went to the helm, and steered her until they were some three hours below Gravesend, when he resigned it to the chief mate, who kept it till about 5.00 pm or half past, when the master again went to the wheel to steer her through the Yarmouth Roads. At about midnight they arrived off Cromer, when the chief officer was called, and the master then went below, saying he should turn out again between 5 and 6 o'clock to do some painting to his cabin. Instead, however, of getting up as he had intended the master did not turn out until about half past 7, and after having his breakfast he went on deck, and relieved the chief officer, who had then been at the wheel since midnight. At this time the steam steering gear was connected, but the master, wishing to give the engineer an opportunity of inspecting it before they entered Sunderland, cut off the steam connection, and proceeded to steer her by the hand wheel.

At 9.00 am the chief officer, having had his breakfast, and knowing that the master had not done what he had intended to do, came on deck and offered to relieve him at the wheel, an offer which the master at once accepted, and he then went down to his own cabin to go on with the painting. They were then about six miles from Scarborough, the weather was perfectly fine and clear, the sea smooth, and there was a light easterly breeze, and the vessel continued her course, keeping at the distance of about four miles from the shore, with her engines going at full speed, and making about 10 ¾ knots. At this time the watch consisted of the chief officer and two seamen; the two seamen, however, were not giving any attention to the navigation of the vessel, but were engaged abaft the bridge, one painting the lower part of the funnel and the engine room casing, the other cleaning out some paint pots, so that the whole duty of navigating the vessel, including steering her, and keeping a look out, devolved upon the chief officer.

At about 11.00 am one of the men spoke to the chief officer from abaft the bridge, telling him that he had finished the work which he had been set to do, and asking what he was to do next; upon which the chief officer turned round, and told him to go and pick out four or five of the best brushes and clean them. How long he was speaking to the man it is not very easy to say, but on his turning round and looking ahead he observed, at a distance, as he says, of about 100 yards, a small boat right ahead of him, the after part of it being alone visible to him from where he was on the port side of the wheel, the fore part being concealed either by the topgallant forecastle or by the foremast. He at once rushed to the telegraph, and signalled to the engine room to 'stop', and in about a minute afterwards he ordered 'full speed astern'. The helm also seems to have been put hard-a-starboard, but it is not quite clear whether this was done before or after the order to full speed astern, and just as the vessel was beginning to answer her helm she struck the boat amidships, turning her over, and so great was her speed that before she could be stopped she had run about a quarter or half a mile beyond the spot. On seeing what had been done the steamer was backed down towards the floating wreckage, and a boat having been lowered search was made for any of the persons who had been in her, but none could be found.

The Inquiry focussed on the issue of whether the **General Havelock** was properly crewed, and the question '*were the owners culpable?*' The fitting of the second wheel, the steam steering wheel, had allowed the owners to sanction reducing the crew complement from six ABs to just four, or two ABs per watch with one officer, the Captain or the first or second mate. In fact on this voyage the second had been left on the quayside at Sunderland as he '*was the worse for liquor*'. Besides, one of the ABs was also the carpenter and he had his own duties to attend to. Not surprisingly the assessors declared the owners also culpable, although the mate should have had at least one of the two ABs on watch on lookout duties.

In due course the ship was fitted with an electric lighting system for the benefit of the passenger accommodation while every effort had been made to keep the otherwise ageing ship in a fit state for passenger trade on the North Sea. By the early 1890s her owners were described as Ralph Milbanke Hudson, of Sunderland, and others, of which William Thompson, of 27 John Street, Sunderland was the managing owner.

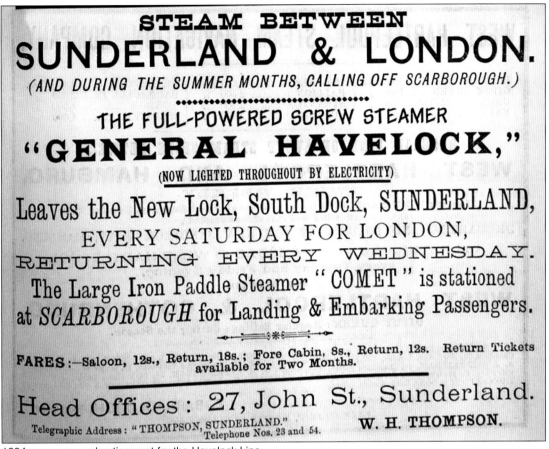

Some ten years after her collision with the coble, on 27 September 1894, the steamer came to grief. Under the banner headline '*General Havelock wrecked*' the *Sunderland Evening Echo* carried the following alarming report:

The **General Havelock** went ashore at 9.40 pm on the rocks near to the old Spelter Works at Hendon. Built in 1868 for passenger and general cargo, she was trading between London and Sunderland calling at Scarborough during the summer months, being occasionally held up for repairs.

On the afternoon of Wednesday she left her wharf in London at about 4.00 pm for the return journey to Sunderland. Pleasant weather was experienced and she called into Scarborough to discharge passengers for the watering place and take other passengers to Sunderland.

The journey was delayed because of contrary winds and she passed Ryhope at 9.00 pm. The tide was low and there was a heavy mist coming from the land. Those on board felt the vessel grating on rocks and soon seen the vessel holed and before they realised the ship was fast, it began to list. Four boats were lowered then the '**Havelock** listed so badly that it was impossible to stand.

Among 30 passengers on board, Captain John Stock and the Officers succeeded in allaying their fears. The Captain and Mate were the last to leave the ship. The second boat, which included passengers and ladies began to fill up with water and the passengers were in a bad plight.

A tug boat, that proved to be the **Norfolk Hero** from Sunderland, was sighted and bore down and enabled everyone to get aboard. It then landed them ashore, some suffering from fright and some fainted when they got ashore. Every assistance was given by the Dock Master and his assistant.

The **General Havelock** filled up with water overnight and the next morning there was very little to see but the engine and boiler. The passengers' and crews' luggage and effects were washed ashore during the early hours and were taken by a crowd of men and women, but the police were called. The vessel belonged to Messrs Hudson of John Street, Sunderland and it was 670 tons.

The subsequent Court of Inquiry stated '*that the stranding was caused by a grave error in judgment on the part of the master, Captain John Stock, in bringing the ship too close to the land, and inshore of the range of the leading light on the Roundhead*'.

Again it is valuable to look in detail at the Annex to the Inquiry to gain insight into the day-to-day workings of the steamer:

She left London about noon on the 26th of September last, having on board a crew of 21 hands all told, and about 50 passengers, and a general cargo, bound for Sunderland, her draught of water at the time being 13 ft 3 ins aft, and 7 ft 9 ins forward. She proceeded on her voyage, and arrived all well at Scarborough at about 1.50 pm of the 27th, where some of her passengers were landed and some others were taken on board, and she then proceeded on to Sunderland, having on board at that time about 50 passengers. At about 6.20 pm Whitby high light was abeam, and a NNW ^{3}/$_4$ W magnetic course was set from Whitby Buoy, which was distant about half a mile. The engines were going full speed, and the vessel was making about 9^1/$_2$ knots. At about 8.30 pm the vessel was abreast of Seaham Harbour, at an estimated distance of a mile, and a N ^{1}/$_2$ W magnetic course was set to bring the vessel to mid-channel, between Hendon Rock Buoy and the Roundhead at the South outlet of the Sunderland Dock. The wind was moderate from the NNW with a NE swell. After running on this course for ten minutes and the master not seeing the light on the Roundhead, he ordered the engines to be eased and the helm to be ported, and the vessel, after paying off to the NNE, struck twice on Hendon Scar, it being about low water at the time.

*The engines were ordered full speed ahead, and then stopped, and the master sent to see if any water was coming in. It was found that there was no water in the engine-room or in the forepeak, but water was rushing into the forehold, and the vessel was settling down fast. Shortly afterwards the second mate reported that there was five feet of water in the fore main hold. Signals of distress were then made by burning blue lights and sounding the steam whistle, and four boats were ordered to be lowered, and the passengers got into them. In answer to the signals the tug **Norfolk Hero**, which was lying in the Sunderland Lock, came out to the assistance of the ship, and the passengers and crew embarked on board of her, all except a passenger named Davis. The chief mate was the last man to leave the **General Havelock**, and before doing so he and one of the passengers named Todd went round the ship's saloon and berths in order to ascertain if anyone was there. They called out several times but received no answer. At this time the electric lights on the vessel were all burning. Upon receiving no answer to their calls they concluded there was no person on board, and they then got into the boat and went on to the tug and were taken to the Sunderland Dock, where they were landed. The man Davis being then missed, the tug with the master and officers of the **General Havelock** returned to the ship with three boats in tow. They went close up to the ship and hailed her several times, but received no answer, the well deck of the ship at that time being level with the water's edge, and the sea breaking over her, it was not considered safe to go on board; and finding that nothing more could be done, the tug returned to the dock and the ship ultimately became a total wreck. The body of the man Davis was subsequently washed on shore at Seaham Harbour.*

Evidence that was teased out during questioning included the fact that the vessel had three compasses, one on the upper bridge by which the course was set and steered, one in the wheel house on the lower bridge, and one on the companion-house top and that these were last adjusted by Mr Postgate, compass adjuster, off the Tyne in June. The master periodically verified the compasses by making good his courses from headland to headland.

It was agreed that the **General Havelock** had been navigated properly but as the Roundhead Light had not been seen as the ship was too close to shore and below its arc, use of the lead would have been prudent. As for the missing passenger:

This man appears to have been imbecile, and he was put in the charge of a steward by his friends in London; he was brought on deck after the vessel struck, and a life-belt fastened on him, and he was told to remain near the main hatch until the boats were ready. It appears he made two attempts to get into the boats, and it was supposed that he had got into one of them, but in the darkness it could not be ascertained, and he was not missed until the passengers were all disembarked at the dock. The mate and one of the passengers went round the ship, all the electric lights being then burning, and examined the cabins and berths, but could find no one.

The stranding of the **General Havelock** and her subsequent wrecking on the Scar left Ralph Hudson without a ship to operate his passenger service. An order was immediately placed with James Laing at Sunderland for the design and construction of a replacement steamer. The third **General Havelock** was launched on 25 May 1895 and delivered ready for her maiden voyage in July. She was a handsome vessel with a steel hull, three masts (schooner rigged) and an elliptical stern. She was 201 feet long by 28 feet breadth. Her engines were built by George Clark of Southwick, Sunderland, of the triple compound inverted direct-acting surface-condensing type, with cylinders of 19½, 30 and 50 inches diameter and a stroke of 36 inches. These provided 200 nominal horse power to sustain a service speed of 12 knots. The two boilers worked at 160 pounds per square inch. The new yacht-like *General Havelock* commenced her career working between Sunderland and Shadwell Basin, London, and quickly became popular with shippers and the travelling public alike.

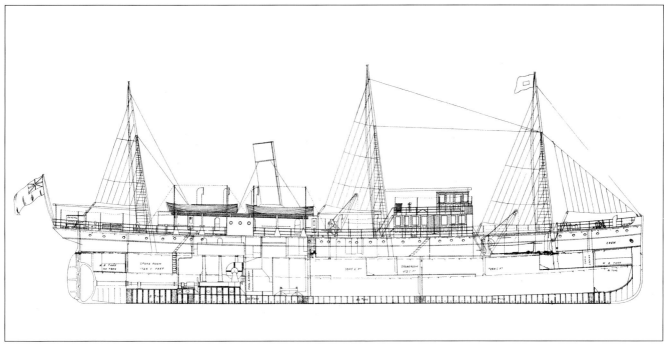

The builder's sectional drawing of the third *General Havelock* (1895).

There was clearly a problem for Hudson in paying the bills as no sooner was the new *General Havelock* launched than he started to sell off 4/20th shares in the ship. At the beginning of July, six weeks after the launch, Ralph Milbanke Hudson sold 4/20th shares respectively to William Hopper Thompson, local ship-owner and James Laing the shipbuilder. Again in December 1898 two further 4/20th parcels were sold by Hudson, this time to George Winlow Hudson, described as a ship-owner and James Laing & Company. On the death of Thompson in 1900, his share was taken up by John Ness and William Edward Sparks, ship-owner and stockbroker respectively. Ralph Hudson also owned a fleet of tramp steamers (see below) which were comparatively successful at this time. In order to shield those interests from potential loss making on the Havelock Line service, the paddle steamer *Comet* and the *General Havelock* and her successor were registered under the ownership of W H Hudson from 1891, certainly through to 1895 and possibly beyond.

Almost a year after she was commissioned, 26 July 1896, the new *General Havelock* was in collision at South Docks, Sunderland, with the collier *County Durham*. The *County Durham* sank while the *General Havelock* suffered only damaged bows; there were no injuries. On 26 June 1897 the *General Havelock* sailed to Southampton to pick up passengers to view the Royal Naval Review at Spithead. The charter fee remained unpaid and litigation followed in the High Court. Later that year, on 24 October, she stranded while on passage up the River Thames in foggy weather but was safely refloated on the flow tide within two hours. On 20 November 1899, while off Rainham in the Thames, she was in collision with the *Fishren*, of Manchester, causing damage to both vessels, but they both continued up river under their own power.

The ship still called off Scarborough in summer and during the main fish-landing season. The *Comet* was sold in May 1897. Local steamers were taken under contract to act as tender. In 1897 the contract for tendering the *General Havelock* was awarded to Captain Evans at a rate of £10 per week. Captain Evans' steamer was the *Mary Ellen*, dating from 1875, but 'thoroughly overhauled in 1896 at a cost of £1,300'. She was sold to J Burns of West Hartlepool that winter and as the *Larmont* again acted as tender to the *General Havelock* throughout 1898 and 1899. In subsequent years the duty of ship's tender fell to locally-owned cobles.

The late Victorian depression had worn away at Hudson's resources and coupled with the loss of one ship and the building of another the Havelock Line was desperate for cash. Despite Hudson having offloaded much of the value of the ship to others he was clearly under pressure to sell her to pay back his investors. As it happened the Royal Mail Steam Packet Company had an urgent need for a small inter-colonial steamer for their Trinidad station to provide connections with the big mail steamers to London and the Pacific. The sale was almost inevitable; the new *General Havelock* was sold to Royal Mail Steam Packet Company, London, in

1901. She was renamed **Kennet**. Royal Mail later sold her in 1915 to Sun Shipping Co Ltd (Mitchell, Cotts & Co, managers), London, and she was given the name **Sunhill**. In September she was taken up for use as an accommodation ship by the Admiralty, only being discharged in June 1920. Michell, Cotts sold her in June 1928 for £20,000 to T W Ward for breaking up.

The **General Havelock** (1895) on her morning approach to the Thames. She was later sold to the Royal Mail Steam Packet Company to become the Caribbean branch liner **Kennet**.

(From an oil painting by the author, by permission L Gowans)

Ralph Hudson had also built up a fleet of seven ships for the global tramp market by 1895 (see Appendix 2 Fleet Lists). In 1895 he took delivery of his third ship to be given the name **Westmeath**, from C S Swan and Hunter at Wallsend on the Tyne. She was a steel-hulled triple expansion engined ship of 6,850 tons gross and modern in every way. Thereafter, the fleet was limited to just a few ships as several had been sold and others lost. Bearing in mind that there was a depression at the time, prices received would have been low. In 1898 Hudson bought two large iron-hulled steamers from William Kish of Sunderland. These were the **Queensland**, 3,892 tons gross and the **Melbourne**, 3,819 tons gross. The **Queensland** was reported on fire at Gibraltar in July 1906 but was insured for £23,000 and was fully repaired and put back into service. In 1913 Hudson's **Leitrim** was wrecked and then in October the **Melbourne** was wrecked in the Philippines. The **Queensland** carried on as before until she was sold for further service in 1913 and R M Hudson ceased to operate as a ship-owner.

But in 1901, Hudson again found himself with an established coastal shipping service, plenty of goodwill but no ship. So in 1901 the coastal company was at a low ebb, although Hudson searched the secondhand market for a suitable ship for his North Sea service, none was forthcoming. Again ships were chartered in to maintain the service as best as possible in order to maintain the goodwill of the company, but the service was erratic and offered only a few passenger berths.

Eventually a deal was struck with the Goole-based shipping company, Gregory B Wadsworth, for the purchase of its steamer **Leona**. The **Leona** had a compound engine and had been built by J Reid & Company at Port Glasgow in 1884. She had a left-handed propeller so that on going forward it turned anticlockwise, rather than clockwise. Initial advertising on the part of Hudson showed a three-masted steamer, but purchase of this ship, whose identity remains unknown, did not take place. Charles Waine describes the two-masted **Leona** in his book *Coastal and Short Sea Liners* (note that the three-masted illustration accompanying this text in Waine's book is the **General Havelock** that was sold in 1901 to become **Kennet** and not the **Leona**):

Leona... [was] completed by J Reid, Port Glasgow for the Humber Steam Shipping Company, Goole which was taken over by the Goole Steam Shipping Company in 1895. Her displacement was about 1,400 tons of which 670 could be cargo. She was purchased by R M Hudson junior, Sunderland and renamed [the General Havelock] in 1904. She became an institution on the London-Sunderland trade...

The layout is basically that of a two hatch, engines aft steamer with accommodation aft and around the after hatch. There were berths for 74 first and 72 second class passengers. She was very well appointed... she had good ballast capacity when carrying light cargoes. She was designed for loading and discharge on the port side. The cranes were primarily rigged to hoist cargo in and out of the holds which had been

The fourth **General Havelock** (1884) at South Dock, Sunderland, awaiting departure.

carried or wheeled aboard through the doors in the bulwarks in the case of the forward hold. The weight of the cranes on the port side was probably offset by displacing the boilers a little to starboard. The steam driven fan, part of Howden's forced draught system for the boilers, just introduced when she was built, was also placed on that side. She was powered by a Kincaid-built compound [engine] with cylinders 19 inch and 10 inch by 36 inch stroke.

She was owned by R M Hudson and Son (Ralph and Alfred Hudson). Alfred George Milbanke Hudson was the son of the Ralph Milbanke Hudson. He married Amelia Maria of Lough Ine, Co Cork. Interestingly her Irish background is reflected in the nomenclature of the associated fleet of tramp steamers owned by the Hudsons (Appendix 2).

No sooner had the latest **General Havelock** taken up service when on 28 May 1904, the local press reported:

*Messrs R. M. Hudson, of Sunderland, on Monday received information that their steamer, the ss **General Havelock**, had collided with the French steamer **Helene**, off Hartlepool, on Saturday night, and that seven of the French seamen were drowned. The **General Havelock** left the Wear on Saturday night on her usual voyage to London, with cargo and passengers. The collision occurred some two or three hours after Sunderland had been left, and it is gathered that the foreign vessel was damaged to such an extent that she went down immediately.*

*The **General Havelock** stood by and picked up several of the sailors belonging to the French vessel. Seven others, it appears, were drowned. The **General Havelock** apparently sustained no very serious damage, for her skipper, Captain Stock, continued his voyage to the Thames. The **Helene** was in command of Captain Teste. She was bound from Rouen to West Hartlepool with iron ore, and was a regular trader to West Hartlepool.*

The steamer did settle into a routine and quickly began to live up to her reputation as an institution in her own right. Advertisements from summer 1909 indicate that the ship sailed from the New Lock, South Dock, on Saturdays at a time between 8.00 am and 1.00 pm depending on tides, and called at Scarborough in the afternoon, and leaving London East Dock (New Gravel Lane Entrance) on Wednesday and calling at Scarborough the following morning. '*Cobles leave the Lighthouse Pier, Scarbro', (weather permitting) half an hour previous to Scarbro' times, landing and embarking passengers FREE OF CHARGE*'. Her regular master for many years was Captain John G Stock; he was presented with a gold watch by the underwriters for navigating his ship safely into Sunderland under difficult conditions on the night of Thursday 7 July 1910 without any assistance. In 1911 the **General Havelock** was reboiled, her original boilers built by Main Wallace & Company of Glasgow having served her well.

Negotiations were carried out during early 1912 by Furness Withy & Company for the purchase of the Havelock Line, its steamer and its goodwill on behalf of the Tyne-Tees Steam Shipping Company. The deal was completed on 1 January 1913. The buff and black-topped funnel of her former owners was over-painted in Tyne-Tees colours although she continued her former trade under the Havelock Line brand complete with seasonal calls at Scarborough. After the Great War she was transferred to the Continental routes while the Middlesbrough steamer called at Sunderland and in season some sailings also called at Scarborough. The **General Havelock** was later deemed uneconomical and sold for further trading under the Algerian flag in 1923. Algeria's gain was very much Sunderland's loss; the Havelock Line was no more and passengers and shippers increasingly turned to Newcastle for a regular link with London.

The **General Havelock** (1884) seen after 1912 when she wore the colours of the Tyne-Tees Steam Shipping Company but still plying her trade from Sunderland.

(National Maritime Museum)

From: *A dictionary of contemporary biographies in Durham at the opening of the twentieth century, 1906*

Ralph Milbanke Hudson – J P, Oak Lea, Sunderland; son of Ralph Hudson of Sunderland; born at Sunderland, 9 December 1813. Senior member of the firm of R M Hudson & Sons, Ship-owners, Tavistock House, Borough Road, Sunderland; Justice of the Peace for the County of Durham, and for Sunderland; Member of the River Wear Commission, and until lately of the Committee of Lloyds; Knight of the Danish order of the Dannebrog; formerly Vice-Consul for the United States, the Hanse towns, and Russia and Denmark. Married Elizabeth, daughter of the late Thomas Robson, author of the *British Herald*, and has issue surviving two sons and five daughters, of whom the two sons, Ralph Milbanke and Alfred George Milbanke, are in partnership with him.

Alfred George Milbanke Hudson – 10, The Cedars, Sunderland; son of Ralph Milbanke Hudson; born at East Boldon, 26 December 1855; educated at Darlington. Member of the firm of R M Hudson & Sons, ship-owners. Married Amelia Maria, fourth daughter of John Richard Hedges Becher, of Lough Ine, Co Cork.

Ralph Milbanke Hudson Junior – Cocken Hall, Fence Houses; son of R M Hudson, Oak Lea, Sunderland; born at Boldon, Co Durham in 1849, educated privately, and abroad. Member of the firm R M Hudson & Sons, ship-owners, Tavistock House, Sunderland; Member of the River Wear Commissioners since 1882; one of the Committee of Lloyds Registry. Married in 1883, Eliza Westropp, daughter of Graham Pallisser, of Prospect House, Plymouth, and has one daughter, Winnifred Milbanke, married to Gerard Chipchase Roberts, of Beechwood House, Sowerby Bridge, Yorkshire, and one son, Ralph Pallisser Milbanke.

CHAPTER 5

THE GREAT WAR

The Admiralty reported on Saturday 22 December 1917 'The British Armed Boarding Steamer **Stephen Furness** *(1,712 tons) has been torpedoed and sunk in the Irish Channel. Six officers and 95 men were lost.'*

At 11.00 pm on 4 August 1914 Britain declared war on Germany in response to the inevitable decline in political relationships in Europe following the assassination of Archduke Franz Ferdinand at Sarajevo on 28 June. The critical Tyne-Tees service at the declaration of war was the Newcastle to Hamburg passenger and cargo sailings operated by the **Juno** and **New Londoner**. James Layton describes the outcome in the *Tees Packet*:

*At the end of her last pre-war voyage she [**New Londoner**] arrived at Newcastle on 30 July 1914 and was expected to sail to Hamburg on 1 August, however, with the threat of war in the air, she remained in the Tyne. Her running mate, the **Juno** of 1882, was not so fortunate. She arrived at Hamburg on 31 July and was due to sail for the Tyne on 1 August but she was delayed and was still at the German port when the war commenced on 4 August. The company was unable to contact the **Juno** in those final days of peace and it was not until 11 August, when they received a telegram from a passenger who had reached Esbjerg, that they were informed that the **Juno** was in German hands, the passengers had been released and had crossed into Denmark and the crew had been taken prisoner. Eventually the crew were taken to a prisoner of war camp at Ruhleben where they spent the next 4¹/₂ years.*

The **New Londoner** (1912) at the eve of the Great War at the passenger terminal at Newcastle beneath the CWS Building.

(National Maritime Museum)

The **Juno** was abandoned to her insurers, the North of England Protection and Indemnity Association of Newcastle, in mid-January 1915. At the end of the war she was returned to Britain and sold by the Insurers through the London brokers Abraham Lazarus to Portuguese owners who renamed her **Afra**. She had numerous subsequent owners and names. She crossed the Atlantic in 1921 when she was bought by the United States Shipping Board and allocated to James R Armstrong of Colon under the Panamanian flag. She later raised the Nicaraguan flag for a variety of different Texas-based owners and was eventually sold for demolition at Pascagoula, Mississippi, in March 1935.

The Rotterdam service operated by the **Teessider** was maintained into the war but was downgraded to two or three round trips a month rather than the peace time weekly service. This was a result of slow turn rounds due to the shortage of dock labour at Newcastle. The **Teessider** was replaced by the **Grenadier** on the single ship service in September 1915.

The *Teessider* (1909) alongside at Schiehaven, Rotterdam.   *(Harold Appleyard collection)*

The day after war was declared, the **Stephen Furness** had left the Tyne for London with 200 passengers aboard. With the Shields still clearly visible astern the steamer was hailed by a Royal Navy warship and ordered to turn about and disembark all passengers before resuming her voyage. While small numbers of passengers were allowed thereafter, none was carried after Christmas 1914 other than military personnel. The **New Londoner**, displaced from the Hamburg run, had joined the **Richard Welford** and **Stephen Furness** on the Newcastle to London service, three ships being needed at war to do the job two could do in peace time, primarily again because of shortages of dock labour. Also during this early period of the war the cargo steamer **Howden** was requisitioned by the Admiralty.

The **Richard Welford** (1908) alongside at Newcastle*.*   *(R Gibson, George Nairn collection)*

In early December both the **Richard Welford** and **Stephen Furness** were chartered by the nation and left the Tyne. HMS **Richard Welford** was commissioned as Armed Boarding Steamer MI.18 and equipped with two 12 pounder guns and painted in a striking dazzle camouflage. For most of her years in service she was stationed at Gibraltar during which time she was torpedoed, but blessed with fortune as the torpedo failed to explode. She returned to Southampton briefly for repairs. Among many acts of bravery HMS **Richard Welford** was able to salvage the Greek steamer **Salaminia**, towing her to safety during 2 and 3 January 1916. **Stephen Furness** initially became a Squadron Supply Ship under the Blue Ensign. In May the following year **Stephen**

Furness became a Store Ship based at Invergordon, and later at Peterhead, and she served as such until 7 March 1916 when she was also taken in hand for conversion to Armed Boarding Ship MI.23. As HMS **Stephen Furness** she was armed with two 4.7 inch guns; she was a far cry from the luxuriously fitted coastal passenger liner that she had been. The weight of the new gun emplacements and the guns themselves required the ships to be heavily ballasted which in turn made them stiff in a heavy sea. Both were sadly missed on the London service, but generous recompense was received by the owners by way of charter fees, and the **Sir William Stephenson** was transferred from the Rotterdam service and placed on the London run in their stead.

An advertising image of the **Stephen Furness** (1910).   *(Harold Appleyard collection)*

Armed Boarding Steamers were essentially sentries posted at strategic locations such as the Western Approaches and the approach to the North Channel in order to intercept and identify shipping that may be operating on behalf of the enemy. They tended to work alongside the Cruiser Squadrons. Their primary role was examination duties. For example, three Armed Boarding Steamers were based at Aden to monitor shipping movements. The job itself was not as hazardous as it seems, the main danger was standing almost hove-to in heavy weather trying to maintain station while the ship sustained damage from the seas and the crew suffered from boredom through the numerous long periods of inactivity. Most of the Armed Boarding Steamers were converted cross-channel ferries, largely railway-owned ships, some from the Isle of Man Steam Packet Company and also the nearly-new **Royal Scot** owned by the Edinburgh & London Shipping Company.

An early Tyne-Tees casualty in 1915 was the **New Oporto** which was wrecked off Haisborough Sands on 8 January. She was a casualty of bad weather and the blackout, a loss that would not have happened in peace time. She had left Middlesbrough the previous day bound for London and was making passage outside Haisborough Sands to avoid known mine fields.

But it was not all bad news. The replacement for the **Juno** had been planned early in 1914 long before the Germans had taken her at Hamburg at the outbreak of war. The order for a third **Teessider**-class ship had been agreed with S P Austin & Sons at Sunderland on 22 April 1914 for a vessel of about 1,400 tons deadweight, equipped to carry 100 passenger and with a service speed of 12$\frac{1}{2}$ knots. The tender for £29,500 stipulated delivery on or before New Year's Eve that same year. However, with war declared in August the shipbuilders reported that the delivery date would have to be put back due to priority work for Government and the loss of men from the yard who had been called to war. Eventually on 22 April 1915 the ship was launched with the name **Novocastrian** by her sponsor Mrs R J Thompson, wife of one of the Tyne-Tees company directors.

The **Novocastrian** was a single deck ship with four watertight compartments. She had the same raised foc'sle and quarterdeck as her two near sisters, was 235 feet long and 34 feet in breadth. Like the **Teessider** she had just two holds, one forward of the bridge and engine compartment, and one aft. These were served by two derricks rigged on the aft side of the foremast, two deck cranes aft of the forward hold, and two derricks on the aft side of the mainmast which was at the after end of the bridge deck. Her triple expansion engines were built by Richardson & Westgarth & Company at Sunderland, with cylinders of 21$\frac{1}{2}$, 35 and 59 inches and the stroke was 39 inches. She differed from the **Teessider** and the earlier **New Londoner** in appearance as the main deck and boat deck were plated in under the bridge giving the ship a squarer profile. She was delivered in wartime grey with three embossed hoops on her funnel ready to define the margins of the white over red bands of her owner's markings. Passenger accommodation was completed to the contract specification and comprised 54 first class and 28 second class berths on the bridge and main decks. Sadly, as events were to unfold, none of this accommodation was ever used and her funnel never carried the company colours.

A remarkable and rare photograph of the **Novocastrian** (1915), probably on trials. She was launched on 3 February 1915 and mined and sunk on 5 October just eight months later.

(Harold Appleyard collection)

The **Novocastrian** was put in the charge of Captain Bruce on delivery and she joined the **New Londoner** and **Sir William Stephenson** running between the Tyne and the Thames with overlong stays in both ports due to the shortage of dock labour. The ships tended to interchange with the Tees to London ships at that time but schedules were difficult to maintain and deliveries for shippers somewhat haphazard. But very quickly two of the three Tyne-based ships were to be lost to enemy action; the **Sir William Stephenson** on 29 August and two months later the brand new **Novocastrian** on 5 October 1915.

The North Sea coast had been repeatedly visited by German minelayers at the start of the war. Initially it was possible to see where the mine fields were being laid, but use of minelayers disguised as innocent merchantmen and discharge of mines by submarines made this more difficult as the year 1915 progressed. The **Sir William Stephenson** was unfortunate to strike one of the mines on 29 August when she was near the Cockle Lightship on a voyage south to London. Two of her crew died when the mine exploded but other injuries were fortunately light. It is believed that the mine detonated by the **Sir William Stephenson** had been laid the night before by UB 6 under the command of Matthias Graf von Schmettow.

Although the **Sir William Stephenson** was disabled, a tow was quickly arranged and she was brought into the shallows adjacent to Great Yarmouth Roads and allowed to settle on the bottom. Ideas of subsequent salvage were thwarted by the early autumn gales and the ship soon became damaged. In December the steamer **Adams** collided with the wreck and the **Sir William Stephenson** was finally declared a total loss. The **Adams** was a substantial cargo steamer of 2,223 tons gross owned by J Adams & Sons; in October 1917 she too was lost to a mine.

The **Novocastrian** was even less fortunate. On leaving the Thames she had been given a message by an Admiralty trawler to stay well outside the buoyed limit of navigation inshore of which were the known minefields. The same message was given by a second armed trawler off the Suffolk coast and again by a third abeam of Lowestoft. Almost immediately, in calm conditions in the late morning, just after the third trawler had left her, the **Novocastrian** hit a floating mine and immediately began to take on water at an alarming rate. Aware that she was sinking fast, Captain Bruce gave the order to abandon the flagship of the Tyne-Tees fleet which sank rapidly; three minutes after exploding the mine all that was left was wreckage and the entire ship's crew. The crew were picked up in record time as well, with the Chief Engineer, ship's carpenter and one of the fireman alone requiring medical attention when they were taken ashore. Again a submarine had been responsible for the attack, German submarine UB 7 commanded by Franz Wäger having previously laid mines 3¹/₂ miles east-south-east of Lowestoft.

These losses meant that Tyne-Tees no longer had enough ships available to maintain the basic London service. A plea was made to the Admiralty to release the **Howden** back to her owners but this was rejected. Tenders were even invited for a replacement for the **Novocastrian**, the company aware that it would otherwise have difficulties in resuming its passenger services once peace reigned again. Costs had escalated and estimates of over £54,000 were received from two Sunderland builders including S P Austin & Sons. Price was clearly an issue and the idea of a new build was dropped in favour of the secondhand market. The overall shortage of ships due to war losses had already almost doubled the cost of new and secondhand ships. The **Wendy** was inspected and deemed suitable for the east coast service and was duly purchased at the seemingly expensive price of £35,000 in November 1915. Her owners were George V Turnbull & Company of Leith, then wholly owned by Furness Withy, so it may be that the price paid was in fact reasonable given the Furness Withy still held some shares in Tyne-Tees. Furness Withy, however, had by then been selling its Tyne-Tees shares for some time on the open market. The two remaining ships in the Turnbull fleet, **Peter Pan** and **Togston**, were merged into the Furness Withy fleet in 1916.

The **Howden** (1909) resplendent in her civilian colours after her post-war refit; the brown superstructure was finally replaced by white.

(From an oil painting by the author)

To make matters even worse for the operation of the Tyne-Tees company, the **Teessider** was requisitioned by the Admiralty early in 1916 to act as a stores carrier. This left the London services from Newcastle, Stockton and Middlesbrough even more difficult to maintain.

On 30 July 1916 the **Claudia** was lost off Lowestoft. She was on a voyage from Middlesbrough to London with general cargo and steel, and was sunk by a mine laid by the German submarine UC-1, commanded by Kurt Ramien, 8¹/₂ miles south east of Lowestoft. Three lives were lost in the incident. Loss of the **Claudia** only served to exacerbate the company's shortage of vessels, but fortunately the **Teessider** had returned from her duties as a stores carrier in June and was able to take up the Middlesbrough to London via Stockton run.

In September 1916 the company tug **WDS** was chartered to J Batey & Son of Newcastle. This was the end of tug operation within the company as the vessel was sold to Batey after the war.

Meanwhile the *Grenadier* had been maintaining the Rotterdam service as best she could. Sadly, on 23 February 1917, she was torpedoed and sunk by an enemy submarine when she was in a position 6 miles east-north-east of the Shipwash Light Vessel. No prior warning of the attack had been given and not surprisingly eight men, including the ship's master, lost their lives. The temptation to return the *Teessider* to the Rotterdam service must have been considerable, but sense prevailed and she was retained on the strategically important coastal service to London. As a consequence, sailings to Rotterdam were suspended and the Tyne-Tees Steam Shipping Company became a coastal operator with no sailings offered to the Continent. The sense in the decision to retain the *Teessider* on the coastal service was underlined when she was again requisitioned in June 1917, putting the London services under even more strain.

The two Armed Boarding Steamers HMS *Richard Welford* and HMS *Stephen Furness*, the latter under the command of Lieutenant Commander T M Winslow, Royal Naval Reserve, remained on duty as before. HMS *Stephen Furness* had been on duty in the White Sea until the summer of 1917 when she returned to home waters. HMS *Stephen Furness*, was on passage from Lerwick, which port she had left at 2.00 pm on 11 December, to Liverpool in order to receive essential repairs and maintenance and many of her crew were looking forward to a well-earned spell of leave. She never made it to Liverpool as at 4.15 pm 13 December she was torpedoed by the German submarine UB-64 some 15 miles north-west of Peel on the Isle of Man. Another five hours steaming and she would have been in the safe waters of Liverpool Bay.

The Armed Boarding Steamer HMS *Richard Welford* in full camouflage.

(Harold Appleyard collection)

The torpedo struck on the starboard side between the bridge and the funnel, and the gallant steamer immediately started sinking. Damage was considerably greater than anticipated and before even the lifeboats could be lowered, she suddenly and without warning sank in only a few minutes. The speed of the sinking was tragic and many of those still on board perished while others died in the sea. A total of 101 lives, ship's company as well as numerous military personnel, including six members of the Royal Canadian Naval Volunteer Reserve, were lost in the sinking (see World War I Casualty Lists at http://www.naval-history.net/xDKCas1917-12Dec.htm). The few survivors held on to wreckage until they were picked up at 6.30 pm by a passing trawler which then took them to Holyhead, some by then suffering from exposure. There were just twelve survivors that reached shore, including one member of the RCNVR.

Tragic though the loss of HMS *Stephen Furness* was it was a double loss to Tyne-Tees. Commercially they lost the charter income from the Admiralty and would have to wait until after the war for compensation for the ship. An end to the war was in sight and Tyne-Tees viewed the *Stephen Furness* as the core of the London passenger service from the Tyne. The Directors worried that it would now be all but impossible to get a passenger service up and running once hostilities ended and a deep concern for the future survival of the company persisted in the Board Room.

The **General Havelock** was in trouble due to severe weather in January 1918. The *Sunderland Evening Echo* later recalled the incident in an article published on 16 October 1987:

*The SS **General Havelock** was driven ashore at Warham Hole, close to Blackeney Harbour, in a north easterly gale. A powerful tug was sent from Immingham in the Humber to tow the steamer off, but soon after the tug had put to sea a terrible gale and blizzard set in, driving the tug ashore about half a mile to the eastward of the **General Havelock**. The Blackeney Lifeboat took the [tug] crew off.*

*After the motor pumps were sent down from London, which no doubt saved the ship, the **General Havelock** was towed off by two Government boats. The tug was still lying ashore but was got afloat afterwards.*

The agreed Armistice between the Allies and Germany came into effect on 11 November 1918 at 11.00 am. It was another six months before the Treaty of Versailles was agreed and signed, but peace once again reigned. Britain had virtually lost a whole generation of men while the survivors slowly headed towards collecting their 'demob' suit and returned home to look for work.

The Tyne-Tees Steam Shipping Company survived with only seven of the thirteen ships it had owned at the start of the war. It had been obliged to suspend all its Continental services and had struggled to maintain even a weekly departure to London. Nevertheless those weekly departures contributed greatly to the war effort by transporting steel, chemicals, and other manufactured goods as well as a great deal of coal south, returning with a variety of essential goods and foodstuffs to nurture the north-east of England. In addition there were many military cargoes to be carried, and these ranged from cased aviation fuel and munitions to less volatile stores, vehicles and other essential military equipment.

The **Teessider** and **Howden** were returned from Admiralty duty in a reasonably fit state to resume civilian duties. The **Richard Welford** meantime, lay in a long queue awaiting decommissioning and was only returned to her owners in August 1919 after extensive refurbishment and renovation of her passenger accommodation. She now had 94 first class berths and 316 second class. She retained extensive support and gun emplacement fittings although the emplacements had been cut down to deck level.

The Tyne-Tees company had received good charter rates from the Admiralty and had held war insurance premiums on all the ships it lost in commercial service save for the **Juno**. It was a company with cash in the bank but too few ships with which to start to rebuild its pre-war business. It was also a company that emerged into a new world where commercial opportunity for international trade was lacking with Britain, Germany and other European nations brought to financial austerity by the costs incurred in the war years. Costs of new ships had doubled during the war and, with the post-war shortage of shipping, secondhand purchases were equally difficult to fund. The company would, for the moment, have to make do with what it had until such time as commercial and trading prospects both in Britain and the Continent, improved. The future looked bleak indeed.

CHAPTER 6

THE POST-WAR YEARS

"...the war ended on the foamy crest of inflation....shipping became a vast speculation."
(From Tynesider, Arthur Monro Sutherland's memoirs)

The Tyne-Tees Steam Shipping Company emerged from the Great War with a sadly depleted fleet having been dependent for much of the War on revenue from its coastal services between Newcastle, Hartlepool, Sunderland and the Tees ports with London, and with charter fees from the Admiralty. It was deprived of its Continental services either through necessity, or in the case of the Dutch services because of a shortage of available ships. If the company was going to survive at all it had to achieve two goals: the first was the reinstatement of the passenger services between the north-east of England and London, and the second was the need to re-establish its cargo and passenger services to the Continent. To do this it still had to overcome its chronic lack of ships, the fleet comprised just seven vessels. Among other war losses were the flagships of the fleet, the **Stephen Furness**, and the brand new passenger and cargo steamer **Novocastrian** which had hardly been allowed to start its career when it was sunk by a mine.

The **New Londoner** was left in charge of the Newcastle to London service which strived to become weekly. In August 1919 she was joined by the **Richard Welford**, freshly refurbished following her military duties, and the London service resumed its pre-war twice-weekly roster. Business slackened into the winter period and from autumn 1919 until the following spring the **New Londoner** made several trips from Newcastle to Rotterdam and Antwerp, from Middlesbrough to Antwerp with pig iron and from Middlesbrough to London with steel products.

The **Richard Welford** (1908) at the passenger terminal at Newcastle Quayside.

When the **Teessider** became available she returned to the Tees to London route. In March 1919 the **General Havelock**, with her large deadweight, resumed the Newcastle to Antwerp and Rotterdam services, the schedule being 'as cargo offers'. Her role as the Sunderland to London passenger and cargo ship was now over. From December 1919 onwards, as cargo shipments increased, the **Teessider** diverted from her London duties to supplement the **General Havelock**'s routine. From March 1920 she made a regular weekly sailing to Rotterdam, her role on the Middlesbrough to London route being taken up by the **Buccaneer** on her release by the Admiralty. The **Buccaneer** called weekly also at Sunderland as the direct successor to the pre-war Havelock Line service that had been operated by the **General Havelock**.

Furness Withy had been systematically selling its ownership in Tyne-Tees while others had been increasing their shareholding. This came to light in 1919 when Newcastle tramp shipowner Sir Arthur Monro Sutherland gained control of the company. New blood on an established board can be difficult but in this case Sutherland appears to have been exactly what was required – forward looking, expansionist, yet not over-bullish, and above all a man who was willing to debate his ideas and who respected his fellow Directors.

Sir Arthur Munro Sutherland was born on 2 October 1867, and was the son of Benjamin John Sutherland. The Sutherland family were originally from Thurso in Caithness. Arthur grew up in Newcastle and was educated at the Royal Grammar School which he left at the age of 16. He took a job as junior clerk and with experience from this first job, which exposed him to ship owning and brokering, he determined to own ships himself. His first ship was the **Sutherland** which he bought for £22,700 with a soft loan from his father. In 1896 Sutherland floated the Sutherland Steam Ship Company and he sold a large part of his fleet during the inflation bubble after the Great War. The cash he now held was partly used to invest in the Tyne-Tees Steam Shipping Company and shortly afterwards also in the *Newcastle Chronicle*. He was elected Lord Mayor of Newcastle in 1918.

Sutherland's Managing Director at Tyne-Tees was Robert Mason, a man of similar disposition to Sutherland himself. The Board comprised some new faces and some old friends: Frederick Whittock, W B van Haansbergen, Robert Milbanke Hudson junior, C E Pease and R J Thompson. Collectively, they were a sage team that spent money wisely with total disregard for extravagance.

One of the first things Sutherland did was to sanction the sale of the company tug, **WDS**, and the steam wherry **Poodle**, recognising the need for a core product and the out-sourcing of marginal tasks. The **WDS** had been on charter to J Batey & Son and they finally bought the vessel in 1919 for £5,500.

Sutherland was against building new ships as he considered the post-war cost of building was inflationary and that it would return to more cost-effective levels in due course. Consequently, in 1921 the company was able to buy the German steamer **Greif**, a modern cargo vessel which was suitable for the bulk coal and grain trades as well as the break bulk and parcel traffic with berths for twelve passengers. She was given the name **Dunstanburgh**, and placed on the recently revived Newcastle to Hamburg service. Another ship was bought on the secondhand market the following year and given the name **Bamburgh**. She was a smaller vessel than the **Dunstanburgh**, of just 648 tons gross, but was an ideal unit to supplement the passenger and cargo ships operating to London and the Continent. The **Bamburgh** or **Wendy** also maintained a bi-weekly cargo service between London and Middlesbrough.

Free Trade Wharf in the early 1920s with the **Richard Welford** (1908) alongside and the **Dunstanburgh** (1912) at anchor off Hubbuck's Wharf.

Also in 1921 a new headquarters building was opened for the Free Trade Wharf Company which by now normally employed about 500 hands each day. Aptly named Sutherland House it was situated at Broad Street, East 1. The company now had river frontage of 920 feet with seven steamer berths. There were eighteen warehouses with a total capacity of 4 million cubic feet. Many of the warehouses were designed for heavy goods including rubber and grain. There was also ample bonded warehousing and offices for HM Customs staff.

But Sutherland's trump card was convincing his Board in the sustainability of the London passenger trade and placing orders for two new passenger and cargo steamers to maintain it. Since summer 1920 the twice-weekly service between Newcastle Quayside and Free Trade Wharf had been operated by the **Richard Welford** and **New Londoner**, and replacement tonnage would allow these ships to be transferred to Rotterdam and Antwerp duties where additional passenger accommodation was much needed. But the order for new passenger and cargo ships for London was a huge commitment which endorsed Sir Arthur Munro Sutherland's conviction that the passenger trade to London was there to stay. The outcome of this decision was the magnificent coal burning steamers **Hadrian** and **Bernicia** which came into service in June 1923. Oddly they were by no means sisterships, the **Hadrian** was built at Swan Hunter's yard and the **Bernicia** came from Hawthorn Leslie. Both ships had an operational speed of 15 knots to maintain the 24 hour voyage to London.

The **Hadrian** could accommodate 176 first class passengers amidships and 260 second class passengers in the poop while the **Bernicia** had 136 first class berths and room for 100 second class passengers aft in dormitory accommodation. Both ships carried 60 portable berths in the 'tween decks aft during the tourist season as an extension to the 40 second class berths available in the poop. First class cabins had hot and cold running water and a grand oak staircase led up one deck to the lounge which was beneath the bridge with the smoke room aft of the engine casing on the same deck. But the pair was no match for the pre-war luxury of first class aboard the **Stephen Furness**, although they were comfortable ships that quickly gained popularity with the travelling public.

The **Hadrian** (1923) coming up the Thames on a high tide. Although not sisters, her profile was almost identical to that of the **Bernicia**.

(F W Hawks)

The **Bernicia** (1923) in the Thames.

(A Duncan)

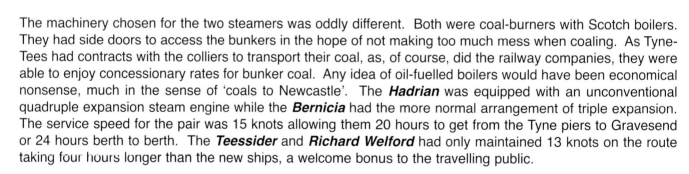

The machinery chosen for the two steamers was oddly different. Both were coal-burners with Scotch boilers. They had side doors to access the bunkers in the hope of not making too much mess when coaling. As Tyne-Tees had contracts with the colliers to transport their coal, as, of course, did the railway companies, they were able to enjoy concessionary rates for bunker coal. Any idea of oil-fuelled boilers would have been economical nonsense, much in the sense of 'coals to Newcastle'. The **Hadrian** was equipped with an unconventional quadruple expansion steam engine while the **Bernicia** had the more normal arrangement of triple expansion. The service speed for the pair was 15 knots allowing them 20 hours to get from the Tyne piers to Gravesend or 24 hours berth to berth. The **Teessider** and **Richard Welford** had only maintained 13 knots on the route taking four hours longer than the new ships, a welcome bonus to the travelling public.

There was cargo space for 100,000 cubic feet on two decks and the shelter deck. There were two hatches forward served by two steam cranes and a 15 ton capacity derrick mounted aft on the foremast. The after hold had one crane and a derrick mounted forward on the mainmast. The ships were attractive to the shippers, both in London and in Newcastle because they had copious holds and rarely had to turn away unbooked cargo and because they tended to stick admirably to their schedule.

Tyne-Tees tended to market the first class accommodation towards the 'Upper Class' clientele and the second class dormitory style accommodation at the 'Lower Class', the working man including members of the armed forces for whom there were concessionary fares. Which end of the ship the 'Middle Class' passenger was supposed to travel in was anybody's guess! One class of traveller was especially canvassed and this was the football fan attending an away match, be he Londoner playing away in the north-east, or Northerner playing away in the south. The fares were cleverly pitched just below the cheap weekend return rail fare while coaches could be arranged at a small increment to the basic fare to get fans to the venue on the ships' arrival at port. The fans had no access to alcohol aboard ship but managed to bring enough aboard most voyages to pass the night away in the appropriate mood; a lost away game was an event that required some steady and concerted drinking as consolation on the way home!

*The Gentleman's Smoke Room aboard **Bernicia** (1923).*

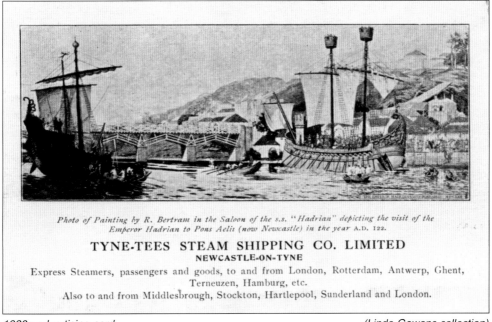

Photo of Painting by R. Bertram in the Saloon of the s.s. "Hadrian" depicting the visit of the Emperor Hadrian to Pons Aelii (now Newcastle) in the year A.D. 122.

TYNE-TEES STEAM SHIPPING CO. LIMITED
NEWCASTLE-ON-TYNE

Express Steamers, passengers and goods, to and from London, Rotterdam, Antwerp, Ghent, Terneuzen, Hamburg, etc.
Also to and from Middlesbrough, Stockton, Hartlepool, Sunderland and London.

1920s advertising card.   *(Linda Gowans collection)*

The new ships displaced the **Teessider** and **Richard Welford** from the London service. They were then deployed on Newcastle to Rotterdam duties upgrading that service to two departures per week with occasional trips to Antwerp. From 23 June 1923 the **New Londoner** became dedicated to the Antwerp service offering a Saturday departure from Newcastle and returning from Antwerp on Tuesdays. She had previously been split between Rotterdam and Antwerp duties. The enhanced passenger capacity on the Antwerp service was very welcome and she often sailed in the summer months with few berths unoccupied.

The morning of 2 August 1923 was one the company could have done without. The **Richard Welford** was discharging cargo from Rotterdam alongside Newcastle Quayside in full view of the company offices and in full view of the comings and goings of the city. With part of her cargo already unloaded, and the remainder no longer evenly distributed, the ship slowly began to list toward the quay until there came a point when it was apparent that the list was not going to recover. Alarm bells were sounded as the ship was rapidly abandoned to the murky waters of the Tyne. And there she lay on her side for all to see, her funnel and masts snapped against the quayside, a deeply embarrassing monument to the Tyne-Tees Steam Shipping Company.

The capsize was caused by a port side cargo door being opened in anticipation of working cargo directly to the quay while discharge proceeded through the hatches. The cargo door at that stage of the tide, however, was still below the level of the quay and could not be used. When the discharge was partly complete and cargo, much of it bagged potatoes, was no longer evenly distributed in the holds, the ship developed a customary list to port and shoreside. As the list increased, little by little, as the unloading proceeded through the hatches, the bottom of the forgotten cargo door became submerged allowing the murky waters of the Tyne to begin to flood the hold. Little could be done to stem the inflow which only served to exacerbate the list and the ship was rapidly evacuated and left to her fate as she heeled over and lay against the quay. She had become quite a delicate ship because of the addition top weight of remnant gun emplacements, an artefact of her service as an Armed Boarding Steamer, and had a common tendency to list slightly to port, but this was by no means the cause of the accident. Sadly one of the firemen, Mr Ralph Hewitt from Wallsend, was drowned as he slept in his bunk. Others fared better and one of the stewardesses reported that she only survived because one of the stewards came to waken her and help her off the ship.

It was not until 23 October 1923 that the **Richard Welford**, mastless, muddy and funnel-less, with a badly damaged bridge deck, was righted and removed to Smith's Dock at North Shields for inspection. The decision was taken to refurbish the ship and after temporary repairs had been effected she left the Tyne on 19 December in tow, bound for Rotterdam and further repairs and rebuilding at a cost of over £12,000. Although little changed in appearance apart from mast heads being reduced by several feet, the ship re-emerged as the **Hethpool** returning to the Tyne in May 1924. Her gross tonnage was significantly increased from the original figure of 1,411 tons to 1,712 tons. The short-lived twice-weekly passenger departure to Rotterdam was maintained as a weekly departure by the **Teessider** assisted by one of the smaller ships, generally cargo only although up to twelve berths were offered depending on which vessel was available. The rebuilt **Hethpool** rejoined the service in time for the summer season minus the majority of her passenger berths.

*Salvaging the **Richard Welford** (1908) at Newcastle Quay, August 1923.*

On the Middlesbrough to London service, calls were resumed at Scarborough in 1923, but for cargo rather than passengers. The Scarborough visits were initiated by the **General Havelock** which had returned to the Middlesbrough to London service in a cargo only capacity. She was occasionally rostered to call into the Fish Dock at Scarborough an hour and a half before high water with a view to having finished her business by one hour after high tide at the latest. On the northward run this meant that she would have to wait off Middlesbrough for the tide so from the end of that year one of the smaller cargo steamers on the Middlesbrough run displaced the **General Havelock** from this duty. The **General Havelock** had become increasingly expensive to operate although her elderly compound engines still maintained a steady 10 knots, and she was put up for sale. Her master, in these her twilight years with the Tyne-Tees company, was Captain R Storm, and it was he who delivered the ship to new owners in Algiers towards the end of the year.

The big cargo steamer **Middlesbro'** was delivered in October 1924 by Hawthorn Leslie at Hebburn. She had been launched at the end of August. She was an imposing looking vessel with two large holds with long hatches forward of the bridge, accommodation and engine compartments, and one hold aft. Each hatch was served by its own derrick, Numbers 1 and 3 mounted aft of the fore and mainmasts, and Number 2 hatch served by a derrick mounted on its own kingpost. The compact crew accommodation was, by all accounts, 'cramped but cosy'. The **Middlesbro'** was equipped with the now ubiquitous triple expansion engine which, of course, was coal-fired. She was an extremely useful vessel being able to deputise both on the Continental routes and on the English coastal services.

The year 1925 saw a number of changes to the fleet. Firstly, C Rowbotham's cargo ship **Helmsman** was purchased and given the name **Cragside**. The **Helmsman** had been completed by Wood Skinner at Bill Quay, Gateshead, in May 1903. She too had a coal-fired triple expansion engine which provided a handsome service speed of 11 knots. She had one long hold forward, suitable for stowing long steel girders, served by two derricks. Engines and accommodation were aft with a vertical funnel placed abaft the bridge. She was a direct replacement for the **Howden**, although six years younger in age, the **Howden** when new could only manage 9 knots and with age could struggle to maintain even that. The **Howden** was sold for further service and hoisted the Norwegian flag; she was wrecked on the coast of south-west France four years later on passage from the Westman Islands, off the south coast of Iceland, on a voyage to Vigo with a cargo of salt cod.

The heavily loaded **Middlesbro'** (1924) showing her cargo handling gear.

(Captain J F Puyvelde, Harold Appleyard collection)

Tyne-Tees also took delivery of a pair of handsome shelter-deck passenger-cargo steamers in 1925, the sisters **Lindisfarne** and **Newminster**. Again built by Hawthorn Leslie, the new ships were designed with a 12 knot cruising speed that schedules now demanded. The **Lindisfarne** was the first to go down the ways on 7 May followed a month later by the **Newminster** on 3 June, and they were delivered in June and July respectively. They had a gross tonnage of 967 tons and were equipped with berths for 12 first class passengers. There were two holds forward and one aft of the central island and they were single deckers with a shelter deck.

The **Lindisfarne** (1925) outward bound, stoking up the boilers.

Passenger accommodation was situated on the main deck and there was a saloon provided for them forward under the bridge. Passengers otherwise had the freedom of the ship except when cargo was being worked on deck. Like the **Middlesbro'** before them, the new sisters were versatile and capable of operating on any of the company services although primarily designed for the Continental routes, but unlike the **Middlesbro'** capable of offering twelve berths in six two-berth cabins.

The introduction of the new ships allowed the elderly **Buccaneer** to be sold, best remembered running for Furness Withy on its Hartlepool to London service. Even though she was 35 years old, she readily attracted a buyer and traded successfully for a further eleven years before being scrapped. With either of the new ships **Newminster** or **Lindisfarne** available to run on the Rotterdam service, the **Hethpool** was surplus to requirements and was sold to Canadian owners in September 1925. James Taylor wrote in the *Tees Packet*, January 1965:

*She crossed the Atlantic and began a new career trading between Canadian and US ports as the **Farnorth**. In 1937 she changed hands again becoming the **Southern Lady** and in 1942 she was acquired by a Jamaican company and renamed **Conister**. She remained under the Canadian flag with these owners but in 1950 she came under the Dominican flag as the **Ciudad Trujilyo**. She changed hands for the last time in 1952 when she was bought by the McCormack Shipping Corporation of Honduras and renamed **Lewis Fraser**. For the next five years she served these owners but in 1957 she was sold to the Patapsco Scrap Company for breaking up. She was delivered at Baltimore and this sale realised $55,000, probably more than she cost when new.*

An unfortunate ship in that she was never able to prove herself in the trade for which she was built, she nevertheless served her owners on the other side of the Atlantic long enough to prove that her accident of August 1923 was a freak and should not be held against her.

Advert in Tyne River Official Handbook, 1925.

The **Farnorth** (1908) formerly the **Richard Welford** / **Hethpool**, seen at her home port of Halifax, Nova Scotia, before she was resold in 1937.

Despite her earlier mishap at Newcastle Quayside, the former **Richard Welford** traded successfully throughout the depressed years of the early 1930s, survived World War II, until she finally went to a breaker's yard just four months short of the fiftieth anniversary of her launch.

Deployment of the passenger ships in 1925 was essentially as follows:

Hadrian and **Bernicia**	-	express Newcastle to London service
Dunstanburgh	-	Newcastle to Hamburg
Teessider and **Newminster** or **Lindisfarne**	-	Newcastle to Rotterdam
New Londoner	-	Newcastle to Antwerp
Buccaneer	-	Middlesbrough and Sunderland to London.

With the retirement of the **Buccaneer** at the end of the summer season, passenger carrying on the Middlesbrough service effectively ceased although a few berths were to be had when suitable vessels deputised at Middlesbrough. Numerous scheduled supplementary cargo services were operated as required and these included Newcastle to Ghent during the flower season and trips to Dunkirk and other northern French ports as required. The company's appointed agents were D Burger & Son at Rotterdam, A Kirsten at Hamburg and John P Best & Company at Antwerp and Ghent. The Free Trade Wharf Company, of course, supported the London end of the business at Ratcliffe in East London.

The buoyant years of the first half of the 1920s had seen the company back onto its feet. New building of passenger and cargo ships as well as several carefully chosen secondhand purchases had brought the fleet up to full strength with a minimum service speed of 12 knots on all its services. The ever popular Newcastle to London express passenger and cargo service was enjoying its new crack steamers the **Bernicia** and **Hadrian** while the Middlesbrough steamers called at Sunderland every other voyage. The Tyne-Tees Steam Shipping Company was on a roll, with the Board turning its attention to the need for yet another new passenger and cargo steamer destined to replace the **Teessider** on the Rotterdam service (Chapter 7).

In his annual statement to the Shareholders dated 17 August 1925, company Chairman Sir Arthur Sutherland reported a good trading year and a final dividend of 1/- per fully paid £1 share. His Managing Director was still Robert Mason, and the rest of the Board now comprised: Ralph Milbanke Hudson, Claud Pease and R J Thompson and Company Secretary, George Charlton.

Annual Report to the shareholders of the Tyne-Tees Steam Shipping Company for the year ending 30 June, 1925. [Continued on the next three pages]

Tyne Steam Shipping Co. Ltd.,
ESTABLISHED 1864.

Tees Union Shipping Co., Ltd.,
ESTABLISHED 1880.

Amalgamated 1903, under the name of the

Tyne-Tees Steam Shipping Company Limited.

Directors' Report, Balance Sheet
AND
Profit and Loss Account.

Year ended 30th June, 1925.

NOTICE IS HEREBY GIVEN

That the ordinary general meeting of Shareholders in the TYNE-TEES STEAM SHIPPING COMPANY LIMITED will be held on Tuesday, the 1st September, 1925, in the Lord Mayor's Chamber, Guildhall, Newcastle-upon-Tyne, at noon.

The Company's Transfer Books are closed from 19th August to 1st September, 1925, inclusive.

By Order of the Board,

GEO. H. B. CHARLTON,
SECRETARY.

18th August, 1925.

TYNE-TEES STEAM SHIPP

PROFIT AND LOSS ACCOUNT for

	£	s.	d.
To Interest on 4½ % Debenture Stock for year ended 30th June, 1925	6,306	15	0
„ Interim Dividend, paid March 1st, 1925	6,820	4	0
„ Interest on New Shares to 30th June, 1925	1,696	11	3
„ Depreciation on Steamers as per Provisions of Debenture Stock Trust Deed	14,552	15	2
„ Depreciation on Freeholds, Leaseholds, Loose Plant, &c.	14,155	12	8
„ Remuneration of Directors and Trustees for Debenture Stock Holders	1,603	16	6
„ Balance carried to Balance Sheet	16,185	0	6
	£61,320	15	1

BALANCE SHEET a

	£	s.	d.	£	s.	d.
SHARE CAPITAL—						
AUTHORISED—						
750,000 Shares of £1 each	750,000	0	0			
ISSUED—						
136,404 Shares of £1 each, issued as fully paid	136,404	0	0			
272,808 Shares of £1 each, upon which 10s. per share has been paid ...	136,404	0	0			
NOTE. By Indenture of Indemnity and Charge, dated 8th April, 1904, the Company has assigned 10s. per Share in respect of each of the above 272,808 partly paid Shares in the Capital of the Company which has been issued and is outstanding, and all calls and sums hereafter made or received in respect thereto to an amount not exceeding £25,200 as a specific security for the purpose of indemnifying the Trustees of the Free Trade Wharf Company's leasehold properties from any liability whatsoever in connection with the leases.						
136,404 Shares of £1 each. Amount received, including payments on account of final call of 10s. per share due 1st July, 1925 ...	117,844	10	0			
				390,652	10	0
(Allotted 6th February, 1925, under terms of circulars to shareholders dated 12th January, 1925.)						
4½ per cent. FIRST MORTGAGE DEBENTURE STOCK—						
Authorised	150,000	0	0			
Issued	...		...	140,150	0	0
DEBTS DUE BY THE COMPANY—						
Sundry Creditors, including provision for Taxation, Repairs, Contingencies, &c.	110,470	4	10			
Unclaimed Dividends and Debenture Stock Interest	143	0	7			
Interest accrued on Debenture Stock for half-year ended 30th June, 1925 ...	3,153	7	6			
„ „ New Shares to 30th June, 1925	1,696	11	3			
				115,463	4	2
DEPRECIATION FUND as per provisions of Debenture Stock Trust Deed ...	...		...	159,628	16	9
COMPANY'S INSURANCE and BOILER FUND, and for GENERAL PURPOSES				29,108	7	9
PROFIT AND LOSS ACCOUNT—						
Amount brought forward from last year	1,109	19	6			
Add Balance as per above Account	16,185	0	6			
				17,295	0	0
				£852,297	18	8

Report of the Auditors to the Shareholders of the Tyne=Tees Steam Shipping Company Limited.

We have audited the above Account and Balance Sheet dated 30th June, 1925, with the books and vouchers have been taken and valued by the Officials of the Company. Subject to the foregoing, in our opinion such Balan to the best of our information and the explanations given to us, and as shown by the books of the Company.

11, IRONMONGER LANE, LONDON, E.C. 2.
AND
GREY'S BUILDING, 53, GREY STREET,
NEWCASTLE-ON-TYNE,
17th August, 1925.

ING COMPANY LIMITED.

the Year ended 30th June, 1925.

	£	s.	d.
By Trading Profit, after providing for Taxation, Repairs, Contingencies, &c.	47,516	5	7
„ Rent of Charrington Properties	8,400	0	0
„ Interest on Investments	5,374	16	6
„ Transfer Fees, &c.	29	13	0
	£61,320	**15**	**1**

t 30th June, 1925.

	£	s.	d.	£	s.	d.
FREEHOLD LAND, PREMISES, LEASES, FIXTURES, SHIPS, WHERRIES, LOOSE PLANT, TOOLS AND OFFICE FURNITURE, &c.—						
Amount as per last Account	567,382	17	2			
Additions, less Sales during year	113,315	3	6			
	680,698	0	8			
Less Depreciation on Freeholds, Leaseholds and Loose Plant	14,155	12	8			
				666,542	8	0
SHARES IN FREE TRADE WHARF COMPANY, LIMITED—						
6,300 Shares of £10 each, at cost				57,000	0	0
STORES IN STOCK				3,691	7	3
CLAIMS ON UNDERWRITERS				6,366	6	2
INSURANCE, &c., paid in advance				587	17	5
DEBTS DUE TO THE COMPANY—						
Sundry Debtors, *less* provision for doubtful debts	46,267	11	11			
Free Trade Wharf Company, Limited	26,894	4	10			
				73,161	16	9
INVESTMENTS—						
In Government and other Securities, at cost				38,256	0	0
CASH—						
At Company's Bankers on Current Account	6,407	16	8			
Do. do. on Dividend and Debenture Stock Interest Accounts	109	5	4			
In hand	175	1	1			
				6,692	3	1

ARTHUR M. SUTHERLAND, ⎫
ROBERT MASON, ⎬ DIRECTORS.
⎭

£852,297 18 8

of the Company, and we have obtained all the information and explanations we have required. The stores in stock
Sheet is properly drawn up so as to exhibit a true and correct view of the state of the Company's affairs according

PEAT, MARWICK, MITCHELL & Co.,
CHARTERED ACCOUNTANTS.

TYNE-TEES STEAM SHIPPING COMPANY LIMITED.

DIRECTORS.

Sir ARTHUR M. SUTHERLAND, Bart., K.B.E., J.P., Chairman.

R. MILBANKE HUDSON, J.P.   CLAUD E. PEASE, J.P.   R. J. THOMPSON, J.P.

ROBT. MASON, J.P., Managing Director.

GEO. H. B. CHARLTON, Secretary.

Trustees for Debenture Stock Holders.

Sir ARTHUR FRANCIS PEASE, Bart.   Sir WILLIAM HENRY PEAT, K.B.E.

DIRECTORS' REPORT.

To the Shareholders of the Tyne-Tees Steam Shipping Company, Limited.

Your Directors present herewith the Company's Balance Sheet and Profit & Loss Account for the year ended 30th June, 1925, together with the Auditors' Report.

The Profit and Loss Account shows a credit balance of £16,185 0s. 6d., which, added to the balance of £1,109 19s. 6d. brought forward from last year, makes a sum of £17,295 0s. 0d., which your Directors recommend be appropriated as follows:—

Final Dividend of 1/- per share (*less* Income Tax) on 136,404 fully paid shares	£6,820 4 0	
Final Dividend of 6d. per share (*less* Income Tax) on 272,808 partly paid shares	£6,820 4 0	
Balance carried forward	£3,654 12 0	
	£17,295 0 0	

In accordance with the Articles of Association, two Directors, Mr. R. Milbanke Hudson and Mr. Claud E. Pease, retire by rotation; they are eligible and offer themselves for re-election.

The Auditors, Messrs. Peat, Marwick, Mitchell & Co., also retire and offer themselves for re-election.

ARTHUR M. SUTHERLAND, Chairman.

ROBT. MASON, Managing Director.

GEO. H. B. CHARLTON, Secretary.

25, *King Street,*
    Newcastle-upon-Tyne,
            17th August, 1925.

THE SUTHERLAND STEAM SHIP COMPANY OF NEWCASTLE

Having served as a clerk in the shipping industry, young Arthur Sutherland persuaded his father Benjamin to invest £22,700 in a new ship to work in the bulk charter market. Benjamin Sutherland was established in the flour and grain industry and could see the potential of such a venture. In 1894 B J Sutherland & Company took delivery of its first ship, the **Sutherland**, from W Dobson & Company on the Tyne. The venture was an immediate success and returned a profit to father and son in a very short time. Two secondhand purchases followed and in 1896 the Sutherland Steam Ship Company was formed to take over the assets and goodwill of B J Sutherland & Company, with Arthur Sutherland in charge.

Sutherland's breakthrough came with the purchase of his first Doxford-built turret ship, named **Caithness**, in 1898 (see Appendix 2 Fleet List). Turret ships had a harbour deck and a raised main deck in order to reduce transit fees in the Suez Canal which were partly based on the width of the main deck rather than the ship's beam. Doxford firmly believed the hulls to be stronger than conventional hulls but was initially up against Lloyds which refused to classify the ships. They did have stability problems if incorrectly loaded and after the first losses Doxfords issued standing instructions to owners to flood the ballast tanks if bulk cargoes were loaded above the harbour deck level.

Sutherland's turret ship **Caithness** (1898) seen on trials in rough weather.

(Sunderland Antiquarian Society)

The first turret ship was commissioned in 1892 and the success of the early ships eventually prompted orders, not least from the Clan Line of Glasgow. Clan Line ordered the first of its eventual fleet of thirty turret ships in 1907 following trial charters of two existing vessels. By then Sutherland already had seven turret ships in service and had become a champion of the design and a recognised sales 'agent' for Doxford. Between 1909 and 1917 Sutherland bought another nine turret ships on the secondhand market, while building only two ships of conventional design for the fleet, which were delivered in 1911. He continued to buy in the early part of the Great War before prices began to inflate due to the increasing lack of available tonnage.

Sutherland's key move was to recognise that the post-Great War inflation boom was not going to last. His fleet book price had quadrupled since 1914 so in 1919 he set about disposing of tonnage before the price bubble inevitably burst. Twelve of the fourteen ships he had bought during the war were sold, ten of them to a new Cardiff ship-owner, Western Counties Shipping, for over £2 million. Western Counties inevitably went bust and Sutherland was able to repossess ships not paid for and buy back others at greatly reduced prices - and then resell them. Sutherland became a very rich man very quickly, but his business acumen and strong nerve were recognised by his peers and he earned his place as one of the great tramp ship owners.

During the rest of the 1920s freight rates were poor and B J Sutherland & Company, to which name the company had reverted post-war, had a fleet of only five ships. In the recession of the early 1930s Sutherland sold his entire fleet, one to the breakers, one to Greeks, and the other three sold as prices once again started to rise in 1932. He was then able to buy four modern tramp steamers at knock down prices from owners keen to sell unwanted and laid up tonnage. These were the **Fife** from Lundegaard & Sons and the **Nairn** from Thomas Law & Company both completed only in 1929 and the **Cromarty** from Woods Tylor Brown and the **Peebles** from James, Muers & Company, both ships built in 1930. At the eve of World War II, B J Sutherland & Company owned seven modern vessels and two more were delivered in 1940, the **Inverness** and **Sutherland**. The company lost only two ships in the war, the **Inverness** in 1941 and the **Ross** the following year.

Sir Arthur Sutherland died at his home in Jesmond on 29 March 1953. The remaining fleet of four ships was sold later in 1953 and in 1954, the **Sutherland** delivered by Doxford in 1940 to the Carlton Steam Ship Company, the **Inverness** completed as **Empire Freetown** in 1945 was sold to Turnbull Scott, the **Dumfries**, built in 1944 as **Empire Rabaul**, to the Chine Shipping Company, and the oldest ship **Cromarty**, dating from 1936, to Swedish ship owners J Larsson. The fifth, the **Argyll** dating from 1939, traded under the Sutherland flag just a little longer, and was sold to Newcastle owners in 1954 but almost immediately resold to Finnish owners.

The **Argyll** (1939) seen at London, was the last ship to fly the Sutherland colours when she was sold in 1954. *(Tom Rayner)*

Sir Arthur Sutherland was truly a canny businessman and a hugely successful tramp shipowner and operator. He brought the skills he learned in the tramp ship market to the Board table at Tyne-Tees and as a consequence the Tyne-Tees Steam Shipping Company benefitted tremendously from his talent for survival and business success. Sutherland was majority owner of Tyne-Tees from 1919 until 1943 when Coast Lines took over.

THE MID-1920s TO THE MID-1930s

The **Hadrian** (1923) departing the Thames with a notice on the main deck that reads '*Newcastle London via Southend*'.

(Harold Appleyard collection)

In summer the **Hadrian** and **Bernicia** called at Southend-on-Sea pier to disembark passengers keen to travel into town by train to save themselves the few remaining hours of the working day or to spend a few days enjoying the seaside. This was also the seasonal practice of the Scottish steamer from Dundee during the late 1920s. Southend to Free Trade Wharf, which is about one mile below Tower Bridge on the north bank of the river, could take as long as four hours when the river was busy. Tyne-Tees threatened to cease the Southend stop in the 1932 season and in May that year a deputation of Southend and Westcliffe councillors went to Newcastle as guests of the company aboard the **Hadrian** to plead successfully their case for local tourism. At Newcastle they were hosted by Sir Arthur Sutherland and the party appear to have been given a very enjoyable stay in the North East.

Northbound the steamers slowed down off the Tyne pier heads where they were met by a launch that took those passengers in a hurry to get to their destinations to the ferry landings at North and South Shields. This was the preferred option of the businessmen keen to get to work while the steamer spent another hour and a half before she was alongside at Newcastle Quayside ready to disembark the main body of passengers. But, for all that, if the weather was inclement and the conditions difficult, the ships could arrive at their final destination anything up to twelve hours late.

Handbill advertising '*Summer Pleasure Steamer Service, Southend-on-Sea to Newcastle and vice versa, by the fast, comfortably appointed screw steamers **Hadrian** and **Bernicia** for the period 18 July to 30 September 1925*'.

(Harold Appleyard collection)

Had the status quo prevailed, the Tyne-Tees Steam Shipping Company would have been well placed for the future. Following the initial postwar boom years, the down-turn in trade that took place in the late 1920s was exacerbated by the General Strike which deteriorated into the Coal Strike during 1926. The working man was faced with a falling wage packet. With less and less buying power he eventually took matters into his own hands and walked out into the sunshine to remonstrate with Government. The General Strike began on 4 May 1926 and was the first of its kind. The number of strikers was an overwhelming 1.7 million people, closing mines, transport, newspapers, docks and power stations. It was called by the Trades Union Congress in response to the 1 million miners that had been locked out of work by refusing to take a 13% drop in wages for an increased working day from seven hours to eight. Although the General Strike lasted only until 13 May, Prime Minister Stanley Baldwin learnt in July that 'there had been no real tendency on the part of the miners to return to work' and that money set aside to improve the mining industry was rapidly being spent on importing foreign coal. North East England was particularly badly hit and the response to strikers derailing the **Flying Scotsman** express train in Northumberland was the arrival of a warship in the Tyne, very much reminiscent of the British gun boat diplomacy of the Victorian era!

The situation in 1926 had three significant effects on Tyne-Tees. Firstly, although it had agreements for the supply of bunker coal with the mine owners, prices rose significantly and care had to be taken to ensure that ships kept a fair reserve in case of difficulties in supply. Secondly, the railway companies drove freight prices down so increasing their share of the carriage of what coal was available so that coastal coal cargoes were barely profitable. Thirdly, and most importantly, it drove a number of shipping companies out of business as they were both deprived of bunkers and suffering from greatly reduced freight rates. This played into the hands of the near Continental shipping companies such as Tyne-Tees, General Steam and the Scottish based Gibson and Rankine lines, all of which were able to capitalise on a greater share of a diminished market.

For the next few years the company schedules were maintained with little change. Some cargo only sailings tended to be as cargo induced rather than to a set schedule, particularly on sailings that supplemented a regular timetabled cargo passenger service.

Conscious that competition had eased, the Tyne-Tees company set about an aggressive expansion programme with the purchase of a succession of secondhand cargo steamers. Between 1926 and 1929 it bought eight steamers ranging from the small **Belford** of just 366 tons gross and completed in 1920 as **War Arun**, to the big single deck colliers **Marden** and **Bilton** dating from 1904 and 1920 respectively. The **Bilton**, built originally for Coombes, Marshall & Company of Middlesbrough was named after the Coombes family home near Harrogate. Her name remained unchanged when she joined the Tyne-Tees fleet in July 1929. The **Marden** had been a war loss when, under her original name of **Main**, she was sunk by gunfire 1½ miles east of Drummore in Luce Bay on 9 October 1917 while on passage from Belfast to Liverpool in ballast. Twelve men lost their lives in the sinking. She was raised in August 1920 and taken to the Ardrossan Dockyard Company for renovation and refurbishment later re-entering service in 1922.

The **Bilton** (1920), registered at Middlesbrough rather than Newcastle, seen working cargo.

(Harold Appleyard collection)

Collectively the new acquisitions allowed the company to maintain its liner trade while competing in the bulk coal export and grain import trade. There was also the import of silver sand from Amsterdam to the glassworks at Sunderland; traditionally imported from the Baltic, Dutch sand was of very high quality and supplied both James Jobling's glass works and Turnbull's glass works at Southwick. An upturn in the steel trade from Middlesbrough to London had the newly-acquired, former Dutch-owned **Ayresome** join the already busy **Cragside**, **Middlesbro'** and **Wendy** on the service. The single deckers were otherwise employed both as back up to the company's cargo liner services and in whatever bulk trade they could attract. The Tyne-Tees flag was consequently flown in numerous ports with which the company had not previously been associated.

In June 1929 a portion of the Tyne-Tees Shipping Company's wharf at Gateshead collapsed into the river. The wharf was used by some of the Continental steamers and fortunately none was alongside the 80 feet section of quay that collapsed. Repairs were put in hand but just over a year later another collapse occurred and it was some time before the entire wharf was reinstated and put back into use.

In 1929 the subsidiary company Free Trade Wharf became ship owners when it purchased the **London Trader** and **Hull Trader** and the goodwill of the London to Hull service operated by James Cook & Company's Bulk Oil Steamship Company of London. Bulk Oil was better known for its coastal steam tankers each with the name **Pass of ...** but the company also ran a twice-weekly service from London to Hull with calls at Grimsby. The two ships **London Trader**, dating from 1904 and only just acquired by Bulk Oil, and **Hull Trader** built in 1917, had the white over purple over white hoops on their black funnels repainted in Tyne-Tees colours and continued trade as normal under the banner of the Free Trade Wharf Company.

By the end of the decade the Tyne-Tees fleet of ships was at its greatest strength. It comprised some eighteen vessels of various types and sizes which provided the company with considerable versatility. Indeed little had changed. While the Continental passenger demand remained buoyant, the passenger receipts on the Newcastle to London service had slowly declined and were beginning to be cause for concern. There were a number of reasons why the travelling public had forsaken the sea journey apart, of course, from the onset of the economic recession. A key factor had been the introduction of the long-distance motor coach which seriously eroded the need for football fans to sail the North Sea; football clubs had also begun to negotiate contracts with the railway companies to supply special football excursion trains as required.

There was one very important new build, the passenger-cargo steamer **Alnwick**. This was the ship the Board so dearly craved for as a replacement for the ageing **Teessider** on the Rotterdam route. The order had been placed with Swan Hunter, Wigham Richardson for a steamer with a service speed of 13 knots, cargo capacity of about 1,400 tons, and with passenger accommodation for 50 in saloon class (the term first class having fallen into disuse) and about 25 in second class. The ship was launched from the Walker-on-Tyne Neptune Yard on 6 March 1929 and the ship's sponsor was Ralph Hudson's granddaughter Miss Violet Chipchase Roberts. Five weeks later the ship attained 14 knots on trials and was handed over to her owners. Lord Ambrose Greenway described the **Alnwick**:

The **Alnwick** (1929) with a fine trail of coal smoke.   (R Gibson, George Nairn collection)

In appearance she was a neat little ship with raised foc'sle and bridge deck and although by this time raked bows and cruiser sterns were becoming generally more prevalent, she retained the old fashioned straight stem and counter stern. Her rather unusual masting arrangement consisted of a foremast in the normal position between Nos. 1 and 2 hatches forward, but her mainmast was placed on the end of her bridge deck and was supplemented by a short kingpost aft. A standard size funnel bearing the company's white and red bands was mounted behind a built-up bridge on a single deck superstructure amidships.

Shortly after her delivery she was one of the first ships to berth at the newly-extended Newcastle Quayside after it had been vacated by ships of both Bergen and Oslo lines in favour of North Shields.

Heyday - Quayside in the early 1930s with the **Alnwick** (1929) to the fore and the **Hadrian** (1923) on the London Wharf two ships behind, with a Tyne-Tees cargo ship beyond her.

(George Nairn collection)

The **Teessider** (1909) was sold in 1929 but maintained the Algeria to France ferry for the next 25 years.

(Harold Appleyard collection)

The **Alnwick** took her maiden voyage from Newcastle to Rotterdam at the end of April and the **Teessider** finally stood down. James Layton described the final years of the **Teessider** under the Red Ensign in an edition of the *Tees Packet*:

However, it was not the end. Throughout the latter part of 1928 and the first part of 1929 she continued regular sailings from the Tyne to Hamburg, Ghent, Amsterdam, Antwerp, London and finally a voyage from the Tees to London. She sailed from Middlesbrough for the last time on 20 July 1929 bound for the Tyne and a new owner.

*On 8 August 1929 she was delivered at Hamburg to Soc. Algérienne de Navigation Pour L'Afrique du Nord (Charles Schiaffino & Compagnie, managers), Algiers, and was renamed **Finistère**. Four years earlier this company had bought the **General Havelock** from the Tyne-Tees company and had renamed her **Finistère**, she had now been sold and renamed so the **Teessider** was able to take her name. As the **Finistère** she spent the next 25 years trading on the North African coast and to ports in the Eastern Mediterranean... Finally in October 1954 she was sold to M Bertorello and was broken up at Savona, Italy. The end of a quite remarkable 45 year career.*

The **Alnwick** quickly settled in on the Rotterdam route. However, it was soon realised that demand for second class berths during that first summer season frequently meant turning away potential passengers. Consequently, an additional 25 second class berths were built into the poop during her guarantee refit the following winter. The **Dunstanburgh** was still the main passenger carrier on the Hamburg service, while the **Newminster** and **Lindisfarne** maintained the Antwerp service and the seasonal route to Ghent.

The **Dunstanburgh** (1912) seen beneath the Tyne Bridge in 1927 during its construction.

(Newcastle Central Library)

On 27 May 1929 the single deck steamer **Marden** was on a voyage from London to Newcastle with a cargo of paper. In poor visibility she collided with **The Sultan**, owned by J Hay & Sons of Glasgow. Both vessels were of similar size, but the **Marden** came off the worse and rapidly started to sink. Her crew were taken aboard **The Sultan**. The **Marden** was the oldest ship in the Tyne-Tees fleet, having been built in 1904 by Mackie & Thomson on the Clyde at Govan as **Main** for the Main Colliery Company of Cardiff. She joined Tyne-Tees to become **Marden** only in 1926.

The 1929 summer timetable advertised 'Reduced fares' on the London service in an attempt to recoup passenger numbers. The first class single to London was 16 shillings (80 pence) and return 26 shillings and second class was just 12 shillings and £1 respectively. A contract meal ticket in first class needed to be pre-booked and cost 7/6d. Departures from Newcastle Quayside and London Free Trade Wharf by the **Hadrian** (Captain Bruce) and **Bernicia** (Captain Little) were still on Saturdays and Wednesdays. In addition there was a twice-weekly cargo service operated by the **Bamburgh**, **Wendy** or **Middlesbro'** between London and Middlesbrough, Stockton, West Hartlepool, and Sunderland with calls also at Scarborough as required. The newly-acquired **Sandhill** (formerly one of Bulk Oil's several ships named **London Trader**, and predecessor to the one purchased by the Free Trade Wharf Company) was scheduled to call at Scarborough on 6 December to part-discharge cargo from London. She was refused permission to dock on the high tide and carried her cargo on to Middlesbrough. It was not long afterwards that the viability of the Scarborough call was being questioned and the stop was discontinued.

The Continental passenger and cargo services had the **Alnwick** leaving Newcastle Quayside for Rotterdam on Tuesdays and returning on Saturdays with '*an extra steamer leaving Rotterdam on Tuesdays as required*'. The **New Londoner** (Captain Flause) left for Antwerp on Saturdays returning from Antwerp on Tuesday nights, again with an additional steamer in service as required that left Antwerp on Saturdays and Newcastle on Tuesdays. There was also a Tuesday departure for Ghent from Newcastle returning on Saturdays and this was generally operated by the **Newminster**. Meanwhile, the **Lindisfarne** and the **Dunstanburgh** left Newcastle for Hamburg on Fridays. The **Lindisfarne** provided the extra supplementary services as advertised. The **New Londoner**, **Dunstanburgh**, **Lindisfarne** and **Newminster** offered saloon class accommodation while the **Alnwick** offered a second class option as well. Saloon fares to Hamburg inclusive of meals were 55 shillings single and 100 shilings (£5) return; to Antwerp and Rotterdam were 45 shillings and 80 shillings (£4) and the second class fares to Rotterdam excluding food were 22/6d single and 40 shillings (£2) return. Saloon class passenger berths to Ghent, when offered, were the same price as those to Antwerp and Rotterdam. Infants were carried free of charge and children between the ages of three and fourteen qualified for half fare.

Cargo-only services were also operated to the Continent. A steamer left Hamburg for Middlesbrough every other Friday, and from Gateshead Quay on the Tyne a steamer sailed for Amsterdam on Tuesdays returning on Saturdays. Additional services to northern French ports were run as required on a demand basis. The United Shipping Agency looked after the company's affairs at Amsterdam, otherwise the Continental port agents remained unchanged.

The basic pattern of services continued more or less unaltered for the next couple of years. The recession worsened considerably as the impact from the American Wall Street Crash of 1929 spread to Europe; freight rates fell in order to chase what freight was available. As time went on the **Hadrian** and **Bernicia** became barely profitable on the express London service as the passenger carrying season had contracted to just the three main summer months. With much of the passenger accommodation unused for the remainder of the year many of the stewards and catering staff were laid off in the winter, a situation that was by no means welcome to either employer or employee. Profitability on the Continental services remained satisfactory although there were fewer back-up cargo-only services. Nevertheless the company was able to keep all its ships in employment.

The **Lindisfarne** collided with the Norwegian freighter **Tancred** on 20 January 1931 in the Nieuwe Waterweg between Schiedam and Vlaardingen. The **Lindisfarne** was holed above and below the waterline and was promptly beached. Later patched and refloated she was soon back in service. One of the big single deck ships from the late 1920s purchasing spree was lost in 1932. The **Gateshead**, built for Dutch owners in 1917, was sunk following a collision with the 1,328 ton gross Norwegian cargo steamer the **Miranda** some 8 nautical miles north-east of Seaham Harbour on 21 December. The **Gateshead** had earlier left Newcastle with a part-cargo of coal and part general cargo bound for Amsterdam.

Earlier in the year, in April 1932, the **Bernicia** ran a special cruise service leaving Newcastle at 10 pm on Wednesday 20 April under the banner 'Wembley Cup Final, make the Tyne-Tees steamer your hotel'. A first class return fare was offered at 25/- and accommodation was offered aboard ship alongside Free Trade Wharf on the Thursday and Friday nights before returning from London at midnight on Saturday. Keys and Smith described her departure:

It was reported that around 4,000 people, many of them singing, assembled on the city's quayside as the **Bernicia** *prepared to sail... The* **Bernicia** *was carrying a six foot high black and white replica of the F A Cup on her funnel. Passing ships signalled 'Good luck!' – it seems a considerable number of captains were Newcastle supporters, including* **Bernicia**'s *Captain A A Lawrence. More than 300 fans made the trip to see their team play at Wembley. Before a vast crowd of 92,000, Newcastle beat Arsenal 2-1.*

The **New Londoner** had done the same trip in 1905 when Newcastle had lost the English Cup Final to Aston Villa at Crystal Palace. The **Tynesider**, with Captain Durham in charge, had hosted fans in April 1906 to see Newcastle play Everton and in April 1908 to see Newcastle play Wolverhampton Wanderers. On both occasions departure from Newcastle was on the Wednesday evening and the return sailing was on the Saturday evening from Free Trade Wharf, saloon return 12/- and with 'provisions' 20/-, second cabin 8/- return and 15/- with provisions. The advertisement for the trip advised that '*There is a regular train service from the Palace, by the East London Line, through the Thames Tunnel to Shadwell Station*'. The **Bernicia**, when brand new, also took 300 fans to Wembley in 1924 to see Newcastle avenged with the defeat of Aston Villa 2-0.

After the 1932 summer season both the **Hadrian** and **Bernicia** were withdrawn from the London service and laid up in the Tyne at the end of September. In their stead came the **New Londoner** transferred from the Antwerp service which she had championed since June 1923 and the four year-old **Alnwick** from the Rotterdam service.

The **Bernica** (1923) along with the **Hadrian** were laid up and replaced by the **Alnwick**.

(Harold Appleyard collection)

76

In November the **New Londoner** was taken off the London service and laid up as well, leaving the **Alnwick** to maintain the twice-weekly passenger service between Newcastle and London in company with the twelve-passenger **Newminster**. The following June the three mothballed ships were recommissioned, the **New Londoner** returning to the Antwerp trade on 3 June, the **Hadrian** and **Bernicia** displacing the **Alnwick** and **Newminster** from the express London service, the **Alnwick** returning to the Rotterdam trade and the **Newminster** to Antwerp.

The **Alnwick** (1929) demonstrating that she really was a coal burner.

(Harold Appleyard collection)

The **New Londoner** stayed on the Antwerp service only another few months and was finally withdrawn. She arrived at Dunston Buoys once again on 7 October. Passenger carrying on the Newcastle to Antwerp route ceased with the departure of the **New Londoner**. She completed a single round trip to Rotterdam in November and a single London trip in mid-February 1934, on both occasions returning to Dunston. She stayed in mid-river for the remainder of 1934. Buyers were found for both the **Hadrian** and **Bernicia** in 1934 and a grateful Tyne-Tees company handed the two ships over to their new owners, the **Hadrian** to the London-based wing of the Egyptian Khedevial Mail Line and the **Bernicia** to the Greek Hellenic Coast Lines.

The **Bernicia** was wrecked on Skiathos in December 1944, but the **Hadrian** continued to serve her new owners until 1961 when she was sold for further employment until 1966 when she was scrapped. The **Alnwick** was again brought back to the London service in 1934 and maintained a weekly round trip. She did not carry any passengers, her public rooms being left unattended. This lasted only for another twelve months when the **Alwick** too was withdrawn and put on the 'For Sale' list. Jim Layton again:

After almost 80 years carrying passengers between the Tyne and London, the service succumbed to the increasing competition of road and rail transport and the pleasure of a voyage along the east coast of England aboard a Tyne-Tees passenger ship disappeared forever. The passenger services from Newcastle to Hamburg and Rotterdam continued but the ships employed had only accommodation for twelve passengers.

The vacancy at Antwerp caused by the withdrawal of the **New Londoner** in September 1933 was taken by the cargo-only steamer **Akeld**. She had been built in 1922 for owners in Dublin but latterly had been working as **The Earl** for J Hay & Sons, Glasgow. Purchased specifically for the Newcastle to Antwerp trade, the **Akeld** became a valuable and reliable unit in the cargo liner fleet, rarely deviating from her core route. She did have a spare twin berth cabin and this was often used by company employees travelling to Antwerp and on rare occasions was used for passengers, often clients of the company, who were attended by the ship's steward.

J Hay & Sons' **The Earl** (1922) was built by Yarrow at Scotstoun as **Mayfield** and only became **Akeld** in March 1933 when she was purchased by Tyne-Tees.

A number of the big single deck cargo ships that had been bought secondhand in the late 1920s were sold from 1934 onwards. The **Wooler** and **Sandhill** were sold to the Stanhope Steamship Company of London in a single deal to become the **Stanmore** and **Stanhope** respectively and were used largely in the coal trade. The following year the Dutch-built **Ayresome**, dating from 1916, was sold to Brook Shipping of Middlesbrough (Comben Longstaff & Company) and renamed **Surreybrook**. This left only the **Lowick** and **Belford** and these were sold shortly afterwards in 1936. A new **Gateshead** entered the fleet in 1933. She had been built by Forth Shipbuilding at Alloa in 1919 as the **War Colne** but was completed for J Leete & Company of London as the **Catherine Annie**. She later become J Hay's **The President**. She was a useful large deadweight vessel whose triple expansion steam engine provided her with a comfortable service speed of 9 knots.

Form of Guarantee to the North of England Protecting and Indemnity Association for the 'protection and indemnifcation' of the steamers **Akeld** and **Gateshead**, newly acquired by the Tyne-Tees Steam Shipping Company, dated 22 March 1933 and signed in person by Arthur M Sutherland.

(Harold Appleyard collection)

The compound-engined steamer **Northgate** was acquired by the Free Trade Wharf Company in 1933 to develop trade to Stockton and Hartlepool from Hull. She had been built by Hawthorn Leslie in 1925 for Pease & Partners of Stockton and was equipped with an old-fashioned compound steam engine. She was not renamed for her new duties. However, the Hull to Stockton and Hartlepool trade was discontinued in 1938 and the **Northgate** was sold and converted into the sand dredger **Garth**. The small motor vessel **Etal** was bought on the stocks from her Dutch builder Gideon Koster at Groningen in 1933. She was followed by another motor ship the **Rock** delivered by Hawthorn Leslie in 1934, both to develop the coastal traffic between London and East Anglia. The **Rock** had a whale-back foc'sle and a long hold before a raised quarter deck. Her engine was a 4-cylinder oil engine made by Humboldt-Deutzmotoren AG, Köln. Like the **Etal** she had two masts with a single derrick mounted on each.

The **London Trader** was renamed **Old Trader** in 1934 in anticipation of the delivery of a new steamer with the name **London Trader** building at Hawthorn Leslie at Hebburn. She was a coal burner and was completed as a single decker with a shelter deck. Engines were aft with the bridge and accommodation. She had two masts, one before the forward hold with a derrick slung aft and one between the holds with derricks slung fore and aft. She was designed for the London to Hull service.

Tyne-Tees took delivery of the new cargo ship **Glen** in July 1935 following her launch from Hawthorn Lesley's yard on 14 June. The order had been placed once Free Trade Wharf Company's little motor ships the **Etal** and **Rock** had settled down into service and demonstrated the viability of this type of ship. The **Glen** was a significant development for Tyne-Tees as the first motor ship and for a short time the only motor ship in a fleet otherwise comprising coal-burning steamers. Her oil engine was built by Humboldt-Deutzmotoren AG, Köln and comprised a single 7-cylinder engine, the cylinders being 11 inches in diameter and the stroke nearly 18 inches. This arrangement provided an output of 82 nominal horse power to provide a service speed of 9 knots. She, like her later consorts, was a single decker. Tyne-Tees retained an option on repeat orders to the same design (see Chapter 8).

The engine was of the direct reversing type, requiring the engine to be stopped and after the reversing lever had been activated, restarted in reverse. Failure to restart was the cause of many a bump against the quayside with this type of engine. After World War II the geared engine was more prevalent but progress had yet to wait for metallurgists to provide gears that were strong enough to withstand the stress. The engineers comprised both new recruits to the company and steam certificated engineers who had asked to be retrained for diesel certificates. The 'guinea pig' motor ship **Glen** was set to work on a variety of tasks having been designed so that she could deputise on any of the company's liner trades and work also in the bulk cargo market and the steel shipment trade. Judgement on the diesel engine was dependent on the performance of the **Glen** – but the outcome, it would seem, was indeed favourable (see Chapter 8).

In June 1935 the **Dunstanburgh** stood down from the Hamburg service to lay up at Dunston Buoys. Her replacement was the brand new cargo steamer **Craster**, launched at Swan Hunter, Wigham Richardson's yard on 2 May. Like the **Dunstanburgh**, the new ship had saloon accommodation for twelve passengers. The **Craster** had her triple expansion engine and accommodation aft, with two long holds and hatches served by derricks mounted on a short foremast and a centrally located main mast. Her funnel had absolutely no rake to it giving the ship an attractive, although business-like, appearance.

In September 1935 the **Lindisfarne** transferred from the Rotterdam route to cover on the Newcastle to London service following the final withdrawal of the **Alnwick**. The **Dunstanburgh** was brought back into action and put into the Rotterdam trade. The **Alnwick** was finally sold to Fred. Olsen (A S Ganger Rolf) who renamed her the **Bali**. She served principally on the Bergen to Rotterdam service for Fred. Olsen. After World War II she was put on the Oslo to Newcastle service until 1951 when she served between Oslo and Antwerp. In 1952 the **Bali** was sold to the Burmese Government and renamed **Pyidawtha**. She went aground while approaching Kyaukpyu on Ramree Island off the Burmese coast in May 1955 and later became a constructive total loss after developing a severe list to starboard.

The faithful **New Londoner** was also sold in 1936. A sale was nearly agreed in May 1934 but Ignazio Messina & Company of Genoa failed to agree on a sale price of £11,000. The **New Londoner** was laid up at the Dunston Buoys for nearly 18 months, from February 1934 until June 1935 when she went to Mercantile Drydock to prepare for a final stint on the Newcastle to London service. On 15 June 1935 she became third ship in the London trade for two weeks and was then deployed as spare ship, visiting Hamburg, Rotterdam and Antwerp and on several occasions loading at Bamletts Wharf or Tyne-Tees Wharf at Middlesbrough for London. This ended in April 1936 when she returned to Dunston-on-Tyne, only coming out of retirement in September to load fertilizer and general cargo at Middlesbrough for London. She sailed north to the Tyne to return to her buoys at Dunston. Meanwhile sale negotiations were completed with J A Billmeir & Company of London and she was handed over on 29 October to become their cargo steamer **Kenwood**. Her Tyne-Tees master, Captain Willam Ainsley, stayed with the ship when she became the **Kenwood**.

The **Alnwick** (1929) spent the majority of her career under the Norwegian flag as the **Bali** in the attractive colours of Fred. Olsen.

The **New Londoner** (1912) working cargo alongside Newcastle Quay.

The period from the mid-1920s to the mid-1930s is best described as messy. Although it had started upbeat with both the London and Continental trades enjoying a boom, the depressed years that followed, coupled with the downturn in Newcastle to London passenger receipts required significant changes to fleet deployment and the premature sale of some of the passenger vessels. Tyne-Tees had nevertheless come through these difficult years successfully and was set to change its trading pattern to ensure profitable years lay ahead. Meanwhile the company lost one of its long-standing staff members, one-time employee of the Tyne Steam Shipping Company, when George Charlton retired from the post of Managing Director in August 1934.

The *Sandhill* (1920)

From a letter to the Editor of *Sea Breezes* by James Layton
first published July 1981:

*...was launched as the **Pekelderdiep,** a small river in Groningen and not **Tekelderdiep** as shown in Lloyd's Register, but was completed as **Estoril** for E Noronha-Barros, of Portugal. In 1923 she was sold to J W Cook & Company, London, was renamed **London Trader** and... spent the next five years running between London Hull and Grimsby. She was sold in May 1928 to the Tyne-Tees Steam Shipping Company for £7,000, was renamed the **Sandhill** and for the next six years ran between London and north-east coast ports with occasional voyages to the Continent. [She was replaced by another **London Trader** which together with the **Hull Trader** was bought in 1929 by the Free Trade Wharf Company along with the goodwill of the London to Grimsby and Hull service.]*

The **London Trader** (1920) in the colours of J W Cook & Company before she was sold to Tyne-Tees in 1928 and renamed **Sandhill**.

*After a period laid up at Stockton in 1934, she was sold to J A Billmeir & Company, London for £2,750 and was renamed **Stanhope**, the name ship of the Stanhope Steamship Company. Under the Billmeir house flag she traded regularly to Spain prior to being sold in December 1936 for £4,525 to Northern Coasters (G T Gillie & Blair) who renamed her **Northern Firth**.*

*In 1939 she was badly damaged at the Trevor Quarry pier, North Wales, after drifting ashore with a rope round her propeller. She was sold to J Lamont & Company, Greenock, who carried out repairs, and with survey passed sold her in October 1939 to Charles Mauritzen, Leith, who renamed her **Baranda**. She commenced trading between Scottish ports and the Faeroe Islands and probably spent most of the war years in this trade.*

*Barline Transports (C R Mauritzen, manager) acquired her in 1943 and in 1946 she was sold to Duff, Herbert & Mitchell, was given her final name, **Juliet Duff**, and went tramping. In 1953 she passed to Dinorwic Slate Quarry Company (O T Williams, manager), and in 1955 was sold to W N Lindsay, Leith, who retained her until 21 January, 1957 when she arrived at Grays, Essex, to be broken up by T W Ward & Company.*

CHAPTER 8

PIONEER MOTOR SHIPS

The recession over, Tyne-Tees took delivery of four new ships during 1935. With the 12-passenger cargo steamer **Craster** established on the Hamburg trade in June and the pioneer motor ship **Glen** in service from July (Chapter 7) with at least one repeat order in the planning stage, Tyne-Tees also took delivery of two more coal-fired triple steam expansion-engined cargo ships. These were the **Cragside** launched at the Furness yard at Haverton Hill in May by Mrs A H Forster, wife of the Tyne-Tees manager at Middlesbrough, (the first time an order had been placed by Tyne-Tees with this yard) and the much larger **Thornaby** which was delivered by Hawthorn Leslie in June.

The **Cragside** was a small single deck steamer designed for the transport of parcels of manufactured steel goods in a single hold forward, serviced by two derricks mounted on the foremast and mainmast. Her bridge and machinery were aft along with the crew accommodation. Her service speed was a steady 9 knots. The **Cragside** was in trouble early in her career when she struck the British India Line's **Madura** in Gallion's Reach on the Thames on 8 August 1935. **Cragside** was in-bound with a cargo of steel girders for use in the construction of the new Chelsea Bridge and she sank within a couple of minutes. All ten members of her crew managed to get safely off the ship and were quickly picked up by boats sent to the rescue by the **Madura**. The **Cragside** was successfully raised on 29 August after most of the steel cargo had been removed from her hold. Temporary repairs allowed her to be towed back to the Tyne where further repairs were carried out, and she was then refurbished ready to restart her career.

The **Elysian Coast** (1935) was built as **Cragside**.

The **Thornaby** was a magnificent single deck cargo steamer with a service speed of 10 knots and of 1,171 tons gross. Her triple cylinders were of 16, 26 and 44 inches diameter and the stroke was 30 inches.   She was a coal-burner with two single-ended boilers made by the North East Marine Engineering Company. She had a well deck forward with numbers one and two hatches providing access to the two forward holds and there was a single hold aft. The forward hatches were served by derricks, a 15 ton capacity derrick forward and a 5 ton derrick aft, mounted on two kingposts, the forward one doubling as the foremast. The aft hold had a 5 ton derrick mounted on the mainmast. She had the Reith system of side coamings which prevented the need for cross-hatch support spars for ease of trimming bulk cargoes and a deadweight of 1,550 tons. Engines, bridge and accommodation were set aft of centre; the funnel had a slight rake and was parallel to the masts and kingposts. The funnel had a patent cowl fitted to help disperse coal smuts. The principal employment for the **Thornaby** was coal shipments south to London or the Continent returning with silver sand from Holland.

The **Northumbrian Coast** (1935) was originally named **Thornaby** and was registered at Middlesbrough.

(Harold Appleyard collection)

The new ships allowed the single-deckers **Lowick** and **Belford** to be disposed of in 1936, both sold for further trading. The venerable **Wendy** was also sold in 1936, taking up service as **Briardale** for the Anglo-Iberian Steamship Company of London. Quickly resold for use as a collier and owned at Newcastle, she reverted to Anglo-Iberian ownership in 1937 before ending up as George Gibson's **Woodstock** in 1940. She was sunk in collision in February 1941 on a voyage from the Tyne to the Thames.

TYNE-TEES STEAM SHIPPING CO., LTD.

REGULAR FAST STEAMERS BETWEEN

LONDON and
{ NEWCASTLE.
SUNDERLAND.
WEST HARTLEPOOL and
SCARBOROUGH.
MIDDLESBROUGH and STOCKTON.
HULL, GRIMSBY, BOSTON, SELBY
and KINGS LYNN.

London Offices: Free Trade Wharf, Ratcliff, London, E.1; and 57, Mark Lane, E.C.3.

Wharfingers and Warehousemen at Free Trade Wharf, Ratcliff, London, E.1, and at Tyne-Tees Wharf, Middlesbrough, Stockton and Gateshead.

NEWCASTLE and
{ ANTWERP.
GHENT.
HAMBURG.
ROTTERDAM.
AMSTERDAM.
DORDRECHT.

For further information apply to HEAD OFFICE, 25, King Street, NEWCASTLE-UPON-TYNE, 1 (Telephone 25111, 6 lines).
Telegraphic Address: "TYNETEES, NEWCASTLE-ON-TYNE."

Or for Local Information to Tavistock House, Borough Road, SUNDERLAND.   Vulcan Street, MIDDLESBROUGH.

AGENTS ABROAD: Antwerp and Ghent, JOHN P. BEST & Co.; Hamburg, A. KIRSTEN, Dovenhof, 68;
Rotterdam, D. BURGER & ZOON, Westerstraat, 7, and Amsterdam, UNITED SHIPPING AGENCY.

THROUGH RATES QUOTED TO ALL POINTS ON APPLICATION.

www.steve-ellwood.org.uk

Advert in Ward's Guide 1936.

The success of the trial motor ship **Glen** and of Free Trade Wharf's little motor ships **Etal** and **Rock** became evident when Hawthorn Leslie launched a sistership to **Glen** on 8 January 1936, the **Beal**, followed in April by another identical triplet which was given the name **Alnwick**. That same month another motor coaster was named **Wooler** on her launch from Smith's Dock at Middlesbrough. In December 1937 Gideon Koster of Groningen delivered the fifth motor vessel which was given the name **Lowick**, and the **Sandhill** was delivered by the same Dutch yard in February 1938 followed a month later by the slightly smaller **Till**, and in April a sister to **Till**, the **Ryal**, both also delivered by Koster to subsidiary company Free Trade Wharf Company for its King's Lynn service. All these ships were single-deckers. The **Till** and **Ryal** displaced the pioneer motor ship **Rock** which was sold for further service.

The **Sylvian Coast**, built as **Beal** (1936), was the second of the motor ships in the fleet.

(John Clarkson)

The **Cyprian Coast** (1936) was built as **Alnwick**, sister of **Wooler**.

This remarkable shopping spree of eight new motor ships in just two years brought Tyne-Tees from potential oblivion, with its big and increasingly inefficient steamships, to the modern age of economic operation with reduced crew numbers. The reason why this had become necessary was competition from the Dutch with their fleets of small, versatile and economic motor ships. They were so successful that they had begun to undercut freight prices in the North Sea trades so making life difficult for Tyne-Tees.

The adopted Free Trade Wharf nomenclature continued from that of Tyne-Tees. Etal, Rock and Ryal are all villages in Northumberland and the River Till is the only tributary of the Tweed in Northumberland.

The Tyne-Tees and Free Trade Wharf motor ships were all engines-aft single-hold vessels, the Tyne-Tees ships designed for the steel trade, and Free Trade Wharf's ships for the coastal trade between London and East Anglian ports. The hold was long enough to accommodate railway lines and girders and was serviced by derricks fore and aft. Including the Free Trade Wharf Company's two purpose-built ships plus the **Etal**, there were nine motor ships comprising one singlet, Free Trade Wharf's **Rock** and three groups of vessels of which groups 2 and 3 were almost identical in appearance save for variations in davits and arrangements for a small deck house right aft:

The **Rock** (Free Trade Wharf), built by Hawthorn Leslie, was 120 feet long by 24 feet beam.

The **Glen**, **Beal**, **Alnwick**, built by Hawthorn Leslie and **Wooler** by Smith's Dock (Tyne-Tees), were 165 feet long by 27 feet beam.

The **Lowick** and **Sandhill** (Tyne-Tees) built by Gideon Koster were 190 feet long by 31 feet beam.

The **Till** and **Ryal**, (Free Trade Wharf), built by Gideon Koster, were 130 feet long by 24 feet beam.

The **Novian Coast** (1936) started life as the **Wooler**. Note the mainmast extension.

(A Duncan)

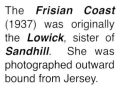

The **Frisian Coast** (1937) was originally the **Lowick**, sister of **Sandhill**. She was photographed outward bound from Jersey.

(Dave Hocquard)

The **Etal** had a minor mishap when she ran onto the beach at Cayton Bay near Scarborough in thick fog one summer night, much to the delight of the holiday makers who found her still sitting high and dry on the beach when the fog cleared. She was refloated on the next tide undamaged, save for the pride of her master as reported in the *Yorkshire Evening Post* on Wednesday 10 August 1938:

*In thick fog early today, the small cargo boat **Etal**, making for Scarborough from London with provisions, ran ashore at Cayton Bay at high tide. She had lost her bearings. Those on board thinking she was at Scarborough Bay, were making for where the harbour should have been when she grounded on a sandy bottom. She was high and dry a low tide, and the crew were able to walk ashore. The vessel was not seriously damaged, and there was no need to launch the lifeboat, though cobles were quickly on the scene from Scarborough ready to lend assistance.*

The **Etal** was carrying a crew of nine... calls at Scarborough twice a week. She runs between London and Middlesbrough. It was expected that there would be little difficulty in refloating her at high tide this evening. Some of the cargo, it was thought, would be landed at Cayton Bay and taken to Scarborough by road to prevent delay in delivery.

This was the fifth vessel to run aground off the Yorkshire coast during 36 hours of dense fog. The fog lifted considerably during the morning and visibility became much better.

As the decade closed, the liner services evolved towards cargo only as James Layton described in *Tees Packet*:

The **Dunstanburgh**... took over the Rotterdam service from the **Lindisfarne** which was transferred to the Newcastle to London cargo service when the **Alnwick** was withdrawn [see Chapter 7]. She remained on the Rotterdam run until the end of 1937 when the new motor ship **Lowick** entered service. The **Lowick** had no passenger accommodation so the passenger trade lapsed until April 1939 when the **Lindisfarne** returned to the Rotterdam run.

The **Akeld** (ex-**The Earl**, ex-**Mayfield**) was the regular ship on the Newcastle to Antwerp service from late 1933 until February 1939 and she had no passenger accommodation. She did have a spare cabin that was occasionally used for passengers but the passenger service to Antwerp virtually ceased when the **New Londoner** was laid up at the end of September 1933. The **Middlesbro'** took over from the **Akeld** in February 1939 but she had no accommodation for passengers.

Layton continues:

In the last week of August 1939 the ships sailing regularly to the Continent were, the **Craster** to Hamburg, the **Lindisfarne** to Rotterdam, the [motor ship] **Sandhill** to Amsterdam and the **Middlesbro'** cargo only to Antwerp.

The declaration of war on Germany in the first week of September was also the precise mid-point of the tenure of the name Tyne-Tees Steam Shipping

STRUCK ROCKS IN FOG

Holiday-makers were surprised to see the motor-ship Etal fast on the rocks when they arrived on the beach at Cayton Bay, near Scarborough, yesterday. The vessel had run ashore in a thick fog in the early hours of the morning.

The **Etal** (1933) perched on the beach at Cayton Bay near Scarborough on 10 August 1938.

(Tyne and Wear Archive)

The **Lindisfarne** (1925) with passengers and well-wishers leaving Newcastle for Rotterdam.

on the Companies Register. Tyne-Tees had come a long way since its foundation 36 years previously but it still had a long way to go in the next 36 years before it disappeared into the mighty jaws of P&O (Chapter 12). Tyne-Tees was a highly respected shipowner with an almost unique business plan. Not only did it maintain a presence in the coastal liner trade to London, albeit now cargo only, it also maintained regular liner services to the Continent and operated a highly successful cargo operation both in the bulk trades, coal, silver sand and grain, as well as the distribution of steel factored goods from north-east ports. It was this very diversity that had enabled the company to flourish and become one of the north-east's most important ship-owners. Credit must be given to the leadership that the company enjoyed throughout the 1920s and 1930s, notably Chairman Sir Arthur Munro Sutherland, his Managing Director for much of this time, Robert Mason, and their dedicated Board of Directors.

At no time had the Board of the Tyne-Tees company veered from their chosen course of a sensible, almost conservative, and thrifty vision. It had weathered the recession following the Wall Street Crash in 1929 and had managed its portfolio of ships to suit the needs of the day. It did have its ups and downs. But even when the **Richard Welford** so publically sank at Newcastle Quayside in 1924, the company saw to it that she was quietly raised and sent away for repairs later to be brought back into service as the **Hethpool**. Although she was sold shortly afterwards she was sold as a ship in top condition that attracted a top price.

Given the conservative management of the company it is notable that coal-fired triple expansion engines were the favoured propulsion system until the mid-1930s. This system was convenient, tried and tested, and drew on a large pool of certificated steam engineers to maintain it. Besides, coal was abundant and cheap given that Tyne-Tees attracted concessionary rates from the colliery owners who maintained contracts with Tyne-Tees to export their coal to London and other ports in the south of England and the near Continent. Coal and steam were, therefore, recognised as the most efficient combination then available.

Why then did some companies in the domestic and Home Trade routes head off towards building motor ships when other companies were content with the triple expansion steam engine? There were two basic reasons, the first was pressure from some commercial tie or former commercial tie and the second was commercial peer pressure. Coast Lines is always recognised as a pioneer developer of the motor coaster, and for that matter of the cross-channel motor ferry. In the latter case the Coast Lines associate company the Belfast Steamship Company put the big **Ulster Monarch**-class of ferry into service from 1929, a class developed through various guises up until 1956 when the last ship based on this same original design concept, the **Scottish Coast**, was commissioned. But Coast Lines' first motor coaster was the **Lochshiel**, commissioned in 1929 by associate company David MacBrayne, complete with a Gardner oil engine that provided her with a speed of 9 knots. The first motor ship in the parent fleet was the **Fife Coast**, delivered by the Ardrossan Dockyard Company in November 1933 and later lost to enemy action in 1940. She was built to the classic Coast Lines profile of bridge and accommodation amidships and engines aft, a profile copied many times over in subsequent years. Associate company Burns & Laird Lines had three motor coasters in service shortly afterwards: the **Lairdswood**, **Lairdscrest** and **Lairdsbank**. These were able to maintain 13.5 knots on the overnight cattle run on the Irish Sea and were novel in that they were equipped with twin 5-cylinder diesel units driving twin screws. From then on steamers became secondary in preference to motor ships throughout the group.

The British & Irish Steam Packet Company's **Glanmire** (1936) was built as **Lairdsbank**, one of three sisters that experimented with twin screws driven by separate oil engines to provide a speed of 13.5 knots.

(Author)

The reason Coast Lines took the motor ship route so early was simply because of the affiliation to the Royal Mail Group which owned Coast Lines until 1936. Royal Mail also owned the Harland & Wolff shipyard at Belfast, and Harland & Wolff had developed an early liaison with the oil engine manufacturer Burmeister & Wain of Copenhagen. This had led to a proliferation of deep sea motor ships built for Royal Mail and its associate companies by Harland & Wolff with Burmeister & Wain oil engines. Perhaps the most famous were the big passenger liners of the Nelson Line built between 1928 and 1931, and Royal Mail had already commissioned numerous cargo ships driven by oil engines. The pros of the early motor ships were essentially lower running costs, instant availability of power, better fuel efficiency and fewer engine room staff. The cons were that the oil engine was limited in power until the opposed piston system was developed by Doxford and by Harland & Wolff, and that the engines were direct drive, gears were only available when metals were developed strong enough to resist the high torques the gear train had to withstand, although some of the smaller ships such as the early Dutch 'schuyts' were geared.

The direct drive engine could be shut down and restarted in reverse. For this engine manoeuvre a bottle of compressed air was always being topped up by an auxiliary air pump to provide sufficient pressure of air to restart the engine either in forward mode or in reverse. Many a pier was bumped as a result of failure of the engine to restart while a frustrated engineer wrestled with the starter valves to coax the engine to refire. But this was an acceptable risk for a ship that was employed on routes that only required berthing manoeuvres once every few days and was, therefore, acceptable to companies operating in the coastal and continental trades.

The Tyne-Tees company took to the oil engine because of commercial peer pressure from its competitors. The Danes, Swedes and Germans were all instrumental in sending the oil engine to sea, but above all the Dutch pioneered the small motor 'schuyts'. These were small cargo ships, low in profile to negotiate canal bridges, with a single hatch before a small poop containing the bridge structure and engine room skylights. Below the poop was the crew accommodation and the all-important engine, a direct drive motor typically of four or six cylinders. The crew comprised the same deck department as a steamer, but the engine room was manned by a Chief and a Second and two engineers. Without the need for firemen there was a saving of five or six men and the little Dutch ships were able to put to sea with a crew of between eight and ten men, providing a considerable saving in the wages bill. By the early 1930s the Tyne-Tees Board had seen the schuyts at work in the North Sea trades creaming business away from the British operators by offering lower freight rates. It was for this reason only that Tyne-Tees was willing, if not eager, to shed its comfort zone and experiment with the motor ship.

Not all British operators in the Home Trade were willing to make the jump from steam to motor but the more discerning did. The General Steam Navigation Company, for example, was one of the first as described in my history of that company:

*… in 1932, the yard of J Koster at Groningen was building a small motor coaster of just 213 tons gross to an accepted engines-aft design. Nearing completion, it became apparent that the intended owners of the vessel would not be able to take delivery due to the recession. The ship was offered to a variety of companies including GSN, and the company directors decided that this was the appropriate opportunity to test the new machinery. Launched as the **Tern**, the vessel had the distinction of being the first motor ship in the fleet and the first GSN vessel to be built at a foreign yard. She had a four-cylinder Deutz engine… The engine controls were in the wheelhouse allowing the engine room to be unattended for lengthy periods, save for checks on pressures, temperatures and the contents of the fuel oil gravity tank. Serving on the near-Continental routes, her success can be judged by the order of a larger vessel of 614 tons gross, the **Fauvette**, which on delivery was placed on the London to Antwerp service in 1934…*

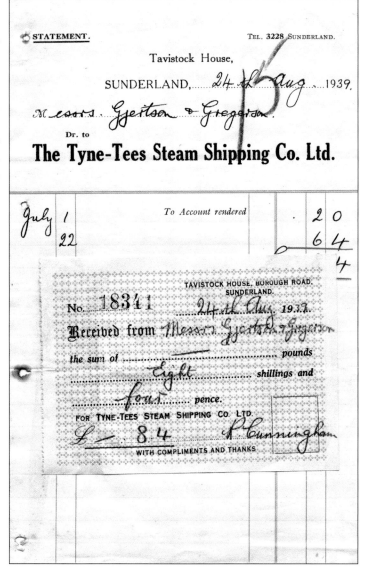

In hindsight, had the Tyne-Tees Board stuck to tradition and the tried and tested technology of the triple steam expansion-engine, the company prospects could have been quite different by 1939. It must nevertheless have been a difficult decision to make, surrounded as they were by owners of numerous collier fleets for which coal-fired steam engines would remain in vogue for another two decades. Had it not also been for the intervention of war with Germany, Tyne-Tees would have been set for a prosperous future. As it was, Britain declared war on Germany following its invasion of Poland and the normal rules of commercial maritime trade were once again suspended.

An historical artefact: statement and receipt for 8/4d to Messrs Gjertson & Gregson, dated 1 July and 24 August 1939 respectively.

(Harold Appleyard collection)

CHAPTER 9

WAR LOSSES

The **Craster** had a lucky escape from internment after she sailed from Newcastle bound for Hamburg on 29 August 1939 under Captain Percy Browitt. On 30 August the company decided that it would be in everybody's best interests to recall her but there was no easy way of imparting this decision to her master. Fortunately she was intercepted by a France Fenwick collier homeward bound from Hamburg and told to return to Newcastle as war with Germany was now inevitable. Chief Engineer George Appleby reported to Jim Layton that he and the rest of the crew were very pleased to receive the recall message, and that they had a very lucky escape. War was declared on Germany on 3 September. Neville Chamberlain's speech to the nation began:

This morning the British Ambassador in Berlin handed the German Government a final note stating that unless we heard from them by 11 am that they were prepared at once to withdraw their troops from Poland, a state of war would exist between us. I have to tell you that no such undertaking has been received, and that consequently this country is at war with Germany.

The first Tyne-Tees casualty of the war was the **Middlesbro'**. She was on a voyage from the Tees to London when she ran into a submerged object about one nautical mile off Flamborough Head on 8 December. The hull of the **Middlesbro'** was ruptured such that the forward compartments immediately began to flood and the order was given to abandon ship. The crew was able to launch the boats and get away from the stricken vessel before she sank and they were all quickly and safely picked up by the small Swedish steamer **Runeborg**.

As it happened, an early casualty in the war on 10 September was the William France Fenwick & Company collier **Goodwood**. She was broken in two by a mine on 10 September while on passage from the Tyne to Bayonne with a cargo of coal and also sank in the shallow waters off Flamborough Head. She was the first Allied loss to a mine in World War II but was followed later in the day by the sinking of T & J Brocklebank's **Magdapur** which struck a mine off Orford Ness on passage from the Tyne to Southampton. In her case the mine was known to have been laid the day after war was declared by U-Boat U.13.

The **Goodwood** was a large state-of-the-art collier of some 2,796 tons gross that had been built by S P Austin & Sons at Wear Dock. The **Goodwood** was launched into the Wear in July 1937. It was some time after the loss of the **Middlesbro'** that the connection was made with the loss of the **Goodwood**, and it was confirmed that the 'unidentified' submerged object that had ruptured the hull of the **Middlesbro'** was in fact part of the wreck of the **Goodwood**. The loss of the **Middlesbro'** was not listed in the official compilation of wartime losses prepared by the Admiralty and published by His Majesty's Stationery Office in 1947; this was one of a number of oversights and errors in this document.

The next loss was that of the **Akeld** on 9 March 1940. She had departed from Rotterdam with general cargo bound for Newcastle under Captain David Lambert, but before the **Akeld** was even out of sight of the Dutch coast she was torpedoed and sunk while in convoy about 30 miles south west of Hook of Holland. She had a crew of twelve men and one RNVR gunner, but none survived the sinking. The gunner, Harold Laws, and one of the ABs, George Wilson, were the youngest crew members and were just 21 years-old.

At 11.30 pm on 9 March 1940, the **Abbotsford**, which was in line aft of the **Akeld**, was hit forward by a torpedo fired by U.14 and immediately caught fire. The **Abbotsford** was owned by George Gibson & Company of Leith and had a crew of nineteen. She was on passage from Ghent to Leith. The **Akeld** turned around to help the torpedoed ship, but at 11.45 pm was herself struck amidships by a torpedo from the same submarine. The **Akeld** sank rapidly allowing no time for her crew to escape. Ten minutes later the **Abbotsford** was hit again and she too sank, again with no time for any of her crew to survive. This had been a tragic night for the two east coast ship owners with many of the ships' crews being local to Tyneside and the Lothians respectively.

The **Sandhill**, one of the Dutch-built motor ships, was dispatched to Dunkirk just prior to the evacuation of the British Expeditionary Force (BEF). She lay in harbour for three days under continual bombardment while she discharged much needed supplies with her own cargo handling gear. Fires burned around the docks and across the nearby industrial area. Opposite the **Sandhill** were two ships; one loaded with cased petrol and the other with ammunition awaiting discharge as the supplies became needed. The **Sandhill** completed discharge safely and was able to reach the comparative safety of the Channel unscathed.

The Tyne-Tees Steam Shipping Company was well represented in the evacuation of the British Expeditionary Force at Dunkirk in May and early June 1940, and later at St Malo and Cherbourg, with the motor ships **Beal**, **Lowick** and **Alnwick** in attendance at Dunkirk as well as the former World War I standard steamship **Gateshead**.

The **Persian Coast** (1919) was built as **War Colne** but was given the name **Gateshead** when she was acquired by Tyne-Tees early in 1933. She was one of several Tyne-Tees and Free Trade Wharf ships attending at Dunkirk.

The **Beal** was next to arrive at Dunkirk with 900 tons of ammunition for the men holding the perimeter of Dunkirk to assist the Operation Dynamo evacuation. The **Beal** was one of the first batch of small motor ships built by Hawthorn Leslie. On arrival off Dunkirk it was realised that no dock facilities remained functional and the cargo of ammunition had to be discharged with her own gear and brought ashore. This was accomplished despite incessant bombing and the ship was made ready to take aboard as many soldiers as was deemed prudent. There was surf over the beach where she was working, but one of the seamen, A D C Hall, of Norman Road, Newcastle, went over the side and swam half a mile to the shore with a line. That rope enabled the loaded lifeboats to be pulled off the beach when the sea made it impossible to handle the boats under oars.

The **Gateshead** was also a Dunkirk survivor receiving telegraphic instruction to proceed to Calais to upload retreating members of the BEF. She made her first run under Captain J R Linn on 2 June. The **Gateshead** was quite close inshore approaching the line of sand dunes to the south west of the Calais harbour entrance channel before Captain Linn realised that the port was already in enemy hands as German gunners began to fire at the approaching ships. Most of the crew of the **Gateshead**, who were all from Tyneside, were at breakfast but were quickly scrambled to action as the ship was turned off the Calais approach channel, avoiding another vessel that was damaged but still under control. The **Gateshead** then sailed along the coast towards Dunkirk and was able to berth alongside Dunkirk East Pier where a ship following her in was hit by a bomb and sank alongside the pier. The enemy had the range of the pier but Chief Officer, Jack Winship, of South Shields, was able quickly to contact the military dispatch office and arrange loading of personnel.

Approaching La Panne the **Gateshead** passed the sinking hospital transport **Paris** with her distress flags still flying. The **Paris** had been a fast day passenger cross-Channel steamer in civilian life, built for the London, Brighton & South Coast Railway in 1913 for service between Newhaven and Dieppe. She was so badly damaged by an air attack off Dunkirk on 2 June that she was abandoned and sank the following day.

Captain J S Stewart, of Ponteland, master of the **Lowick**, described how he passed a motor cruiser in the dark in mid-Channel on his way to La Panne beaches: '*We saw something white and we suspected it might be an enemy craft. It was a little motor cruiser. The old man and the boy on board asked for a tow which was impossible in the circumstances. We had to give them a bearing as they had no compass.*' Captain Stewart had some 900 tons of ammunitions on board but these were not discharged and were safely returned to Britain.

Captain Graber, later a South Shields Pilot Master for the Tyne pilots, was master of the **Alnwick** when she attended at Cherbourg to evacuate troops in mid-June 1940. Typical of the improvisation of his galley was a new ash bin mounted on the stove to make 20 gallons of tea at a time. Tins of tomatoes were used to make soup for the troops on the return journey. The **Alnwick** took 500 men out of Cherbourg. One soldier that arrived had an Alsatian pup in his arms. On being told that the dog could not accompany him to England he replied: '*We really are going home?*' He was exhausted but quite ready to move on to carry on the fight.

The little motor ship **Lowick** was sent to Le Havre as the evacuation continued towards its final day on 27 June. The ship's crew helped disable trucks and tanks, some of the younger crew members having their first driving lessons as vehicles were brought in ready for destruction. The **Lowick** did several trips also to St Malo until her engine failed off Falmouth where repairs were later put in hand.

On 26 July 1940, Free Trade Wharf's **London Trader** was torpedoed and sank 13 miles south-west of Shoreham. This was the second day of attacks on westbound Convoy CW 8 which came from several E-boats supported by low-flying fighter planes, the latter outnumbering the British Spitfires and Hurricanes by up to five to one. One man was killed in the explosion aboard the **London Trader** while the remainder of the crew were saved. Over the two days 25 and 26 July, eleven of the colliers in the 21 ship convoy were sunk in the English Channel, most within sight of the English Coast and two British destroyers were also lost – these were the bleakest days in the Battle of Britain.

Free Trade Wharf's little East Anglian motor ship **Till** was mined in the Thames estuary on 10 October 1940 but was able to complete her voyage into London under tow. She was quickly repaired and put back into service. The **Ryal** was the next casualty when she struck a mine in the lower Thames estuary some 8 miles north of Whitstable on 24 November 1940. Seven of her crew lost their lives. The ship sank in about 60 feet of water. The **Till** was lost shortly afterwards when she was involved in a collision on 1 February 1941 on a voyage from the Tees to King's Lynn in convoy.

The **Sandhill**, which survived the war, was largely deployed in the Irish Sea from early 1941 onwards as Robert Sinclair describes in his history of the Belfast Steamship Company (**Sandhill** was later deployed at Belfast as **Ulster Chieftain**):

*…on a voyage from Belfast to Preston in January 1941 [the **Sandhill**] was severely damaged by a mine near the English coast. Disabled, she had drifted helplessly for two days until taken in tow near the Northern Irish coast. Then in November 1941, off the west coast of Scotland, fire broke out in her after 'tween decks and she was carrying 800 tons of high explosives…*

With two of its fleet already lost in the war, the Free Trade Wharf Company maintained the **Hull Trader** on duty between London and Hull as best it was able. In a northbound convoy from the Thames the ship hit a mine off Cromer, 1 mile east of 57C Buoy, on 23 June 1941 and sank rapidly. Eleven of her crew of fourteen lost their lives. The company was forced to withdraw from the coastal service for much of the remainder of the war. The loss of the **Hull Trader** left the company with only the **Etal** in service although it was then given the little **Empire Isle** to manage for the Ministry of War Transport.

The **Bilton**, in the Tyne-Tees fleet, served as a collier on the east coast until 1942 when she was allocated by the Ministry of War Transport to John Kelly of Belfast. Under Kelly's management she was deployed on the Irish Sea bringing coal from the Lancashire coalfield to Northern Ireland; Ireland, north and south, has only very minor reserves of coal centred on Coalisland west of Loch Neagh and these are insufficient for power, gas and coke generation let alone fuelling the major industry of the Belfast area. By 1944 the **Bilton** had swapped her Irish crew for a normal Tyne-Tees crew again.

The steamer **Lindisfarne** was the third and final loss to the Tyne-Tees company in the war. She was sunk in a northbound east coast convoy on 12 December 1942. Convoy FN 889 had assembled off Southend in the lower Thames and was bound for Methil on the Firth of Forth with ships joining and leaving at intermediate ports. The convoy was first attacked by at least 15 E-boats at 2035 hours in a position about 20 miles north east of Lowestoft. At the time the convoy columns were 5 miles long, there being 38 ships in the convoy. Five ships were quickly sunk by torpedo, four British, the **Avonwood**, **Lindisfarne**, **Glen Tilt** and **Knitsley**, and one Norwegian, the **Marianne**. **Lindisfarne** was hit three nautical miles from the Lowestoft No. 4 buoy marking the navigation channel cleared of mines.

The **Bilton** (1920), seen after World War II as **Coleraine** when owned by J Kelly of Belfast.

The destroyer HMS **Wallace** escorting ahead, turned down the seaward side of the convoy when the attack began, firing starshell to seaward from 340 degrees to 160 degrees, but saw nothing. At 8.45 pm one torpedo crossed her bows on an easterly course, and almost immediately another passed on a westerly course. At 8.54 pm she turned north-east, and engaged three E-boats on an easterly course until 9.04 pm when she again turned north-east. Almost immediately two more E-boats were engaged both by HMS **Wallace** and HMS **Meynell**, hits being claimed by the latter. The action lasted only a few minutes. HMS **Wallace** then turned back to ensure that survivors were being rescued, and resumed her position at the head of the convoy at 10.12 pm. After 11.00 pm, the weather deteriorated, and coastal forces, which had been augmented by British motor gun boats were, of necessity, recalled. Four ABs were killed in the sinking of the **Lindisfarne**: Clifford Hodges, Richard Martin, Norman Moore and John Walls; the remainder of the crew were able to get away from the stricken ship and were picked up safely. The Commander-in-Chief, Nore, later acknowledged that there was no easy way of defending such a large convoy faced with an attack of this magnitude.

Management of the **Empire Cape** was vested in the company in 1943. She was a motor ship built by Scott & Sons at Bowling on the Clyde, one of a class of six ships built during 1941 for the Ministry of War Transport. She had a gross tonnage of 872 and her 5-cylinder British Auxiliaries oil engine provided a speed of 10 knots in a fair sea. The bridge and accommodation was amidships and engines aft with two long holds one forward and one aft of the bridge each serviced by a single derrick. Initially managed by William Robertson of Glasgow, management was transferred to Tyne-Tees in 1943. In July 1944 the Dundee, Perth & London Shipping Company took over the management of the ship for the Ministry of War Transport. At the end of the war she was bought by the Dundee, Perth & London Shipping Company and renamed **Gowrie**, and later renamed **Lochee**, serving her Scottish owners until sold for further service in 1966.

The former German steamer **Empire Conifer** was put under Tyne-Tees management in 1945. Two years later her Tyne-Tees crew handed her over to the Commonwealth of Australia (Department of Shipping Transport) who renamed her **Nyora**. She was a motor ship completed as **Adrian** in in 1935 for E Komrowski. She eventually foundered in 1978 after several subsequent changes of name.

Free Trade Wharf managed three ships for the Ministry of War Transport. Between 1941 and 1943 the **Empire Isle** was under company management, passing to Comben Longstaff & Company in 1943 and later bought by them and renamed **Suffolkbrook** in 1945. They sold her in 1946 to Cardiff owners Lovering & Sons who renamed her **Fennel** and four years later she became **Hindlea** for the Hindlea Shipping Company. She was wrecked in Moelfre Bay off Anglesey in October 1959 when she dragged her anchor in stormy conditions, having earlier sailed from Weston Point in ballast for Newport. She was a small, engines-aft motor ship with a deadweight of just 480 tons.

The **Empire Cape** (1941) was managed for the Ministry of War Transport by the Tyne-Tees company between 1943 and 1944. After the war she was bought by the Dundee, Perth & London Shipping Company and renamed **Lochee** as seen here.

In 1944 both the **Empire Drover** and **Empire Marksman** came under Free Trade Wharf management, the latter transferred to William Coombs & Sons of Cardiff during the late stages of the war. She later became their **Afon Morlais**. In 1956 she was sold to John S Monks of Liverpool and renamed **Cliffville**. Approaching Glasgow from Liverpool with a cargo of grain that had shifted badly, she rolled over and capsized on 12 May 1958 and was later broken up at Dublin. The **Empire Drover** was sold to Queenship Navigation Company in 1946 and renamed **Roman Queen**, eventually being sold for demolition in 1961. Both the **Empire Drover** and **Empire Marksman** were part of the **Tudor Queen**-class, styled on the lines of the steamship **Tudor Queen** completed by the Burntisland Shipbuilding Company in 1941 for Queenship Navigation Company with a deadweight of approximately 1,100 tons. The **Stuart Queen** later became the **Hampshire Coast** when she joined the Tyne-Tees fleet in 1952. Another ship was the **Empire Atoll**, managed by Coast Lines in the war and later becoming an important unit under Tyne-Tees as the **Hadrian Coast** working also for the subsidiary Aberdeen Steam Navigation Company (see Chapter 11).

A wartime picture of the steamship **Stuart Queen** (1940) owned by British Channel Island Shipping Company, later Coast Lines and then Tyne-Tees as the **Hampshire Coast**.

The **Thornaby** was one of the first ships to discharge at the prefabricated 'Mulberry' port of Arromanches, built immediately subsequent to the Normandy Landings. Port Winston, as it was known, was opened for business on 9 June 1944 despite storm damage that occurred during its assembly. Over the next ten months the artificial port was used to land over 2.5 million men, 4 million tons of supplies and 0.5 million vehicles, all of which had to find their way to shore along the narrow and confined roadway built over the caissons.

The previous year, 1943, was the year when the Coast Lines Group of Liverpool acquired the Tyne-Tees company. The fortunes of war had begun to turn and the Allies were beginning to see a positive future. The disastrous losses of 1940 and 1941, when Germany clearly had the upper hand over Allied merchant shipping were history, and commercial futures could at last again be postulated.

Coast Lines dominated the west coast domestic trades between Liverpool via the Bristol Channel or Dublin and Cork to London as well as routes north about to Newcastle. The round-Scotland passenger and cargo route was originally operated by Langlands of Liverpool until this family firm was acquired by Coast Lines in 1918.

Langlands' services were operated in collaboration with Tyne-Tees for onward shipment of freight via Newcastle to the Continent. Tyne-Tees also collaborated with the Antrim Iron Ore Company whose ships returned to Ireland empty from Stockton to Belfast apart from goods transhipped from Tyne-Tees Continental steamers in the Tees. This two-ship service was taken over by Coast Lines in 1929, the **Glendun** becoming the **Aberdeen Coast** and **Glentaise** the **Antrim Coast**, while in both cases Coast Lines continued to encourage transhipment via Tyne-Tees vessels. The service called at Stornoway and on inducement also at Leith and Aberdeen on the return to Belfast. The service was finally closed in December 1963.

Coast Lines' **Aberdeen Coast** (1909) was formerly the Antrim Iron Ore Company's **Glendun**. She served under both names on the Belfast to Stockton service with freight connections with the Tyne-Tees company's Continental services.

For all its might, Coast Lines had never had a proper foothold on the east coast and for this it dearly yearned. Acquisition of the Tyne-Tees Steam Shipping Company would also give the Coast Lines group that vital opening to the North Sea Continental trades. Although the company Chairman and Managing Director Alfred Read openly stated that 'Coast Lines owned the Irish Sea', the group, known then as Coast Lines Seaway, held little business on the east coast and Read considered this to be an obvious area for his group to expand. Coast Line's collaboration with the Tyne-Tees company over the years led it to respect the Newcastle company and eventually to view it through the eyes of a predator as a means of getting a grasp on the east coast trade.

Overtures by Coast Line's Chairman were at first rejected by the Tyne-Tees Board. Nevertheless, the Board recognised the difficulties that a relatively small independent shipping company would face in the uncertain trading conditions that would prevail following the eventual declaration of peace. After considerable deliberation it was agreed the Tyne-Tees Steam Shipping Company would become a part of the Coast Lines empire with purchase of all the share issue recommended by the Tyne-Tees Board to its shareholders at a total price of £1.3 million. This sum was to be paid both in cash and in shares in the parent group. The deal was completed in December 1943. For the moment the Tyne-Tees Directors were left to carry on much as before with one of the Coast Lines' Directors appointed to the Board as an observer rather than an agent for the new owners.

Under the watchful eye of Coast Lines, the Tyne-Tees Steam Shipping Company suffered no further casualties in the war and emerged into the grey dawn of peace two years later having lost three ships including the crews of two of them. Compensation for the losses was poor and despite good charter fees for Admiralty duties the company was not as well off as it had been at the end of the Great War. But its new masters had a powerful and diverse portfolio of interests and Tyne-Tees Directors, answerable now to Liverpool, were nevertheless grateful that their company was no longer independent but a part of a vibrant and diverse group of companies. An early consolidation of the two companies was merging the London offices of Coast Lines and the Free Trade Wharf Company under one roof at Seaway House, 338 The Highway, E1.

COAST LINES

F H Powell & Company, John Bacon Limited and Samuel Hough Limited amalgamated their services, many of which were shared routes, to form Powell, Bacon and Hough Lines in 1913, under the directorship of Chairman Sir Alfred Read (also a Colonel). The company was rebranded Coast Lines in April 1917 when Read, now appointed company Chairman, oversaw the majority shareholding being acquired by the Royal Mail group. Read took Powell, Bacon and Hough into Royal Mail ownership in order to cement the coastal feeder deal for the Royal Mail group's network of deep sea cargo liners, and to draw on the massive resources of the Royal Mail empire to develop the Coast Lines network. Read went on a shopping spree using resources from the Royal Mail group to buy, for example M Langlands & Sons and British & Irish and the City of Cork company in 1917 and 1918, Belfast Steamship Company in 1919, and Burns and Laird was formed soon afterwards with the purchase of the Laird Line and G & J Burns in 1920. George Bazeley & Sons at Penzance and its three ships were bought out, also in 1920. Sir Alfred Read was invested as a Knight Bachelor in 1919. Ernest Reader wrote in *Sea Breezes*, February 1949:

Operating the world's largest fleet of coastal liners, Coast Lines, although not one of long-standing under its present title, has routes which extend back into the early nineteenth century. Pioneer of the motor coaster, the firm operates some of the finest ships of their types in the world, being as they are, well-built, well-found, and well-manned.

The core Coast Lines service was Liverpool to London calling at a variety of ports including Falmouth and Southampton or Dublin and Plymouth. It also maintained the passenger ferry links between Liverpool and Dublin, Belfast and Cork, between Fishguard and Cork, between Glasgow and Belfast, Dublin and 'Derry. The Coast Lines' partners flourished in the 1920s, despite the downturn in the Irish trade during 'The Troubles' and the subsequent partitioning of Ireland. But the parent Royal Mail Line group, under Lord Kylsant (Owen Philipps as was, who once tried to buy the Tyne Steam Shipping Company, see Chapter 3), began to suffer financial difficulties. A number of measures were taken by Alfred Read to isolate Coast Lines from its parent and the inevitable collapse of the Royal Mail group of companies. The collapse, when it came, was aided by the intransigence of Lord Kylsant, the group's Chairman, to refinance the company in 1922. The inevitable fall of both Lord Kylsant and Royal Mail occurred in 1931, but Coast Lines and its associate companies had become sufficiently independent by then to ride out the storm. In 1936 Coast Lines was able to buy itself out of Royal Mail altogether by floating the company on the Stock Exchange. Coast Lines acquired the British Channel Islands Shipping Company in 1936; the Plymouth, Channel Islands & Brittany Steamship Company in 1937; the Merchants Line and Fisher Renwick in 1939; and Gilchrist's Steamers and Tyne-Tees Steam Shipping Company in 1943. Coast Lines went from strength to strength, and became the dominant major independent coastal sea carrier in steadfast competition with the railway owned, and cross subsidised, ferry fleets as Charles Waine recounts in his book on coastal liners:

Proliferation of Coast Lines services was immense, quite apart from the services of other members of the group like the Belfast Steamship Company. In 1933, for example, the company, based at Liverpool, could offer services from Liverpool to Aberdeen, Bristol, Cardiff, Dover, Dundee, Falmouth (where cargo was discharged over-side to the company's barges), Glasgow, Greenock, Inverness, Kirkcaldy, Llanelli, Leith, London, Middlesbrough, Newcastle, Penzance, Plymouth, Poole, Portsmouth, Shoreham, Southampton, Swansea, Teignmouth and Weymouth. Ships totally within the company carried the old Powell funnel, black with a white chevron, while group members kept their own funnel colours. Names were standardised with a Coast suffix mainly for Coast Lines own vessels although many group members kept their naming styles. There was much switching of ships within the group as trades demanded. Fortunately, during the 1930s Depression, the parent company was financially strong enough to save group members who would otherwise have perished. Complete restructuring of the British & Irish Steam Packet Company took place in 1936...

*Coast Lines was able to supply more tonnage throughout the group, the Harland & Wolff passenger motor ships for Belfast, Dublin and Cork services [William Denny & Brothers built the post-war **Innisfallen**], engines-aft motor coasters for its own fleet and for its subsidiaries. Some new steamers were built for Coast Lines itself... but most of is steam fleet was acquired from the companies it took over. The first motor coaster was **Fife Coast** (1933), but the twin screw **British Coast** (1933) and **Atlantic Coast** (1934) were a great improvement with accommodation for twelve passengers.*

The **British Coast** (1933) was a pioneer motor coaster in the Coast Lines fleet with the classic bridge amidships engines aft profile.

Sir Alfred Read was quite a remarkable man. He was born in July 1871 at Liverpool. He was the son of Colonel Alfred Read and Emily Blanche Musgrave. He married Agnes Mary Parry in July 1895 at Chester. He and Agnes had four children but were divorced before 1917. He remarried, in 1918, Jane Charlotte Macneal at Chelsea. Jane gave him a son. He was married a third time to Elsa Elena Fisher in 1920 at St Malo. Read stood down as Managing Director of Coast Lines in 1946 and as Chairman in 1950. He died on 6 March 1955 aged 83 at Lisbon and his body was brought home aboard the **Adriatic Coast**. He had been Chairman and Managing Director of Coast Lines; Chairman of the Liverpool Marine and General Insurance Company; Managing Director of the City of Cork Steam Packet Company and of the British and Irish Steam Packet Company. Ernest Reader wrote in *Sea Breezes* February 1949:

The dynamic and outstanding personality of the Chairman, Sir Alfred Read, has provided the driving force behind the creation of what is recognised as the largest coastal liner organisation. With a character founded on the generosity of greatness, and knowing by name most of the members of his vast staff ashore and afloat, partaking of their joys and sorrow, he is held in the highest esteem by all who have been fortunate enough to meet him…

From 1904-1920 he was a member of the Mersey Docks and Harbour Board; in 1912, Chairman of the Liverpool Steam Ship Owners association; from 1917-1919 he served as Director of Home Trade Services, Ministry of Shipping, and was knighted in 1919. He was also a member of the Port of London Authority during the years 1934-1941, and President of the Institute of Transport in 1936.

At the end of his career he was Chairman of Coast Lines, British & Irish Steam Packet Company, Burns & Laird Lines, Belfast Steamship Company, Tyne-Tees Steam Shipping Company, British Channel Islands Shipping Company, David MacBrayne, Ardrossan Harbour Company and Ardrossan Dockyard, and Managing Director of several of these companies as well as others within the Coast Lines group.

CHAPTER 10

UNDER ORDERS FROM LIVERPOOL

On 2 February 1946 *The Times* reported:

*The 7,157-ton cargo ship **Fort Massac**, bound from Middlesbrough to Cape Town, sank in shallow water off Harwich last night after a collision with another vessel. Thirty-three of the crew were taken off by the Walton-on-Naze lifeboat, but the captain remained on board the partly-submerged vessel. One man is missing.*

The other vessel was the **Thornaby**. On the 1 February 1946 the **Thornaby** ran into the British Ministry of War Transport's **Fort Massac** off the Sunk Light Vessel 10 nautical miles east south east of Harwich. The weather was mild for the time of year, blustery but with brief and intense rain storms occurring throughout the day. The **Fort Massac**, carrying general cargo including a railway locomotive, sank rapidly while the lifeboat from Walton and the Trinity House pilot vessel **Pioneer** picked up survivors. The bows of the **Thornaby** were ruptured back to the forward water-tight bulkhead in the impact, but the bulkhead fortunately held allowing the crippled ship to reach the safety of Harwich, later to be fully repaired. The **Fort Massac** was built in 1943 at Vancouver as one of the many 'Victory' type standard wartime ships. The loss of the **Fort Massac** from collision with a much smaller ship may relate to structural deficiencies in the Victory ship's part-welded hull. At the time of the sinking she was under the management of John Cory & Sons of Cardiff. Sadly on 9 April the coaster **Empire Bridge** (Springwell Shipping Company), which had been helping salvage cargo from the wreck, was holed and sank alongside the big Victory ship. Finally, in July 1949, the collier **Corcrest**, dating from 1918 and owned by William Cory of London, struck the wreck of the **Fort Massac** and sank alongside her and the **Empire Bridge**. The wrecks are still a hazard to shipping and are marked by the Fort Massac Buoy.

Sir Alfred Read took his Chair on the Board of Tyne-Tees at the end of the war and wasted no time in bringing the Tyne-Tees Steam Shipping Company into the appropriate corporate style. Like many of his subsidiaries the company was allowed to retain its own livery but the fleet's endearing Northumbrian nomenclature was replaced by 'Coast' names. The only concession towards some sort of Tyne-Tees identity was that all the first names could end in –*ian*. The fleet was duly renamed early in 1946:

The steamships:

Newminster to **Dorian Coast**
Gateshead to **Persian Coast**
Craster to **Caspian Coast**
Cragside to **Elysian Coast**
Thornaby to **Northumbrian Coast**

The motor ships:

Glen to **Belgian Coast**
Beal to **Sylvian Coast**
Alnwick to **Cyprian Coast**
Wooler to **Novian Coast**
Lowick to **Frisian Coast**
Sandhill to Valerian Coast

The old collier **Bilton** was not renamed but was sold to John Kelly of Belfast. She had been assigned to Kelly for much of the war and she became a useful vessel in the Irish Sea collier fleet despite her age. Kelly renamed her **Coleraine**, and later **Ballyhalbert**, in keeping with their own nomenclature newly adopted in the early 1950s. The **Dorian Coast**, formerly the **Newminster** was also sold for further service, going to Indian owners although she was sold for demolition at Bombay in November 1951.

Just as the Tyne-Tees company had been nervous about post-war trading conditions so too had several of the other east coast coastal liner operators. During 1944 the concept of a new consortium to be called the London Scottish Lines was drawn up by the London & Edinburgh Shipping Company, General Steam Navigation Company, Clyde Shipping Company and the Carron Company. The new private joint stock company was incorporated on 1 December 1944. This was first discussed in 1939 but its development had to be shelved during the war. Invitations to join the new company were issued to the Aberdeen Steam Navigation Company, the Dundee, Perth & London company and the Aberdeen, Newcastle & Hull Shipping Company. Each rejected the prospect as not being in the best interests. The Aberdeen, Newcastle & Hull company went into liquidation and the Dundee company planned a cargo-only future.

The **Sylvian Coast** (1936), newly renamed, looking very clean and tidy while on trials following her post-war refit.

The **Novian Coast** (1936), newly renamed in September 1946, passing the John Fraser Millwall boiler works on the Thames. Note the mainmast extension for the new masthead light had not then been added.

(Richard Danielson collection)

The Aberdeen Steam Navigation Company was not to remain isolated for long as Coast Lines made an initial approach for control of the company as soon as Germany had surrendered on 2 May 1945. Graeme Somner takes up the story in his history of the Aberdeen Steam Navigation Company:

...in May 1945 an approach to the [Aberdeen] company was made by the Coast Lines group of Liverpool as to the possibility of buying out the company. A firm offer was received in June 1945 from the Tyne-Tees Steam Shipping Company of Newcastle (a company within the Coast Lines group) to take the [Aberdeen] company over, and this offer was accepted. It was all part of a move to rationalise coastal shipping in the light of the drift of passenger and cargo traffic from the sea to road and rail...

Sir Alfred Read funded the purchase from Liverpool and cleverly put Tyne-Tees in between Liverpool and Aberdeen so creating a single line of management for Coast Line's North Sea interests. Somner again:

The [Aberdeen] company had already decided that passenger sailings would not be resumed when peace came because of the changed trading conditions, and the fact that the transportation of livestock at sea was no longer acceptable, further reducing the potential revenue of the company. The age and condition of the three passenger steamers anyway was such that to reintroduce them into service would be expensive, so steps were put in hand to sell them by Coast Lines.

The transfer of control to the Tyne-Tees Steam Shipping Company came about in November 1945, with the [Aberdeen] company then becoming Coast Lines' group agents at the same time. The new managers found that they had taken over an old and uneconomical fleet of four steamers, all heavily worked during the war, and all requiring extensive refurbishment.

The fleet that Tyne-Tees had acquired comprised the passenger cargo ships **Aberdonian**, built in 1909, the **Harlaw** built in 1911 as GSN's **Swift** and the **Lochnagar** which was G & J Burns' Ardrossan steamer **Woodcock** when first commissioned in 1906. There was also the venerable cargo steamer **Koolga** acquired by the Aberdeen company in 1918 and built for Thomas Cowan of Leith in 1910. **Harlaw** and **Koolga** were put back into traffic with a new intermediate call at Newcastle now that the Aberdeen, Newcastle & Hull Steam Company had withdrawn. The **Lochnagar** was returned to Aberdeen from her official duties in February 1946 and was laid up until sold in August. The **Aberdonian**, meanwhile, lay at Plymouth awaiting Government funded refurbishment and was sold as lying at Southampton in August 1946.

The **Aberdonian** (1909) entering the Pontoon No 3 dry dock at Aberdeen.   *(Aberdeen Library)*

The **Harlaw** was sold to Chinese owners and became the **Min Chih** and in 1947 to other Chinese owners and renamed the **Hai Yang**. In 1949 she raised the Panamanian flag and was renamed **Chepo**, one year later with new owners again she became the **Holina**, still registered at Panama and still working the Chinese coast trades. In August 1953 she made the headlines when she was seized by her Chinese Nationalist crew and taken to Formosa (now Taiwan) where her cargo was landed and looted. It turned out the cargo was not destined for the Chinese Communists at all but had been paid for by the South Koreans. Intervention by the Panamanian Consul General in China forced the return of the ship to her owners but there was never another word said about the cargo. The old steamer was eventually broken up in 1963 in Hong Kong.

The **Harlaw** and **Koolga** were displaced in October 1946 when the **Valerian Coast** was transferred from Newcastle to Aberdeen to maintain the weekly round trip between Aberdeen and London. The maiden departure of the **Valerian Coast** from Aberdeen took place on 24 October 1946. She sported a new funnel design with the traditional all yellow funnel of the Aberdeen company defaced by a broad green band.

One ship was inadequate for the service and provided no cover for departures following delayed arrivals. At times either the **Frisian Coast** or **Olivian Coast** was also drafted in to support the service. Meanwhile two new ships had been ordered by Coast Lines and were being built at the local shipyard of Hall, Russell & Company with their twin oil engines under construction at the British Polar works in Glasgow. The pair was an upgraded successor of the pioneer **British Coast** and **Atlantic Coast** built in 1933 and 1934. The new ships had accommodation for eleven passengers and were expected to take over the service to London by early 1948. In the meantime the make-do service operated by the Tyne-Tees ships was continued.

The **Frisian Coast** (1937) was drafted on to the Aberdeen service in the early post-war period.

(A Duncan)

Building of the two new ships for the Aberdeen Steam Navigation Company was slow as materials in post-war Britain were in short supply. Nevertheless, the first of the pair was launched on 27 September 1946, resplendent with a spotless white hull, and christened the **Aberdonian Coast**. The local press reported the launch in the excited tones of heralding a new beginning of the Aberdeen to London service. Fitting out proceeded slowly but the new ship was finally set to take her maiden voyage via Newcastle to the company's new London terminal at Free Trade Wharf on 1 June 1947, while the **Frisian Coast** had already left for Liverpool on 28 May in anticipation of the new incumbent. The **Aberdonian Coast** had been built at a cost of £178,072. Her twin 4-cylinder oil engines were designed to provide a service speed of 14 knots.

There were two holds forward of the central bridge island and between the forward hatches was the foremast with twin derricks mounted fore and aft. No 3 hatch between the bridge structure and the poop was served by twin derricks mounted on the mainmast stepped at the front of the poop, and by twin derricks on Samson posts at the fore end of the hatch. By September it was realised that the cargo handling gear was not coping with the demands placed on it and the **Aberdonian Coast** was withdrawn and returned to her builders.

The **Valerian Coast** was hastily dispatched back to Aberdeen to resume the abandoned service. The **Valerian Coast** was again stood down when the **Aberdonian Coast** returned to duty on 16 December 1947, her masts and derricks suitably strengthened.

The **Hibernian Coast** (1947) originally commissioned for the Aberdeen to London service of the Aberdeen Steam Navigation Company as **Aberdonian Coast**.

(J K Byass)

New tonnage came to Tyne-Tees in the form of the **Hadrian Coast** and **Olivian Coast**. The **Hadrian Coast** had been ordered by Coast Lines for the refrigerated carcass trade but was delivered to the Ministry of War Transport in 1941 as **Empire Atoll**. Coast Lines were managers of the ship throughout the war and finally became her owners in 1946. She was transferred to Tyne-Tees in December 1946 and renamed **Hadrian Coast**. As the **Empire Atoll** she had large refrigerated compartments but these were removed along with the refrigeration plant before coming to the Tyne. The **Olivian Coast** was new, completed by the Ardrossan Dockyard Company in November 1946 to the order of Tyne-Tees Steam Shipping Company. She was of the same pedigree as the first Coast Lines' cargo motor ship **Fife Coast** which had been delivered by the Ardrossan Dockyard Company in 1933. Of 749 gross tons with a service speed of 12 knots and deadweight capacity of 965 tons, the **Olivian Coast** was a valuable addition to the company for both the bulk and general cargo trades. As it turned out, she was to spend her entire career working under the Tyne-Tees house flag.

ABOVE: The **Hadrian Coast** (1941) in the colours of the Aberdeen Steam Navigation Company. She had a white hull in 1948 but this was deemed impractical and she quickly reverted to black.

RIGHT: Deck view of the **Hadrian Coast** (1941) clearly showing the defaced Aberdeen company funnel colours with the addition of broad green band.

(E J Charman)

On 8 July 1946 the **Frisian Coast** inaugurated a new service to the Channel Islands. This was at the request of the Ministry of Food as part of its food allocation programme. The maiden inbound voyage brought 250 tons of tomatoes to Gateshead Quay. The service continued thereafter with coal carried south and vegetables in season northbound.

At the end of 1946 Sir Alfred Read stood down as Managing Director of Coast Lines and its associated companies and was succeeded by Arnett Robinson. Sir Alfred retained the Chair until 31 March 1950 when he was succeeded by Captain Nutting. Nutting immediately placed an order for a relief ferry for Irish Sea duties, an order which Read had resisted as extravagant and unnecessary. The new ship was the **Irish Coast** and amazingly she was followed by a second extravagance, the sistership **Scottish Coast**. The careful and reserved management of the group was, it seems, now out of the window.

Two ships were required to inaugurate the new service of London Scottish Lines which commenced on 1 October 1946 between London and Leith with road connections to Glasgow and Grangemouth. The service initially used vessels ceded from the parent companies. The first ship acquired by London Scottish Lines and dedicated to the new service was the steamer **Caspian Coast**, the former **Craster**, which was sold by Tyne-Tees to London Scottish in 1947. She was joined in 1950 by the motor ship **Scottish Co-operator** built in 1939 for the Scottish Co-operative Wholesale Society. The pair was renamed **London Merchant** and **Scottish Merchant** respectively.

The **Craster** (1935) was sold in 1947 to London Scottish Lines and renamed **London Merchant**. She served in this guise until she was resold in 1959.

In March 1947 another exchange took place within the Coast Lines group when the **Belgian Coast**, the first of the Hawthorn Leslie motor ships in the Tyne-Tees fleet and originally named **Glen**, was transferred to Burns & Laird Lines. She was renamed **Lairdsrock** on 3 April. Her long hold designed for carriage of steel goods was in demand on the Greenock to Belfast service supplying steel plate and factored goods mainly to Harland & Wolff. The **Lairdsrock** joined the **Lairdsoak**, previously, the Merchants Line's **Silver Coast**. She was replaced within the Tyne-Tees fleet by the **Grampian Coast**. She had been ordered by Coast Lines from De Noord at Alblasserdam as **Welsh Coast** in 1937 but delivered as **Emerald Queen** for the Plymouth Channel Islands & Brittany Steamship Company then newly acquired by Coast Lines. The **Grampian Coast** was a useful motor ship with a service speed of 9 knots and of 481 tons gross.

The first motor ship in the Tyne-Tees fleet was the **Glen** (1935). Renamed **Belgian Coast** in 1946, she was transferred shortly afterwards to Burns & Laird Lines and renamed **Lairdsrock** (1935) for the Greenock to Belfast steel run.

The **Grampian Coast** (1937) was a valuable addition to the Tyne-Tees fleet when she was transferred from the Plymouth, Channel Islands & Brittany Steamship Company in 1947.

Three large and elderly colliers were purchased in 1947, seemingly unlikely units for the Tyne-Tees fleet, but two of the three proved to be profitable for some years in the bulk trades, particularly coal. James Layton described the three colliers in the *Tees Packet*:

*The years following the 1939-1945 War saw some remarkable changes in the fleet of the Tyne-Tees Steam Shipping Company, none more so than the purchase of three 2,500 tons deadweight colliers from Richard Hughes & Company (Liverpool), the **Dorothy Rose** of 1929, **Dennis Rose** and **Maurice Rose** both of 1930. The ships came round to the Tyne in February and March 1947 and the first two were renamed **Belgian Coast** and **Virginian Coast**. The **Maurice Rose** arrived in the Tyne on 17 March and remained in the river until May when she was sold to A Coker & Company, Liverpool [another Coast Lines associate company] and renamed **Baltic King**. She left the river on 19 May never having carried a cargo for the Tyne-Tees company.*

*The **Belgian Coast** and **Virginian Coast** arrived on the east coast during the very cold weather of early 1947. Collier sailings from the north-east coast to the Thames and other south country ports had been disrupted for a considerable period by very bad weather at sea and snow and freezing conditions at the collieries, and coal staithes had virtually stopped the movement of coal to the ships. Coal stocks in the south of England fell to a very low level and when the weather did improve the two ships joined other East Coast colliers in a race to replenish the depleted stock piles.*

The second of the new motor ships built at Aberdeen for the Aberdeen Steam Navigation Company, the **Caledonian Coast**, was commissioned in 1948. Completion was seriously delayed when the casting of her engine bed plate was dropped at the iron works and had to be replaced. She was launched on 30 September 1947 but was ready for her maiden voyage south on 21 April 1948, this time with a black hull, the 'spotless' white of her sister having quickly been deemed impractical. The **Caledonian Coast** like her earlier sister, had been built with a winch platform between Numbers 1 and 2 hatches. Given the early problems with cargo handling experienced by the **Aberdonian Coast**, this platform was removed before completion of the **Caledonian Coast** and in due course removed also from the **Aberdonian Coast**.

The **Virginian Coast** (1930), formerly the collier **Dennis Rose**, provided much needed bulk cargo capacity in the post-war years.

The **Belgian Coast** (1929) was formerly the collier **Dorothy Rose** until bought by Tyne-Tees in 1947.

(A Duncan)

But the new service offered by the twins was plagued with problems at Free Trade Wharf and it was found that the published timetable was impossible to maintain. Letters to the local press reported how poor the new service had become and the company found it difficult to fill the passenger berths even in this first two-ship summer season. Shippers too questioned the reliability of their deliveries and some began to turn to overland transport. In little over two months the two 'Prides of Aberdeen' were withdrawn while a decision was awaited about their future. The whole experience had become a costly mistake on the part of Coast Lines, perhaps judging the east coast conditions from their own predominantly west coast knowledge without first taking counsel from the locals. Graeme Somner tells the story:

It was soon found that post-war labour conditions in the port of London made it difficult to maintain a passenger schedule, and when a fifteen-day strike took place in that port at the end of June 1948, the company decided to withdraw the passenger ships permanently. The sisterships were transferred to the ownership of the parent company, Coast Lines, at the beginning of July 1948, and then employed on the Liverpool-Dublin-South Coast-London sailings instead.

The question needs asking why Coast Lines believed the ships would fare any better on the west coast as they still ended up running to strike-prone London. The answer is that Liverpool saw the pair as too valuable an asset to be running out of Aberdeen where cargo on offer was continuing to decline and passengers were unwilling to test the unreliable schedule. In hindsight Coast Lines made the right decision, but at the time Coast Lines was hailed in Aberdeen as an ogre for removing the new ships. The **Caledonian Coast** retained her name on the west coast service but the **Aberdonian Coast** was renamed **Hibernian Coast**. Somner again:

*The [Aberdeen] company was invited by the Tyne-Tees Steam Shipping Company to then select two out of three vessels from their fleet for transfer to them. On offer were the cargo motor vessels **Hadrian Coast** at a book value of £44,6000, **Valerian Coast**, book value £12,500, and **Olivian Coast** book value £91,000. The first two vessels were selected by the company on 1 July 1948.*

*As a temporary measure, the **Frisian Coast** arrived back again at Aberdeen on 2 July to take up the sailings once more, the first being on 4 July. She was joined on 7 July by the **Valerian Coast** (which was shortly* *afterwards more suitably renamed **Hebridean Coast**). In September 1948 the **Hadrian Coast** relieved **Frisian Coast**. Passenger sailings between Aberdeen and London were now a thing of the past.*

From the outset both the **Hadrian Coast** and **Hebridean Coast** wore the new yellow funnel with a broad green band. At her next refit the **Hadrian Coast** was given an all-white hull to emulate the **Aberdonian Coast** but more purposefully in an attempt to woo shippers back to the London service. Sadly the shippers stayed away and there was work enough for only one ship. The **Hebridean Coast** was returned to Tyne-Tees in April 1949, initially on time charter but latterly reverting back to Tyne-Tees ownership. She remained the designated relief ship at Aberdeen during the annual two week overhaul periods of the **Hadrian Coast**, and as her new name very nearly fitted the Tyne-Tees nomenclature it remained unchanged.

As the decade ended, the Tyne-Tees fleet stood at eleven units, over half of which were motor ships:

Steamships:
Persian Coast, formerly **Gateshead**
Elysian Coast, formerly **Cragside**
Northumbrian Coast, formerly **Thornaby**
Virginian Coast ex-Richard Hughes & Company, Liverpool
Belgian Coast ex-Richard Hughes & Company, Liverpool

Motor ships:
Sylvian Coast, formerly **Beal**
Cyprian Coast, formerly **Alnwick**
Novian coast, formerly **Wooler**
Frisian Coast, formerly **Lowick**
Olivian Coast
Grampian Coast, Coast Lines transfer.

In addition, the Aberdeen Steam Navigation Company had the **Hadrian Coast**.

The Free Trade Wharf Company, having lost three of its ships in the war, decided not to renew the London to King's Lynn link and sold the small steamer **Etal** in 1945. In so doing it ceased to be a shipowner. The company continued in the London to Hull trade with the **Cragside** from Tyne-Tees and **Empire Drover**. However, on 26 April that year Free Trade Wharf signed an agreement with the General Steam Navigation Company to the effect that each company would use only one ship on the Hull service with all takings pooled and shared equally:

*We endorse herewith copy of the Agreement which has been made between the General Steam Navigation Company and ourselves in respect of our Hull trade. This will no doubt be signed in due course, and the vessels concerned, the **Ortolan** and **Cragside** will commence their first voyages under this agreement on Saturday 4 May.*

It was agreed that the Free Trade Wharf Company would load the ships at London and GSN at Hull. There was a six months termination notification but the agreement was designed with a 21 year tenure. The **Empire Drover** passed to Queenship Navigation through the auspices of parent company Coast Lines in late 1946.

Free Trade Wharf's business as wharfingers increased since it too had become part of the Coast Lines group in 1943. Free Trade Wharf was now the London terminal for Coast Lines and for the British Channel Islands Shipping Company in addition to Tyne-Tees ships while it also serviced a number of other companies including GSNC which used Free Trade Wharf largely for its domestic services.

The Tyne-Tees company had metamorphosed considerably during the first four years of peace while under orders from Liverpool. The fleet had grown by one motor ship but was now better placed to service the bulk cargo trade, principally coal outward, silver sand back to Middlesbrough and occasionally grain from the continent to any of the north-east ports. The small pre-war built motor ships were well placed to service the steel trade with their long hatches while the **Northumbrian Coast** was well suited to the general cargo trade with London. The Continental trade was variously dealt with by the smaller motor ships and the **Olivian Coast**. Trade with Hamburg was resumed postwar with business at a high level with provision of stores to the British and American forces stationed in Germany. As German industry again got back on its feet, goods were also available for import. The same was largely the case with the Dutch and Belgian trades, which by 1949 had also resumed a satisfying tempo. The coal run to the Channel Islands, returning in season with potatoes and other vegetables kept the big colliers occupied. It was business as usual.

Passengers were no longer carried by Tyne-Tees ships, the last passenger ship, the **Newminster/Dorian Coast** having been sold in 1946. However, a few of the motor ships had spare twin berth cabins and these were available to company staff travelling on business and were occasionally let for promotional purposes to 'friends of the company'.

THE ABERDEEN STEAM NAVIGATION COMPANY

The seed of the Aberdeen Steam Navigation Company was the foundation of the Aberdeen and London New Shipping Company by a group of Aberdeen Merchants in 1821. The first wooden paddle steamship, the **Queen of Scotland**, was introduced to the Aberdeen to London route by the Aberdeen & London Steam Navigation Company in 1827. A second steamer, the **Duke of Wellington**, joined the service in 1929 and a third, the **City of Aberdeen**, in 1835. Competition between the two companies, sail and steam, was fierce, but as there were many joint shareholders the majority were persuaded to join forces to create the Aberdeen Steam Navigation Company in autumn 1836. The inaugural London service was taken by the **Queen of Scotland** in October with the sailing vessel **Nimrod** taking the next sailing. However, within a year there was only one sailing ship left in the fleet and she was used only for relief cargo purposes.

A new service to Hull was commenced with the **Duke of Wellington** in 1836 and calls started at Sunderland in early 1837. The steamer **Duchess of Sutherland** was purchased in 1938 from the Moray Firth & London Steam Packet Company. The Aberdeen & Hull Shipping Company, and its three sailing smacks, was taken over in 1839. A new schooner-rigged sailing ship was built for the Hull service in 1842 and named the **Paragon**. In 1843 the **Duke of Wellington** transferred to the London service leaving Hull in the charge of the sailing smacks. Three schooners were bought along with the goodwill of Nicol & Munro of Aberdeen in 1844, so giving the Aberdeen Steam Navigation Company a monopoly on the London route.

The first iron-hulled paddle steamer in the fleet was the **City of London** built by Robert Napier on the Clyde in 1844. The first iron-hulled screw steamship was the **Duke of Rothesay** built by William Denny at Dumbarton and completed in 1857, although she was sold two years later to the Spanish Government. Her sale was the result of severe competition and loss of revenue, and the loss of one of the three remaining paddle steamers in September 1859 left just two iron-hulled paddle steamers, the **City of London** and **Earl of Aberdeen** with no back up for the London service. The situation was resolved in 1863 when the Aberdeen company bought the rival Northern Steam Company's vessels **Gambia** and **Stanley**, although the latter was wrecked off Tynemouth the following year.

New tonnage was clearly needed, and following various charters, an order was placed with R Duncan & Company of Port Glasgow for the screw steamer **City of Aberdeen**. She took her maiden voyage south from Aberdeen in November 1865 but was never reliable and she suffered boiler problems throughout her career at Aberdeen. The London service was finally put on a firm footing with the delivery of the famous steamers **Ban-Righ** and a second **City of London** both built by John Elder & Company at Glasgow. In 1873 the **City of Aberdeen** was delivered to provide a third back-up ship for the twice-weekly departures north and south between Aberdeen and London.

Sailings to Moray Firth ports and Inverness sailings had been maintained intermittently over the years as dictated by demand. Chartered ships were mainly used and latterly the small steamer **Harlaw** was in charge of the route. The Inverness service was withdrawn in 1882 when competition made the company withdraw the **Harlaw** and charter her out. She was too small to be used on the London run.

The steel-hulled steamer **Hogarth** joined the fleet in February 1892, a product of the local Aberdeen shipbuilders Hall Russell & Company. The **Hogarth** and **Ban-Righ** became the mainstay of the London service with the **City of London** and **City of Aberdeen** in reserve. Cargo back-up was provided by a new **Harlaw**, bought in 1899 from the Goole Steam Shipping Company.

By late 1906 the fleet was again reduced to three ships: the **City of London** dating from 1871, the **Hogarth** built in 1893 and **Harlaw** delivered in 1895. New tonnage was introduced to the passenger service in 1909 when the **Aberdonian** was delivered by D W Henderson & Company at Glasgow at a cost of £39,800. She was a magnificent ship with accommodation for 100 first class and 200 second class passengers and her triple steam-expansion engines were able to maintain a tidy 14 knots. As always with a new and advanced ship in the fleet she had no consort. Plans for a second ship were put back on 6 January 1910 when the **Aberdonian** collided with, and sank, the collier **Holmwood** off Orfordness, and the owners of the **Aberdonian** were fined £14,820. Sale of the **Harlaw** recouped £3,500, but it was clear now that a new ship was no longer feasible. The finances of the company were further stretched by the coal strikes and the London dockers' strikes in 1912.

During the Great War the **Aberdonian** was converted for service as a hospital carrier in 1915 and then designated as an ambulance transport in 1917. During the period until her return to the Aberdeen company in 1919 she yielded much-needed charter revenues. The **Hogarth** and **City of London** maintained the domestic service until in May 1917 they were obliged to wait for convoys so inhibiting the revenue earning potential of the company. The **Hogarth** received a DEMS (Defensively Equipped Merchant Ship) gun in 1918 which allowed her free passage once again but in June she was sunk by torpedo off the Farne Islands. Only one survivor was picked up alive out of the full crew complement of 27.

The London sailings were suspended in the summer of 1918. The **City of London** was away on charter initially to Charles Mauritzen of Leith and latterly to the Carron Company for its service between Grangemouth and London. The eight year-old cargo steamer **Koolga** was purchased in 1918 and she took her first Aberdeen to London sailing in January 1919. Although the **Aberdonian** was back in port in May it was September before refurbishment was complete and she was able to resume service, now with berths for 80 first and 120 second class passengers. The **City of London** was returned from charter and in May 1920 received an extensive refit and upgrade so that the elderly ship could be maintained in service alongside the **Aberdonian**.

Post-war strikes plagued the operation of the company and the **Koolga** was even sent off to Antwerp on one occasion in search of bunker coal. As a consequence, the passenger departures were reduced to one per week from London and Aberdeen. The six-passenger berth **Swift** was bought from General Steam Navigation in 1929 and renamed **Harlaw**. She became the winter steamer in place of the **Aberdonian** and ran alongside the **Koolga**.

By 1930 business had improved sufficiently for the company to look for a running mate for the **Aberdonian** in the summer months. This was the **Lairdswood**, owned by Burns & Laird Lines, formerly the **Woodcock** built in 1906 for the Ardrossan to Belfast day passenger service of G & J Burns. She was renamed the **Lochnagar** and entered service on her maiden run south to London on 4 June 1931 offering 140 saloon berths and additional unberthed accommodation aft. This allowed the venerable **City of London** to be sold – but not for scrap – to David MacBrayne's West of Scotland service as the **Lochbroom**, eventually going to the breakers in 1937 having served a total of 66 years to the month. In summer the **Aberdonian** and **Lochnagar** ruled the roost as passenger numbers swelled in the late 1930s and in winter the **Harlaw** came out to run alongside the **Koolga**. The company was at last a profitable and buoyant concern with a realistic business plan that suited the trade available.

Commercial services were suspended after war broke out in 1939, but were soon reinstated by the **Harlaw** and **Koolga**. Both ships suffered air attacks but both survived with minor damage. The **Aberdonian** went off to the Admiralty as depot ship, followed by the **Lochnagar** which went first to Scapa Flow then to the evacuation of Norway and by May 1940 was back ferrying supplies to Iceland. The London tug/tender **Ich Dien** (see Chapter 3) was sold for £1,500 in 1942. This, then, was the state of the company when a firm offer was received from the Tyne-Tees Steam Shipping Company leading to transfer of control to Newcastle with effect from November 1945.

CHAPTER 11

THE 1950s – BUSINESS AS USUAL

The decade started with the signing of a lucrative contract to bring much of the heavy engineering equipment down from Middlesbrough to the new Bankside Power Station then being built at the South Bank in London (now the site of the Tate Modern).

There was even more shuffling of fleet members, within the Coast Lines group. The **Sandringham Queen** had been ordered for Coast Lines' associate Queenship Navigation Company from George Brown & Company, shipbuilders at Greenock. Queenship Navigation maintained cargo services from various UK ports to northern Europe, a direct service linking French and German ports and an important spot charter business. The **Sandringham Queen** was launched on 21 December 1949. Early in the New Year it was decided by HQ that she was better suited to the current trade of the Tyne-Tees Steam Shipping Company than she was to Queenship Navigation and her name was duly painted out and replaced by **Iberian Coast** of Newcastle. The full Tyne-Tees livery was applied: the pink Queenship boot topping was over-painted in black and the original buff funnel, thin red band and black top was replaced by the black funnel with the white over red bands of Tyne-Tees. The Tyne-Tees livery had always been unique in that the hull was all black and, until the early 1960s, the boot topping remained black. The **Hadrian Coast** on the Aberdeen Steam Navigation Company service always had red boot topping.

The **Iberian Coast** (1950) had the typical Queenship Navigation Company design of engines aft, bridge between holds 2 and 3 and well deck forward.

(A Duncan)

The **Iberian Coast** was a valuable vessel. She had a large deadweight of 1,503 tons and was suitable for the carriage of steel goods and general cargo, but her deep holds were also capable of supporting the bulk cargo trades. Her oil engine was aft and she was capable of 11 knots. Bridge and accommodation was forward of midships with Number 1 hatch before the bridge structure and numbers 2 and 3 on a raised quarter deck between the bridge and the poop. Each hatch was served by a single derrick mounted on the foremast at the aft end of the foc'sle or fore and aft on the mainmast between hatches 2 and 3. She arrived at Newcastle fresh from the builders in June 1950 and was admired both for her businesslike appearance and her fresh and modern post-war design.

The oldest member in the Tyne-Tees fleet was the **Persian Coast,** formerly the **Gateshead**. Commissioned in 1919 as the **War Colne**, she had come into Tyne-Tees ownership in 1933 and had proved a valuable fleet member capable of delivering in the steel factor trade, bulk cargo trades and in the carriage of general cargo. As such she had often made the circuit south to London with steel and coal, across to the Continent to load silver sand and general cargo and back to the north-east to start over again. By 1951 the old steamer had seen better days and was no match for the efficiency of the newer motor ships in the fleet. But her career was not over yet as she was sold to the Mersey Ports Stevedoring Company in 1951, renamed **Celia Mary** and used for coastal transhipments to and from the Mersey. Her final year of service ended in April 1956 when her last owners, the Glynwood Navigation Company of Hull, sold her for demolition in the Netherlands.

One additional ship was drafted into the Tyne-Tees fleet in 1951. This was the **Suffolk Coast** which retained her Coast Lines name as the first ship to break the *–ian* suffix nomenclature of the first name. The **Suffolk Coast** was built in the Netherlands, and completed in February 1938. She was bought by Coast Lines in 1939 from her Dutch owners, and was a motor ship, re-engined in April 1948, with a deadweight capacity of 535 tons.

The **Suffolk Coast** (1938) was built for Dutch owners and bought by Coast Lines in 1939.   (*FotoFlite*)

More Coast Lines transfers followed in 1952 when the **Elysian Coast**, formerly the **Cragside**, was transferred to the Zillah Shipping Company and renamed **Westfield**. This was an odd move as the old steamer joined a fleet of motor coasters working in the Irish Sea trades with occasional charters. However, she was joined by a second steamer in 1954 when the one year-old Dutch-owned **Medusa** was purchased to become **Fallowfield**. Whereas the old **Cragside** was sold for demolition at Preston in June 1956, the **Fallowfield** served Zillah and then Coast Lines until 1971 before raising the Irish flag as **Arklow Bay**.

Both the **Persian Coast** and **Elysian Coast** were effectively replaced by the **Hampshire Coast**, formerly **Stuart Queen**, which transferred to the Tyne-Tees fleet from British Channel Traders, formerly Merchants Line, during 1952. Coast Lines bought British Channel Islands Shipping in 1942 and created British Channel Traders the following year out of the nucleus of the Merchants Line. A number of the British Channel Island company's ships were transferred into the new company which was initially dedicated to the tramp market, and later became Queenship Navigation. The **Stuart Queen** was one of five 'Queen' ships involved in supplying the Normandy Mulberry harbours in 1944. She had been launched in November 1940 as **Stuart Queen**. Transferred to Coast Lines in 1946 and renamed **Hampshire Coast**, she was next destined for Tyne-Tees. Like the **Iberian Coast** she had a big deadweight tonnage but, unlike her, the **Hampshire Coast**, of course, was a steamship.

By 1952 services had been consolidated as:

London to Newcastle, Sunderland and Middlesbrough and to Hull and Grimsby (the latter operated by the Free Trade Wharf Company in collaboration with GSN).

Newcastle to Hamburg, Bremen, Amsterdam, Rotterdam, Antwerp, Ghent and North French ports and Channel Islands.

Middlesbrough to Hamburg and Bremen.

The **Virginian Coast** (1930), formerly the collier **Dennis Rose**, seen arriving at St Helier, Jersey.

(Harold Appleyard/Dave Hocquard collections)

The **Sandhill**, which had become **Valerian Coast** in 1946, transferred to Coast Lines in 1948 to become **Hebridean Coast** before joining the Aberdeen Steam Navigation Company fleet soon afterwards. Once **Hadrian Coast** had been established at Aberdeen (Chapter 10), the **Hebridean Coast** returned to Tyne-Tees on time charter in 1949 and to Tyne-Tees ownership in 1951. Each year she took her Tyne-Tees livery north to Aberdeen for two weeks to relieve the **Hadrian Coast** for her annual refit. But in 1953, in true nomadic style, she was transferred to another Coast Lines associate, the Belfast Steamship Company, and renamed **Ulster Chieftain**. Now with a shiny black-topped crimson funnel, the **Ulster Chieftain** served on the Liverpool to Belfast cargo service, her relief duties at Aberdeen thereafter undertaken by the **Frisian Coast**.

At Belfast, 1953 or 1954, from left to right, Belfast Steamship Company's **Ulster Hero** (1920) and originally ordered by M Langlands & Sons, the hoops on the funnel being for the Langlands' two white bands on a black background, the British cargo steamer **Venta** (1908) and Belfast Steamship Company's **Ulster Chieftain** (1938) in one of the many manifestations of the **Sandhill**.

(H M Rae, Richard Danielson collection)

In her stead came the brand new **Netherlands Coast,** built for the company by George Brown (Marine) Company with a deadweight of 1,008 tons. Launched at Greenock on 3 April 1953, she was in service with Tyne-Tees in early June. Her 8-cylinder British Polar oil engine was situated right aft and provided a service speed of 12 knots. Bridge and accommodation were also aft, with twin Samson posts fitted to her bridge front to support a single derrick serving Number 2 hatch while the mainmast supported derricks fore and aft to serve Numbers 1 and 2 hatches. The foremast also supported another derrick to serve Number 1 hatch. The **Netherlands Coast** was a neat workmanlike looking ship which always gave the appearance of being too short in length to support all the cargo handling gear she carried.

The **Netherlands Coast** was designed for the Rotterdam and Amsterdam weekly round trip. She often loaded silver sand at Rotterdam which meant a first call in the north-east at Corporation Quay, Sunderland, to discharge the sand before proceeding to Gateshead Quay to unload the remainder of the cargo, including Dutch fruit and vegetables for Newcastle market, before commencing loading again. Sunday night was usually spent tied up at Amsterdam and the old hands insisted on a quiet ship with even the generator shut down. Woe betide any of the younger crew members, a few litres of Amstel lager later, noisily arriving back on board after the rest had turned in. Captain Fisher was the master in the late 1950s and he drove an old Rolls Royce which was left under the Tyne Bridge while he was at sea. Each week, to the crew's amazement, the car would still be there waiting for him with nobody having had the wit at least to steal the wheels and leave the old Roller standing on bricks.

The **Netherlands Coast** (1953) served just fifteen years with Tyne-Tees before she was sold.

(A Duncan)

The business of the company carried on much as before with twice weekly sailings to Rotterdam and weekly services to Hamburg, Bremen, Amsterdam, Antwerp and Ghent, with additional sailings as required. Other Continental ports were served on inducement and the London cargo route continued also to a regular twice weekly schedule while the Jersey and Guernsey coal runs continued usually with the **Belgian Coast**.

The tenure of the big collier **Virginian Coast**, which had been bought by Tyne-Tees in 1946 as one of a group of three similar ships, came to an end in 1953. Although no longer an economically viable vessel in the Tyne-Tees fleet, she saw five further years of service under foreign ownership. Her sister, **Belgian Coast**, continued to ply the bulk trades in the North Sea, but she was eventually sold for demolition at Boom, near Antwerp, in October 1957. Coincidentally, the third sister, now named the **Richmond Queen**, one-time **Maurice Rose**, and briefly a member of the Tyne-Tees fleet, arrived at Dunston for demolition within days of the **Belgian Coast** departing the Tyne for the last time.

The company's ships had to navigate some of the world's busiest rivers so it is not surprising that accidents continued to occur despite modern aids and more manoeuvrable ships. On 4 March 1953 the steamer **Northumbrian Coast** collided in thick fog with the **Egyptian Prince** in the lower Thames estuary. The **Northumbrian Coast** was badly holed and making water in the engine room so the decision was made to run her ashore onto the Mucking Flats on the Essex coast of the Thames estuary as reported in *Sea Breezes*, May 1953:

*Her trouble occurred when she was on passage from Middlesbrough to London and was in collision with the Prince Line's motor ship **Egyptian Prince** in the Lower Hope. Her consort, the **Sylvian Coast**, stood by her in the fog until she was beached on the Mucking Flats with a big hole in her port side through which the engine room had been flooded. She was patched as she lay and refloated within a few days to be towed up river to dry dock.*

This situation could so easily have become a tragic loss of both life and ship. As it was, there was enough time and steam to beach the ship despite the flooding of the engine room. The **Sylvian Coast** was in the area and was able to assist as the **Northumbrian Coast** ran for the shore and then remained off shore until the salvage teams arrived. The **Egyptian Prince** was largely undamaged but was of too large a draught to offer any help and she remained hove-to in the channel until the fog lifted.

The **Hadrian Coast** was in trouble on 1 September 1954 when her engine failed on passage north to Aberdeen. The elements were kind to her and she was able to make her own way slowly into Immingham where repairs were put in hand. She was finally able to resume her voyage on 20 September.

The following year, an altogether more serious incident occurred to the **Cyprian Coast** when she was struck and sunk by the large motor cargo ship **Arabert** in the Tyne off Gateshead Quay. The **Arabert** was built in 1954 for A R Appelqvist A/B of Stockholm and was of 3,045 tons gross. Under the front page banner headline '**Cyprian Coast** sank in Five Minutes', the Newcastle Journal reported on 24 December:

She rested on the river bottom opposite Newcastle Milk Market in the middle of the fairway partly blocking the channel. The ship lay with her masts towards Newcastle Quay and her bow was showing about 3 feet of plating above water. Later she sank lower and only a foot was showing. By midnight the **Cyprian Coast**'s *bow was afloat but the stern was touching the river bed about 35 feet below the surface.*

The **Cyprian Coast** (1936) riding peacefully at anchor once more.   (Harold Appleyard collection)

The article was accompanied by a large photograph of the ship on her side taken with the help of the headlights of strategically placed lorries with an exposure of three minutes. The wreck was later pulled out of the channel towards Newcastle Quay by hawsers attached to bollards on Newcastle Quayside and with the aid of a powerful tug.

The Evening Chronicle, 14 June 2012, later recalled the incident:

Many life-threatening dramas have unfolded on the River Tyne, but one such happening must have been a horrific event for the crew of the **Cyprian Coast** *on the night of 23 December 1955. An attempt to turn the coaster, between Newcastle and Gateshead Quays, ended with it being hit by the Swedish vessel* **Arabert**, *which resulted in the* **Cyprian Coast** *sinking within five minutes. Luckily, all the crew of 10 managed to scramble to safety, either by dinghy or swimming.*

The **Cyprian Coast**, *was formerly the Tyne-Tees Steam Shipping Company's* **Alnwick** *and had been turning towards Gateshead Quay to berth when the collision occurred. The* **Arabert** *was on her way to sea with an escort of tugs.*

Following the impact, some of the crew of the **Cyprian Coast** were rescued from the water by men from the **Arabert**; one man jumped into a tug, and two others managed to reach a dinghy. The whole event happened in less than 10 minutes, and ended with part of the bow of the **Cyprian Coast** protruding above the water.

Members of her crew were: Captain J P Hall, of Liverpool; First Officer A McMath, of Hexham; Chief Engineer George Ballard, of North Shields; Second Engineer W Cunningham, of South Shields; steward J Hindmarch, of West Moor; H Kainins, of Felling; C Cooper of Brixton and M Moodey. The watchman was Harry Kennedy, of Newcastle, who when he scrambled aboard a tug which was attending the **Arabert**, lost his belongings, including his pay packet and spectacles. Other members of the crew suffered more serious losses in property, including Christmas gifts, when they had to jump for their lives.

The raising of the vessel from her watery grave began on 22 January 1956, in driving rain and snow. The 500 ton vessel began to lurch to the surface with the aid of air compressors on the quayside, which pumped air into 'camels' floating above the vessel. The water boiled as air disturbed the surface and the ship's hull lurched into view. A few days later she was back on the surface before being taken to Cleland's Yard at Willington Quay to be repaired. She put to sea again for sea trials on 11 June 1956.

The Newcastle to Aberdeen cargo service operated by the Dundee, Perth & London Shipping Company was suspended in 1955. The link between Newcastle and Aberdeen was then resumed by Coast Lines using a variety of ships from both the parent company fleet and the Tyne-Tees fleet from time to time. The service was originally the bailiwick of the Aberdeen, Newcastle and Hull Steam Company, whose steamers **Earl of Aberdeen** and **Norwood** and their successor the **Highlander** are perhaps best remembered as they all offered substantial passenger accommodation, the first pair until the Great War, the latter until World War II. The Aberdeen, Newcastle & Hull Steam Company was bought by the Dundee company in 1929 and formally dissolved in 1946.

The **Earl of Aberdeen** (1889), seen below the Swing Bridge, supported the Aberdeen, Newcastle & Hull Steam Company's passenger and cargo service between those same ports until she was sold in 1915.

(R Gibson, George Nairn collection)

On 21 November 1955 the *Evening Gazette* announced a totally new venture for the Tyne-Tees Steam Shipping Company, which was to flirt briefly with the aviation industry:

Mr Clive Hunting, Director of Hunting-Clan Air Transport announced at Newcastle today that Elder Dempster Lines and the Tyne-Tees Steam Shipping Company have joined with them through the medium of Dragon Airways of Liverpool for the purpose of developing the northern network services run by Hunting-Clan Air Transport and centred at Newcastle Airport.

Dragon Airways is now controlled by the three companies as equal partners and will be renamed. Its base will be moved from Speke Airport, Liverpool, to Newcastle.

The new arrangements make available to the Newcastle based services 4-engined Heron aircraft seating 14 or 16 passengers. The winter schedule provides two flights to and from London daily, and daily to and from Amsterdam, and Düsseldorf three times a week and Belfast twice a week.

The northern network of Hunting-Clan, a joint venture between Hunting and the Clan Line of Glasgow, was never profitable and was closed in 1957. The withdrawal from Newcastle Airport put an end to the Tyne-Tees company vision to become an airline.

In 1956 the **Hebridean Coast** was returned from Coast Lines to Tyne-Tees adopting the new name **Durham Coast**. She again took up responsibility as relief ship for the one ship Aberdeen Steam Navigation Company service normally operated by the **Hadrian Coast**.

The routine continued uninterrupted through 1957 and 1958. The company reported a drop in demand for the London service but made this up by taking a greater part of the manifest in the form of coal from Pelaw Staithes and steel goods from Dent's Wharf. Just how long this could be maintained in the face of an increasing number of modern specialised colliers in the trade remained to be seen. The Continental trades were still buoyant but freight rates were falling due to severe competition from Dutch and German shipowners operating small, modern and economical vessels with crews of just eight men.

The economics of the triple expansion steam-engine collier **Hampshire Coast**, formerly **Stuart Queen**, were no longer viable and she was sold for scrap in 1959. She was delivered to the breaker's yard at Hendrik-Ido-Ambacht on the River Maas in March. Her sale was brought about by competition from modern colliers with self-trimming coamings and other aids to efficient cargo handling. Her departure from the fleet left only one remaining steamer, the **Northumbrian Coast**, flying the Tyne-Tees flag.

An aerial view showing the **Northumbrian Coast** (1935) at her best.   *(Harold Appleyard collection)*

The next new ship was the **Yorkshire Coast**, an improved version of the **Netherlands Coast**, both being products of the Greenock yard of George Brown & Company (Marine). The **Yorkshire Coast** was of similar design save that her British Polar engine was 6-cylinder rather than the 8-cylinder type in the **Netherlands Coast**, and the new ship only had two derricks, one mounted on the bridge front supported by two Samson posts, and the other mounted on the foremast. Her design service speed was 11 knots and her deadweight capacity was 967 tons. The **Yorkshire Coast** was launched on 18 June 1959 and arrived at Newcastle ready to start work in the London trade in October.

The **Yorkshire Coast** (1959) served less than thirteen years with the Tyne-Tees company before being sold.

(Dave Hocquard)

The arrival of the **Yorkshire Coast** allowed the **Sylvian Coast** to be transferred within the Coast Lines group to Burns & Laird who renamed her **Lairdsburn**. During her refit for her new employer her engine was replaced by new 6-cylinder engine made by Klöckner-Humboldt-Deutz AG, Köln. Her original 7-cylinder Humboldt-Deutzmotoren AG engine, had come from the same factory at Köln back in 1936. Her new role was the steel trade between Greenock and Belfast with manufactured goods mainly destined for Harland & Wolff. Her running mate was the **Lairdsrock**, none other than her near sister formerly the **Belgian Coast**, ex-**Glen**, transferred to Burns & Laird back in 1946 and having worked the steel trade from Greenock ever since. She had already received a new 6-cylinder Klöckner-Humboldt-Deutz AG engine back in 1957. Both the original German-made engines had served satisfactorily for well over 20 years.

The Belfast steel trade transferred to Ardrossan in 1963 and in 1966 was upgraded when the two former Tyne-Tees ships were replaced by the **Foxfield** and **Greenfield** from the fleet of associate company W A Savage. They each had their two hatch covers removed and replaced by a single long 'Cargospeed' folding hatch cover and took up service between Ardrossan and Belfast in the summer as the **Lairdsfox** and **Lairdsfield** respectively. The two old Tyne-Tees motor ships were put on the 'For Sale' list and a deal was struck on 12 October 1966 whereby both ships went to Greek buyers, the **Lairdsrock** becoming **Georgis** for P K Varvates and **Lairdsburn** becoming the **Agia Sofia** for M Koutlakis.

As the decade closed, Tyne-Tees Steam Shipping Company was still operating from Newcastle and Middlesbrough to the same ports in Germany, Holland and Belgium, with the Hamburg/Bremen service maintained on a twice-weekly departure while the other routes were down to just weekly services. The Newcastle to London cargo liner service continued as before usually with the **Northumbrian Coast** or **Yorkshire Coast** supported as required by one of the pre-war-built motor ships. Thus, on 31 December 1959 the fleet comprised:

Cyprian Coast - built 1936 as **Anwick**
Durham Coast - built 1938 as **Sandhill**, later **Valerian Coast** and **Hebridean Coast**
Frisian Coast - built 1937 as **Lowick**
Grampian Coast - built 1937 as **Welsh Coast**, delivered as **Emerald Queen**
Iberian Coast - built 1950 as **Sandringham Queen**
Netherlands Coast - built 1953
Northumbrian Coast - built 1935 as **Thornaby**
Novian Coast - built 1936 as **Wooler**
Olivian Coast - built 1946
Suffolk Coast - built 1938 as **Marili**
Yorkshire Coast - built 1959.

In addition, the Aberdeen Steam Navigation Company operated the **Hadrian Coast** between Aberdeen and London.

The North Sea trades were beginning to change. Competition from various directions kept freight rates down while some shipowners also pursued door-to-door services with integrated onward road haulage to the port of departure and from the port of arrival. In addition the concept of container traffic was beginning to hit the North Sea trades with companies such as the General Steam Navigation Company offering 'boxes' for shipment of goods that could be packed at the factory and unpacked by the importer. The obvious advantages to the shipper included, above all, that of security with goods remaining untouched throughout the journey save for any inspection that Customs officers saw fit to make.

There was also another rather disturbing development on the North Sea, namely that of the vehicle ferry. Pioneer Frank Bustard had inaugurated sailings between Tilbury and Rotterdam in 1946 using otherwise unwanted former military tank landing ships under the banner Atlantic Steam Navigation Company. His service thrived with the transfer of military vehicles and stores between UK and Germany. In 1948 Bustard opened a second route, this time on the Irish Sea, operating between Preston and Larne. This incurred the wrath of Alfred Read at Coast Lines HQ, who saw the new service as an unwanted intruder. Read made no attempt to emulate the roll-on/roll-off idea or even to investigate its long-term commercial prospects.

In 1957 two purpose-built, stern-loading, roll-on/roll-off ferries were commissioned for the Atlantic Steam Navigation Company, the **Ionic Ferry** for the Irish Sea and the **Bardic Ferry** to operate between Tilbury and Antwerp after a brief inaugural spell on the Preston service. Both ships had comfortable accommodation in 55 berths for vehicle drivers and other passengers. The success of the new ships can be judged by orders that were placed for two further specialist vehicle ferries during 1959. But, like Alfred Read before them, neither the Board of Coast Lines nor that of the Tyne-Tees Steam Shipping Company recognised the threat that was being presented to them by the vehicle ferry and both companies still believed in the future of break-bulk cargo shipments between the UK and the near Continent, and for that matter across the Irish Sea. Their judgement was later to become their undoing.

Atlantic Steam Navigation Company's **Bardic Ferry** (1957) was operating the freight vehicle ferry service between Tilbury and Antwerp in the late 1950s. This service was not then perceived to be a threat to break-bulk freight carriers such as Tyne-Tees.

(Author)

THE COAST LINES SEAWAY POST-WAR

Parent company Coast Lines quickly recovered after World War II. The various associate companies of the Coast Lines group were soon back to strength collectively with over 100 ships. In 1951 more than 4 million tons of cargo was carried, along with over one million passengers and a similar number of livestock, principally cattle on the Irish Sea.

Coast Lines bought William Sloan & Company in 1958, and the North of Scotland, Orkney and Shetland Shipping Company Limited in 1961. Both companies were then suffering financing problems, the latter also faced with the issue of how to enter the roll-on roll-off vehicle trade without the capital to buy into the new technology. The Coast Lines group's ships were then mostly general cargo coasters, a few of which still offered a handful of passenger berths in season, along with a selection of conventional passenger ferries with cargo facilities on the Irish Sea and Orkney and Shetland services.

Time was moving on, and already purpose-built vehicle ferries were operating in the Irish and North seas, while the Coast Lines' directors plodded on oblivious to either the roll-on roll-off innovation or the introduction of the container. When Frank Bustard arrived at Preston with his former military vessels to run a commercial roll-on roll-off service to Larne, Alfred Read was incensed and instructed his manager at Belfast to see to it that they were put out of business. Had Read paid more attention to the ideas Bustard was putting forward, the Coast Lines story might well have been very different and its future better assured.

A number of extravagances were made in post-war years when not only was the relief ferry **Irish Coast** commissioned but a quasi-sister, the **Scottish Coast,** was commissioned in 1957. The massive investments for what were effectively relief ferries '*to provide the luxury at relief periods served by the incumbent ferries year round*' paid a short term return and then became a significant drain on resources. The two ships maintained summer services out of Ardrossan and between Dublin and Glasgow but these only lasted a few years. The decline in the cattle on the hoof import from Ireland in favour of the refrigerated carcass trade did little for the fortunes of the company either. The Coast Lines brand was slowly set to decline. It was not, however, alone in its intransigence and the Chairman of the General Steam Navigation Company at London reported to his shareholders '*We have let one hundred years of tradition get in the way of progress*', but both companies had left it too late to act on their own, although together they were to become significant components of a new and exciting initiative that still trades today (Chapter 12).

Coast Lines' **Irish Coast** (1952) seen leaving Glasgow in July 1967 was one of an extravagant pair of Irish Sea ferries built largely for relief duties and support of a seasonal Glasgow to Dublin service.

(Author)

CHAPTER 12

THE FINAL CHAPTER

The 1960s started with the transfer of the **Durham Coast** to the Irish Sea. She had already had a long and varied career, starting with Tyne-Tees as the **Sandhill** when she was commissioned in 1938. In the Coast Lines renaming fest in 1946 she became **Valerian Coast**, but two years later wore Coast Lines colours as **Hebridean Coast** before moving to Aberdeen to adopt their yellow funnel and broad green band later in the year. From Aberdeen she was returned to Tyne-Tees then in 1953 she was sent off to the Belfast Steam Ship Company to become **Ulster Chieftain**. But three years later, as if by some homing instinct, she was back at Newcastle with the new name of **Durham Coast**. As such she again served Tyne-Tees until the Coast Lines bosses decided that she would better suit the trade of the British & Irish Steam Packet Company. So, in 1960, she raised the Irish Tricolor and was given the name **Wicklow**. The following year she was given a new Humboldt-Deutzmotoren engine.

The main employment of the **Wicklow** was on the cargo service between Liverpool and Dublin, but she also operated to Cork, Dundalk and Drogheda and from Manchester occasionally. Indeed it was a trip to Manchester in late September 1964, when her engineers could not put her almost brand new machinery in reverse, and she collided with lock gates so closing the Manchester Ship Canal to navigation for the next three days. The **Wicklow** was undamaged and two weeks after her 'three days of fame' she took the very last sailing from Manchester to Dublin for the British & Irish company.

With the departure of the **Durham Coast** from the Newcastle fleet there was to be no replacement vessel forthcoming from Coast Lines. This was a pattern set for much of the 1960s. The Tyne-Tees company still served all its traditional liner and bulk cargo routes, the prestige service still being that between Newcastle and Hamburg. It also ran occasional trips from Newcastle, sometimes via London, to the Channel Islands, a service it had maintained since 1946, on a seasonal basis with coal taken to the islands and potatoes and flowers brought back to the north-east.

The **Durham Coast** (1938) was a ship of many names, starting life as Tyne-Tees' **Sandhill**, then becoming **Valerian Coast** before passing to the Aberdeen Steam Navigation Company. She returned twice to Tyne-Tees, the second time as **Durham Coast**.

(A Duncan)

On 21 October 1960 it was announced that Tyne-Tees had bought the Middlesbrough company T Roddam Dent & Son, owners of Dent's Wharf adjacent to the Tyne-Tees Wharf. This gave Tyne-Tees a larger wharfage which was equipped with state-of-the-art cranes and warehousing. Regular users of the wharf included liner companies such as Ben Line and P&O.

The Aberdeen to London cargo service was still maintained by the **Hadrian Coast** under the auspices of the Aberdeen Steam Navigation Company. It was increasingly difficult to make the ship pay her way as shippers took to railway and road transport in preference to sea and transhipping at London. In 1961 the **Hadrian Coast** commenced calls at Kirkcaldy for the linoleum trade (the Dundee, Perth and London Shipping Company having withdrawn from the route in 1957), and at Middlesbrough, Hull and Grimsby agented by Tyne-Tees. She then generally returned to Aberdeen direct, but it was now anything but the 'express' service it once was.

Next summer the linoleum trade collapsed and the service provided by the **Hadrian Coast** was declared untenable. After a short spell on the London to Channel Islands service of British Channel Islands Shipping Company she returned to make a few final Aberdeen to London round voyages returning to Aberdeen for the last time on 11 July 1962. She spent much of the next five years working between London and the Channel Islands and was then sold out of the Coast Lines group for further service under the Greek flag. In February 1964 the London and Aberdeen shore assets of the Aberdeen Steam Navigation Company were respectively distributed between the Tyne-Tees company and the North of Scotland, Orkney & Shetland Shipping Company, based at Aberdeen, which had been taken over by Coast Lines in 1961. At the same time the **Hadrian Coast** was registered under the ownership of Coast Lines at Liverpool, and the Aberdeen trading name was formally dissolved.

During 1962 the General Steam Navigation Company was exploring the possibilities of a containerised unit load corridor across the North Sea. GSN recognised that this could not sensibly be done in isolation and called a seminar in Amsterdam to explore likely routes, types of vessels and potential partners. Various companies from the UK, Holland and Germany attended and a variety of companies showed considerable interest in forming a consortium. Belgian operators were not invited due to the politics surrounding the delayed independence of the Belgian Congo. The delegates considered routes between the Wash and Portsmouth in Britain and between Rotterdam and Zeebrugge on the Continent. The main discussion centred on the difficult issue of how best to cope both with containers and roll-on, roll-off traffic, a problem that was incorrectly resolved by Belfast Steamship Company and by Ellerman's Wilson Line when new composite ferries were completed in due course as the **Ulster Prince**, **Ulster Queen** and **Spero**. Their owners, like several others, grossly underestimated the demand for roll-on/roll-off business and overlooked the possibility of carrying containers on trailers.

One of the invited British companies was, unsurprisingly, Coast Lines, and delegates from both Liverpool and Newcastle attended. Further talks were put on hold for the moment because of the imminent sale of the shipping interests of the British Transport Commission. The fall-out from that sale needed to be understood before ideas could be firmed up. Nevertheless, in 1963, Ian Churcher, the GSN General Manager in Holland, held another meeting with those parties that had shown interest the previous year. Mr Churcher had committed himself to the idea of going down the roll-on, roll-off route without any provision for unit load containers at all. In hindsight, of course, he had got the business case exactly right, whereas Belfast Steamship and Ellerman's Wilson compromised, making their new ferries quickly unsuitable to the trade on offer. Churcher was also convinced that the optimum route should be Hull to Rotterdam and he even identified suitable wharves for conversion to fit his plan.

The men from Liverpool, who were already committed to a compromise container and vehicle composite ferry design for the replacement Belfast to Liverpool ferries, were not at all convinced by Churcher's ferry design. But Coast Lines recognised the potential for the route could be massive if the plan was right for the trade on offer. Coast Lines did a very clever thing, by confirming to Churcher that it wanted in and nominating its subsidiary company the Tyne-Tees Steam Shipping Company as its stakeholder. This achieved two objectives. Firstly, the Directors at Newcastle knew and understood the North Sea trades better than the Coast Lines' staff and secondly, should the venture fail then Tyne-Tees could easily be liquidated along with its debts to the consortium without any tenable liability to Coast Lines.

By May 1964 the new overnight ferry between Hull and Rotterdam, to be known as North Sea Ferries, had an agreed funding consortium. This was the Dutch companies Hollandsche Stoomboot Maatschappij and Phs. Van Ommeren collectively with a 40% stake, GSN with a majority 35% stake, the German owned Argo Line joining with A Kirsten in a 20% stake and the Tyne-Tees Steam Shipping Company a 5% stake. The new service would be carried out by two purpose-built ferries which would compete directly with the Associated Humber Lines conventional overnight unit load service operated by the 80 passenger **Melrose Abbey** and **Bolton Abbey**. The vehicle ferries would be built to an innovative design with a drive through vehicle deck extending the length of the ships, passenger berths and reclining seats for about 250 and a capacity of about 1,900 tons deadweight. Orders were placed for two identical ships with A G Weser, Seebeckwerft at Bremerhaven.

The year 1963 was to become a turning point for the Tyne-Tees company when its fleet was reduced by 30% with the sale of three of its larger units. It begs the question whether these sales were necessary in order to reduce non-profitable services operated by Tyne-Tees or whether the sale was necessary to fund the 5% share in the new GSN vehicle ferry consortium. The departing ships were the faithful old steamer **Northumbrian Coast**, which started her days with Tyne-Tees as **Thornaby**, and the motor ships **Grampian Coast** and **Suffolk Coast** which had joined the fleet in the immediate post-war years. The move basically spelled the withdrawal of the company from the bulk cargo trades which had by then become so specialised that Tyne-Tees ships had begun to struggle. The coal burning **Northumbrian Coast** had finally become uneconomical and she was sold in January 1963 and towed up river to the breaker's yard at Dunston. The **Suffolk Coast** and **Grampian Coast** were both sold later in the year for further service under the Italian flag, but with different shipowners.

The **Thornaby/Northumbrian Coast** had enjoyed among others two celebrated masters, Captain D K Wight and Captain Tim Healy who collectively served on the ship for well over 20 years. Even more remarkable was the service of the ship's steward Koih Maenami, known as Joe. Joe came from Japan after World War I and settled in the north-east gaining employment as steward aboard the **Wendy**. In 1935 he transferred to the newly-commissioned **Thornaby** where he stayed until she was sold in 1963.

Tyne-Tees enjoyed a degree of stability until 1966. Although patterns of trade were beginning to change, with an increasing preference for door-to-door shipment of goods, the traditional break-bulk service offered to the continent by the company was still in demand and providing a much needed service.

Long and hard negotiations between parent company Coast Lines and the Irish Government were concluded on 1 January 1965. The focus of interest had been the purchase price and conditions of sale of the British & Irish Steam Packet Company and its subsidiary the City of Cork Steam Packet Company. The sale realised £3.6 million; none of this money was destined for the Tyne-Tees company. Instead the cash was earmarked to support the cost of building three roll-on, roll-off passenger and vehicle ferries. One of these, the **Lion**, was designed to run between Ardrossan and Belfast as a direct replacement for the conventional overnight Glasgow to Belfast ferry service and the other two, **Ulster Prince** and **Ulster Queen**, to replace the aging prototype motor ferry **Ulster Monarch** and her younger consort **Ulster Prince** on the nightly Liverpool to Belfast service. Sadly the two new Liverpool ships were obsolescent before they were commissioned as their vehicle decks were incapable of taking the high-rise lorries that were increasingly wanting to cross the Irish Sea, and the forward hold designed for containers was in little demand – but that is another story.

On 17 December 1965 the new North Sea Ferries service between King George Dock at Hull and Beneluxhaven at Rotterdam commenced with the maiden voyage of the Hull-registered **Norwave** from Hull.

A clear view of the stern door of the **Norwave** (1965) in the Humber, off King George Dock, Hull, August 1967.

(Author)

Her sister **Norwind** was registered under the ownership of Nordzee Veerdiensten NV at Rotterdam and arrived in service three months later with a maiden departure from Rotterdam on 21 March 1966. The two ships maintained a nightly departure from each port save for a lay-over at their respective home ports every Sunday night. With each departure there sailed a 5% stake held by Tyne-Tees. Despite the ill-founded predictions of all the sceptics, the route was found to be the optimum service, drawing as it did on the English Midlands and the north-east of England, and at Rotterdam it was equally well placed to service the huge port hinterland which includes much of Germany and Belgium. The ships were the right capacity to develop the new trade and it was quickly demonstrated that unit load containers could easily be accommodated on trailers. The new service had a devastating impact on the operation of the conventional crane-loaded **Bolton Abbey** and **Melrose Abbey** as shippers lined up to send lorry and trailer loads door-to-door while passengers opted to take their own cars abroad with them. Tyne-Tees received a most satisfactory dividend on its investment at the end of the year, a return that was hooked into the ailing coffers of the Coast Lines parent as soon as it was received.

On the Irish Sea the Burns & Laird Lines steel carriers to Belfast, the **Lairdsrock**, formerly **Glen/Belgian Coast**, and **Lairdsburn**, formerly **Beal/Sylvian Coast**, had been replaced in 1966 by the **Lairdsfield** and **Lairdsfox**. A stark reminder of the dangers of steel cargoes in the North Sea trades occurred when a decline in demand for steel by Harland & Wolff at Belfast allowed the **Lairdsfield** onto the charter market to undertake a voyage from Middlesbrough to Cork with a full cargo of steel goods. On 6 February 1970, under the command of Captain R W Purvis, within an hour of leaving the quayside and having just left the confines of the Tees, the ship rapidly developed a noticeable list and suddenly heeled right over. The incident happened so quickly that none of her crew of ten survived. W Paul Clegg reported on the subsequent Inquiry in *Sea Breezes*, July 1971:

The charterers, John S Braid & Company of Glasgow, were severely censured and ordered to contribute £3,000 towards the cost of the Inquiry... The Lairdsfield had sailed from Middlesbrough with a full cargo of steel plates and hollow columns destined for Cork and Passage West respectively. Within an hour the ship rolled over and sank without warning... Burns & Laird Lines were ordered to contribute £750 towards costs. It was decided that the loss of the ship was due to the improper loading and stowage of the cargo leading to inadequate stability. Fault was found with the loading of 254 tons of steel plates on deck, it being claimed that this move 'defied common sense to any person with a rudimentary knowledge of ship stability or practical experience in loading cargoes'.

The plates were loaded thus because the charterers wanted them off-loading first at Cork. It was, however, stated that the ship was well maintained and that the crew included three experienced and well-qualified deck officers, but the owners were criticised for not ensuring that the latest stability data were posted on board the ship, and the old data removed.

In 1966 the Tyne-Tees fleet was subject to more change in order to optimise services and to provide a degree of unit load capacity onto the Dutch routes. This was partly a reflection of its own competition from the Hull to Rotterdam ferry service operated by North Sea Ferries. The **Iberian Coast** had been laid up for several months when it was announced in August that she had been sold. The buyers were again Italian and they renamed her **Pupi**. Her disposal was brought about by the transfer of the **Stormont** later in the year from Coast Lines. She had previously operated for several associate companies and it was the Belfast, Mersey and Manchester Steamship Company that gave her the name **Stormont** although she had previously operated as **Fruin** for William Sloan and was commissioned originally as the **Fife Coast**. Economic considerations within the Coast Lines group now prevented the renaming of ships transferred between associate companies. Times were indeed hard for the group.

The **Stormont** was initially placed on the Newcastle to Hamburg service taking her first sailing from the Tyne on 4 November 1966. However, she was switched to the Rotterdam and Amsterdam weekly service in late December instead of the **Netherlands Coast**. The attraction of the new ship was that she had been adapted for partial unit load operation while she was working on the Irish Sea. This was the carriage of unitised cargo gathered together at the road hauliers' depots into aluminium containers for onward shipment to the Continent, there to be divided into separate parcels once again ready for delivery. The **Stormont** was switched to a combined Antwerp and Rotterdam service in May 1967 with the **Netherlands Coast** taking up the German trade. Coast Lines was very proud of the network of road haulage companies it had acquired over the years, a development undertaken to match the support given to railway-owned ships operated by state-owned British Railways and more particularly, with the increased demand for door-to-door shipments, by the overland link provided by state-owned British Road Services.

The **Iberian Coast** (1950) working cargo alongside H Hogarth & Sons' **Baron Renfrew** (1935) on the Thames in the late 1950s.

(Malcolm Cranfield)

A picture taken in 1963 by school teacher H M Rae at Belfast with the **Stormont** (1954) flying the Belfast Steamship Company's house flag and registered in Belfast but still wearing William Sloan's colours.

(Richard Danielson collection)

The **Stormont** (1954) was the last ship of the line to wear the corporate Tyne-Tees livery.

A further depletion in fleet strength occurred when the **Frisian Coast** was sold to Greek owners in 1967. She was one of the two larger Dutch-built motor ships commissioned originally as **Lowick**. Her departure reflected the downturn in the Continental cargo liner trades, much of which was finding cheaper options of crossing the North Sea using foreign-owned ships and by the new roll-on/roll-off services.

At the beginning of 1968 the fleet comprised just six ships:

Cyprian Coast - built 1936 as **Anwick**   **Olivian Coast** - built 1946
Netherlands Coast - built 1953   **Stormont** - built 1954 as **Fife Coast**
Novian Coast - built 1936 as **Wooler**   **Yorkshire Coast** - built 1959.

Routes were still maintained to Hamburg and Bremen, to Rotterdam and Amsterdam to Antwerp and Northern French ports and to London and the Channel Islands, although not necessarily at weekly intervals while none was twice weekly any more. Head office at Liverpool had been concerned about the profitability of some of the services and indeed some of the ships for some time and early in the year sent a team from the accountant's office to inspect the books. The Coast Lines' suspicions proved to be largely correct, and the accountants came away with the feeling that there was a genuine risk that Tyne-Tees would start to become a drain on resources if left on its present course. There were two immediate outcomes: replace the **Netherlands Coast** with something smaller and start to downsize both fleet and routes.

The **Netherlands Coast**, with her capacious holds, had indeed become difficult to fill and she rarely sailed loaded down to her marks. She was listed 'For Sale' early in the year and in her place was transferred the smaller **Grangefield**. She had been built in 1954 as the **Statensingel** for Invoer-en Transportonderneming 'Invotra', Rotterdam and had spent some years in the Coast Lines group as **Grangefield** with the Zillah Shipping Company of Liverpool. Her deadweight capacity was a modest 762 tons whereas that of the **Netherlands Coast** was just over 1,000 tons.

The **Grangefield** (1954), on the New Waterway, 31 May 1969. She joined the Zillah Shipping Company in 1955 and was transferred for a brief period into the Tyne-Tees fleet in 1968.

(World Ship Society Photo Library / Les Ring)

The **Netherlands Coast** was still a young ship with plenty of life left in her and she sold quickly to Mediterranean Lines of Haifa to become **Bat Harim**. Mediterranean Lines was on a shopping spree and during 1968 it also bought General Steam Navigation Company's **Philomel** and **Sheldrake** (formerly Manchester Liners' **Manchester Venture** and **Manchester Vanguard**) and the **Talisker** from Coast Lines' associate company William Sloan.

Downsizing was accomplished with the brutal severity that only accountants seem to have authority to make. Both the last of the pre-war motor ships were sold, the **Cyprian Coast** for scrap whereas the **Novian Coast** was immediately transferred to Coast Lines ownership but sold for breaking up a few months later. The final duties of the **Cyprian Coast** were on the last few runs of the London to Channel Islands service of the British Channel Islands Shipping Company working alongside Coast Lines' **Mountstewart**. The service was withdrawn in May 1968 and replaced by a joint link operated partly overland by Commodore and British Rail. The **Cyprian Coast** was sold shortly afterwards. In addition the **Olivian Coast**, built for Tyne-Tees immediately after the war, and for many years the mainstay of the Antwerp service, was also sold for demolition. She too had spent part of her last few years in service with the British Channel Islands Shipping Company running between London, St Peter Port and St Helier. But like so many fine ships before her she went to Ghent to be broken up at Van Heyghen Frères' yard.

The **Olivian Coast** (1946) on charter to the British Channel Islands Shipping Company (red funnel, black top and narrow blue band) in the latter part of her career on 5 July 1967.

(FotoFlite)

The fleet reductions left a three-ship fleet: the **Stormont**, **Yorkshire Coast** and **Grangefield**. So what else had gone? Many of the sea going personnel had transferred to the local collier fleets and none found difficulty in gaining employment elsewhere. Shore-based office staff were reduced by natural wastage with replacement of posts withheld since the start of the year. Some of the younger staff could see little future with the company and left of their own accord. And what of the core shipping services? At a stroke, these were reduced to Newcastle and Middlesbrough sailings to Antwerp and on to Rotterdam and to Hamburg and on to Bremen. Occasional trips were advertised to other continental ports if a ship was available and cargo was on offer. But even that came to an end in 1969 when the **Grangefield** too was disposed of, raising the Panamanian flag but retaining her name until 1973. For the meantime the **Stormont** continued to service the Dutch and Belgian trade with a round trip to Antwerp and Rotterdam, and the **Yorkshire Coast** the German trade. The accountants at Liverpool were happy men, knowing that they had virtually destroyed one of their subsidiary companies yet best of all knowing that they had made what little that was left capable of turning a profit.

The two ships continued to offer weekly round trips to Antwerp/Rotterdam and Hamburg/Bremen, with breaks in service to allow for downtime of each ship for annual maintenance and survey.

In August 1971, following a meeting between John Turner, Chairman of Coast Lines, and Donald Anderson of P&O, Coast Lines agreed to a cash buy-out by P&O valued at £5.6 million. In their agreement to the deal, the Coast Lines' Directors were confident that P&O would allow Coast Lines to continue to trade independently, much as it had allowed GSN its own vision and identity since it was purchased by P&O in 1920. How wrong they were as there followed an almost immediate merger of Coast Lines staff and assets with those of GSN to form P&O European and Air Transport Division in October 1971. Britain was on the verge of entering the European Common Market and P&O recognised the increased trade this would create and wanted just two things from Coast Lines. Firstly, P&O wanted the 5% share in North Sea Ferries held by the Tyne-Tees Steam Shipping Company and secondly, it wanted the vast network of road haulage companies developed by Coast Lines over the years. The remaining assets it saw little future for. Tyne-Tees Steam Shipping Company retained ownership of its share in North Sea Ferries, as did GSN until October 1972 when they were both taken over by P&O.

Coast Lines' **Bison** was renamed **Norbank** when Coast Lines chartered her to North Sea Ferries to commence running a container service between Hull and Rotterdam in late October 1971. Sistership **Buffalo** was later renamed **Norbrae** and joined the **Norbank** on the service in February 1972. They were cellular container ships that had previously been operating on the Irish Sea. Interestingly during 1972 the two ships were re-registered under the ownership of the Tyne-Tees Steam Shipping Company although neither was ever to serve that company.

The **Norbank** (1962), photographed on 24 February 1973, in the corporate livery of P&O (General European).

(Roy Cressey)

The two new North Sea Ferries container ships were intended to provide a supplementary cargo service to the already hard-pressed drive-through vehicle and passenger ferries **Norwave** and **Norwind**. However, the two container ships were dogged by labour problems at Hull and in March 1973 the **Norbank** stood down and was sub-chartered to MacAndrews Shipping Company (MacAndrews & Company) for its Liverpool to Bilbao container service. Things did not improve at Hull and in December 1973 the **Norbrae** was also withdrawn. She was painted in European Unit Routes colours, given the new name **Roe Deer** and commenced on the Tilbury to Antwerp route on 15 January 1974. The two ships were subsumed into P&O Ferries (General European) in March 1976. European Unit Routes was originally championed by GSN but was very much a P&O initiative.

The **Norbrae** (1962) on the New Waterway, 11 July 1972.

(*World Ship Society Photo Library / George Garwood*)

The **Yorkshire Coast** was sold during 1972 and the Antwerp and Rotterdam service was reduced to fortnightly. The **Stormont** left Newcastle and sometimes also Middlesbrough every other week for Hamburg and Bremen and fitted the Antwerp and Rotterdam circuit into the alternate weeks. In June 1976 ownership of the **Stormont** transferred from Tyne-Tees Steam Shipping Company to P&O Ferries (General European) and she was then obliged to adopt the bland corporate pale blue funnel of P&O Ferries as the Tyne-Tees livery disappeared from the North Sea for ever. On 19 September 1976 the **Stormont** returned to the Tyne from Bremen for the last time, sailing two days later for Delfzijl to be handed over to her new Lebanese owners on 14 October. Her passing represented the closure of 149 years of North Sea trading by Tyne-Tees and its antecedent companies.

The **Stormont** (1954) wearing the corporate, but bland, pale blue funnel colours of P&O Ferries.

(*John Clarkson*)

Stormont was replaced at Newcastle in late September by the **Ortolan**, one of the small 'push button' ships formerly of the GSN fleet which were operated by a crew of just five men. **Ortolan** was found to be a little too small and in December 1976 was replaced by another of the former GSN 'push button' fleet, the **Petrel**, the latter offering a deadweight capacity of 536 tons whereas the **Ortolan** could only manage 460 tons. The service was closed shortly afterwards without ceremony and without even a whisper of its ending reported by the local press.

The **Ortolan** (1964) replaced **Stormont** on the German service. Note the GSN house flag at the masthead and the P&O house flag on the jack-staff.

The **Petrel** (1963), formerly of the General Steam Navigation Company's fleet, was deployed on the very last Tyne-Tees Steam Shipping Company sailings from Newcastle to Hamburg and Bremen.

(Author)

Middlesbrough had a linkspan for some years to deal with imports of Datsun cars. In June 1974 the linkspan was also used for a new roll-on, roll-off service to Holland by Norfolk Line. This initiative was followed in August 1974 by a new service to Esbjerg by the UK-Scandinavia Express Company. The final irony was North Sea Ferries moving also into the Middlesbrough trade, starting a commercial vehicle ferry service from Middlesbrough to Zeebrugge in 1988 and to Rotterdam in 1995. Today, North Sea Ferries is rebranded as P&O Ferries and remains a hugely successful enterprise.

The Tyne-Tees company office at 25 King Street is now home to Sabatini's Restaurant still sporting the old advertising board of the Tyne-Tees Steam Shipping Company, while the stores and workshops in City Road overlooking the river, latterly known as Allan House, have been converted for use as a luxury hotel. At London, Free Trade Wharf is now the site of an up market condominium 'Free Trade Wharf, offering fine views up and down the river'.

The company advertising board still on display outside the old offices at Newcastle Quayside.

(Author)

Tyne-Tees Steam Shipping Company and its many associate companies are now just a memory. But when we recall that memory we should not just think of the many fine ships that served these companies but also of their crews, the shore staff and the office workers, the agents and of course the shippers and the passengers who paid for the services the company provided. We must also remember those that died in two world wars in the service of the nation and those that lost their lives at sea during peace time while serving their employer. And finally, we should thank all these people for contributing to the wealth creation of the north-east of England and for helping to make that region a part of England we are all now so proud of.

REFERENCES

Admiralty 1947 *British merchant vessels lost or damaged by enemy action during the Second World War*
His Majesty's Stationery Office, London

Green E & Moss M S 1982 *A business of national importance: the Royal Mail Shipping Group 1902-1937*
Methuen & Co, York

Greenway A 1986 *A century of North Sea passenger steamers*
Ian Allan, Shepperton

Jamieson J & Pike W T 1906 *Durham at the opening of the twentieth Century, 1906*
Pike's New Century Series No 17. W T Pike, Brighton. Reprinted 1985, Peter Bell, Edinburgh

Keys R & Smith K 2006 *Tales from the Tyne*
Tyne Bridge Publishing, Newcastle-upon-Tyne

Lillie W 1968 *The history of Middlesbrough, an illustration of the evolution of English industry*
Middlesbrough Corporation, Middlesbrough

Milne G J 2006 *North East England 1850-1914; the dynamics of a maritime industrial region*
The Boydell Press, Woodbridge

Northway A M 1972 *The Tyne Steam Shipping Co: a late nineteenth century shipping line*
Maritime History, 2, 69-88

Robins N S 2007 *Birds of the Sea, 150 years of the General Steam Navigation Company*
Coastal Shipping Publications, Portishead, Bristol

Robins N S 2011 *Coastal passenger liners of the British Isles*
Seaforth Publishing, Barnsley

Somner G 2000 *The Aberdeen Steam Navigation Company Ltd*
World Ship Society, Gravesend

Sutherland A M 1947 *Tynesider: Some recollections and thoughts of Sir Arthur Munro Sutherland after a lifetime in Tyneside shipping, commercial and civic affairs*
Northumberland Press

The **Bison** (1962), at Liverpool on 16 February 1970.   *(Jim McFaul)*

FLEET LISTS: COASTAL AND NEAR CONTINENTAL SERVICES

Secondhand ships show the previous names and ownership, and ships sold for further service show the name of the purchaser, if known, but not of any subsequent owners. Companies are listed alphabetically.

Aberdeen Steam Navigation Company (acquired by Tyne-Tees Steam Shipping Company 1945) under Tyne-Tees Steam Shipping Company ownership

Name	ASNC service	Gross tons	Comments
Aberdonian	1909-1946	1,648	Hospital ship in WWI, Depot ship in WWII; sold to Peak Shipping Co (Lambert Brothers) Hong Kong and renamed **Taishan Peak**; sold to Shah Steamship Co, Panama 1948 and renamed **Parviz**; damaged in typhoon at Hong Kong July 1948 and scrapped 1950
Koolga	1918-1946	1,110	Built 1910 as **Koolga** for Thomas Cowan, Leith; sold to Aberdeen Steam Navigation Co; sold to Min Kiang Steamship Co., Shanghai 1946 and renamed **Min Yung**; several subsequent owners; scrapped 1953
Harlaw	1929-1946	1,141	Built in 1911 as **Swift** for General Steam Navigation Co; sold to Aberdeen Steam Navigation Co; sold to Min Kiang Steam Ship Co, Shanghai and renamed **Min Chih**; several subsequent owners; scrapped 1963
Lochnagar	1930-1946	1,619	Built in 1906 as **Woodcock** for G & J Burns; chartered as armed Boarding Ship **Woodnut**; returned to G & J Burns 1919 and renamed **Woodcock**; ownership to merged Burns & Laird Lines; renamed **Lairdswood** 1928; sold to Aberdeen Steam Navigation Co 1930 and renamed **Lochnagar**; sold to Rena Cia. De Navigacion, Panama, and renamed **Rena**, renamed **Bluestar** 1951; scrapped 1952

The venerable **Lochnagar** (1906) was one of four steamers acquired with the purchase of the Aberdeen Steam Navigation Company. She had been built for the Ardrossan to Belfast service of G & J Burns as the **Woodcock**.

Name			Comments
Aberdonian Coast	1947-1948	1,258	Transferred to Coast Lines, Liverpool, and renamed **Hibernian Coast**; sold to Alomar Mechanical Engineering Co and renamed **Port Said Coast**; sold 1947 to Kuwait Coast Line Co, no change of name; scrapped 1974
Caledonian Coast	1948	1,265	Transferred to Coast Lines, Liverpool, no change of name; renamed **Makalla** on charter to T & J Brocklebank 1967; sold to Alomar Mechanical Engineering Co, Kuwait and renamed **Ahmadi Coast**; sold 1947 to Kuwait Coast Line Co, no change of name; scrapped 1974
Hebridean Coast	1948-1951	586	Built 1938 as **Sandhill** for Tyne-Tees Steam Shipping Co; renamed **Valerian Coast** 1946 and chartered to Aberdeen Steam Navigation Co between October 1946 and April 1947; to Coast Lines as **Hebridean Coast**; sold to Aberdeen Steam Navigation Co; chartered to Tyne-Tees Steam Shipping Co 1949; sold to Tyne-Tees Steam Shipping Co 1951; to Belfast Steamship Company as **Ulster Chieftain** in 1953; back to Tyne-Tees Steam Shipping Co in 1956 as **Durham Coast**; to British & Irish Steam Packet Co as **Wicklow**; sold to G A Callitsis Sccrs, Nicosia 1970 and renamed **Sinergasia**; several subsequent owners; scrapped in 1980
Hadrian Coast	1948-1964	692	Built 1941 as **Empire Atoll** for Ministry of War Transport (ordered by Coast Lines); to Tyne-Tees Steam Shipping Co and renamed **Hadrian Coast**, 1946; September 1948 to Aberdeen Steam Navigation Co, no change of name; transferred to Coast Lines 1964, no change of name; sold to Daviou Agoudimos & Klissiaunis, Piraeus and renamed **Elda**; wrecked off Morocco 10 January 1970

For earlier fleet list see Somner (2000)

Coast Lines

The core fleet list of the parent company Coast Lines is given in Duckworth & Langmuir's book *Clyde and other coastal steamers*. Ships were often sent to associate companies and then returned to the parent. The Coast Lines group ruling was that if a ship was owned by one company in the group but served another company for six months then ownership passed to that company.

Free Trade Wharf Company

Name	FTWC service	Gross tons	Comments
London Trader / *Old Trader*	1929-1934	600	Built as *Grasmere* 1904 for Grasmere Steamship Co Newcastle; sold to Coombes Marshall & Co, Middlesbrough 1916, no change of name; sold to T G Beatley & Son Middlesbrough and renamed *Mademoiselle Edmere* 1918; sold to Fonteine et Compagnie, Rouen 1921 and renamed *Edmee*; sold to Edmee Steamship Company 1922, no change of name; sold to Bulk Oil Steamship Co 1928 and renamed *London Trader*; sold to Free Trade Wharf Co and renamed *Old Trader* in 1934; sold to Side Shipping Co, London and renamed *Fellside*; several further owners; posted missing 25 November 1937 on voyage Alexandroupolis to Piraeus
Hull Trader	1929-1941	710	Built 1917 as *Edith* for G R Haller, Hull; sold 1917 to Trimsaran Co, Hull, no change of name; sold 1925 to Hannevig Brothers, Hull, no change of name; sold 1925 to D/S Martha A/S, Horten (Norway), no change in name; sold to Bulk Oil Steamship Co, London 1925, partly converted to tanker and renamed *Hull Trader*; sold to Free Trade Wharf Co, London, no change in name; mined 23 June 1941 off Cromer on passage London to Hull
Northgate	1933-1938	425	Built 1925 as *Northgate* for Pease & Partners, Stockton; bought by Free Trade Wharf Co; sold to Bristol Sand & Gravel Co and renamed *Garth*; wrecked following collision in Redcliffe Bay in the Bristol Channel 26 November 1946
Etal	1933-1945	207	Bought on the stocks from Gideon Koster at Groningen; sold and renamed *Farndale*, later resold to Costa Rican owners, no change of name
London Trader	1934-1940	646	Sunk by torpedo from E-boat off Shoreham 26 July 1940
Rock	1934-1938	250	Sold 1938 to Cherbourgeoise and renamed *Cotentin*; numerous subsequent owners; lengthened 1958; scrapped 1980
Ryal	1938-1940	367	Sunk by mine 24 November 1940 in the Thames estuary
Till	1938-1941	367	Sank in collision 1 February 1941 on voyage Tees to King's Lynn

Christopher Furness/Furness Withy & Company

Name	FW service	Gross tons	Comments
Scandinavia	1888-1891	851	Built 1876 as *Columbia*, later named *Sirius*; sold to Christopher Furness and renamed *Scandinavia*; sold 1891 and renamed *Sirius*; scrapped 1893
Chanticleer	1889	539	Built 1853; sold to Christopher Furness; posted missing 23 September 1889
Zebra	1894-1896	551	Built 1851; sold to Furness Withy & Co; scrapped
Albert	1895-1896	525	Built as *Visconde di Attogonia* 1856; sold to Furness Withy & Co; sold and renamed *Guillaume le Conquerant*; several subsequent owners; scrapped
Oporto	1896-1902	570	Built as *Oporto* 1870 for John Bibby & Sons, Liverpool; sold 1873 to Frederick R Leyland, Liverpool; sold 1880 to Coverley & Westray, London; sold 1893 to James E Scott, London; sold to Furness Withy & Co; damaged in collision 14 August 1902 and scrapped
Buccaneer	1902-1904	925	Built 1890 for Tatham Bromage; sold to Furness Withy & Co; to Tyne-Tees Steam Shipping Co
New Oporto	1903-1904	502	To Tyne-Tees Steam Shipping Co

Havelock Line (R M Hudson/R M Hudson & Sons)
(Acquired by Tyne-Tees Steam Shipping Company 1913)

Name	HL service	Gross tons	Comments
General Havelock	1867-1868	473	Built 1861 as *Italia* for James Laing, Sunderland; sold to R R Hudson (Havelock Line brand) and renamed *General Havelock*; sold to James Laing, Sunderland and renamed *Teesdale*; wrecked on Shingles Bank, Isle of Wight, 28 March 1872
General Havelock	1868-1894	673	Wrecked on Hendon Scar, Sunderland Bay, 27 September 1894
Comet (tug)	1882-1897	132	Built 1876 as *Comet* for Star Tug Co, Great Yarmouth; sold 1880 to J Corkhill, Liverpool; to R M Hudson & Sons; sold to Lawson Steam Tug Co, South Shields; 1920 to Lawson Batey Tugs and 1952 Blyth Tug Co; scrapped in 1953
General Havelock	1895-1901	827	Sold to Royal Mail Steam Packet Co and renamed *Kennet*; sold to Mitchell Cotts & Co, London (Sun Shipping) 1915 and renamed *Sunhill*; used by Admiralty as accommodation ship 1915-1920; scrapped 1928
General Havelock	1904-1913	733	Built 1884 as *Leona* for Humber Steam Shipping Co, Goole; sold 1895 to Gregory B Wadsworth & Co, Goole; bought by R M Hudson and Son (Ralph & Alfred Hudson) and renamed *General Havelock*; sold to Tyne-Tees Steam Shipping Co

London & Middlesbrough Steam Shipping Company / Middlesbrough & London Screw Steam Shipping Company / Middlesbrough & London Steam Shipping Company / HWF Bolckow / John Vaughan / J W Pearse / James Taylor

Name	M&L service	Gross tons	Comments
Advance	1854-1869	394	Sold to W Perry; foundered on passage Hartlepool to Gothenburg 23 March 1872 after cargo had shifted
Ann	1860-1870	468	Registered owner H W F Bolckow, Middlesbrough; sold
Ironmaster	1856-1867	394	Registered owner John Vaughan, Stockton; sold 1860 to Bolckow & Vaughan; sunk in collision at Rotterdam, October 1867, later raised and sold for service under Dutch flag as *Martinus & Henriette*
Onward	1861-1862	662	Registered owner H W F Bolckow, Middlesbrough; sank off Flamborough Head 21 March 1862 on passage Middlesbrough to London
Gladstone	1863-1875	650	Built 1863 for J W Pearse, Middlesbrough; sold 1869 to James Taylor, Middlesbrough (London & Middlesbrough Steam Shipping Co); wrecked on Haisborough Beach 12 March 1875 on passage Middlesbrough to London
Dione	1879-1880	849	Built 1868 for Joseph Richardson, Hull; sold 1870 to R C Byrne, Hull; sold 1875 to J Johannsen Linen, London; bought by London & Middlesbrough Steamship Company and to Tees Union Shipping Co

P&O

P&O had diverse interests including the General Steam Navigation Company and Moss Hutcheson Line (for fleet lists see Robins, 2007). Following the take-over of Coast Lines and its various associate companies, it retained diverse interests in the coastal and near Continental routes using both company owned and chartered ships. It later developed roll-on/roll-off vehicle ferry traffic notably at Hull, Southampton and Dover.

Stockton & London Steam Shipping Company

Name	S&SLSSC service	Gross tons	Comments
Stockton	1857-1880	392	Sold to George Bazeley, Penzance, no change of name; sold 1897 to George Toyne, Carter & Co, Fowey; sold to owners in Hull 1907; out of register 1909
Tees	1857-1870	311	Sold to Charles C Duncan, Stockton, still in service 1875
Thames	1866-1884	399	Sold to George Bazeley, Penzance, no change of name; wrecked near Portland Bill, 2 January 1891

Tees Union Shipping Company

Name	TUSC service	Gross tons	Comments
Cobden	1880-1898	672	Built 1866 for James Taylor, Middlesbrough; bought by London & Middlesbrough Steamship Company 1875; to Tees Union Shipping Co; sold to German owners and renamed *Titus*; missing August 1899
Dione	1880-1903	849	Built 1868 for J Johannsen Linen; bought by London & Middlesbrough Steamship Company 1879; to Tees Union Shipping Co; to Tyne-Tees Steam Shipping Co
Andalusia	1893-1898	274	Built 1863 as *Andalusia* for Mories & Munroe, Glasgow; sold 1868 to William Gifford, Leith, no change of name; lengthened 1879; sold 1880 to Scarborough Steam Shipping Co; to Tees Union; sold to Boye Joachim Flood, London, no change of name; several subsequent owners; scrapped 1924
Tees	1893-1896	569	Sold 1896 to Hudson's Bay Co, Stockton, no change of name; several subsequent owners; scrapped 1937
Claudia	1897-1903	1,144	To Tyne-Tees Steam Shipping Co

Tyne Steam Shipping Company

Name	TSSgC service	Gross tons	Comments
Chevy Chase	1864-1881	345	Built 1848 for John Ormston and partners; sold to John Ormston 1858; sold to Tyne Steam Shipping Co; sold to Norwegian owners and later condemned after collision in 1896
Earl Percy	1864-1865	376	Built 1849; wrecked Tynemouth 3 February 1865
Ocean Queen	1864-1865	195	Built 1854 as *Ocean Queen* for Messrs Depledge & Duncan, Hull; sold 1857 to W N Depledge, Hull; sold 1863 to W H Stephenson, Newcastle; sold to Tyne Steam Shipping Co; wrecked 19 April 1865 on Whitby Rocks, 1 mile south of Whitby
Brigadier	1864-1877	444	Built 1855 for W Laing and W D Stephens; sold 1858 to W Laing; sold 1862 to W D Stephens; sold to Tyne Steam Shipping Co; wrecked in the Kattegat 16 March 1877 off Anholt on passage Copenhagen to the Tyne
Otter	1864-1873	475	Built 1855 for John Ormston and John Dobson; sold to John Ormston 1861; sold to Tyne Steam Shipping Co; foundered off Yarmouth in the Wold 20 February 1873 on passage Newcastle to Antwerp
Sentinel	1864-1881	551	Built as *Sentinel* 1860 for Laing and Davies; sold to W D Stephens 1862; sold to Tyne Steam Shipping Co; lengthened 1865; lost
Admiral	1864-1903	625	To Tyne-Tees Steam Shipping Co
Lord Raglan	1864-1886	516	Built 1855 as *Lord Raglan* for John Ormston; sold to Tyne Steam Shipping Co; sold for breaking up 1886; scrapped 1888
Dragoon	1864-1888	744	Lengthened 1873; lost in Scheldt on 3 September 1888 on passage Newcastle to Antwerp
Fusilier	1864-1868	323	Sold to J Laing, Newcastle; resold 1868 to R Fell, no change of name; sold 1881 to French owners 1881 and renamed *St Jean*; broken up 1911
Hussar (tug)	1865-1869	87	Sold to John Ormston jnr, Newcastle; later sold to Robert Redhead and renamed *Dundee*
Kitten (wherry)	1865-1875	25	Built as *Kitten* 1865 for Laing & Davies, Newcastle; sold 1862 to W D Stephens, Newcastle; sold to Tyne Steam Shipping Company; sold 1875
Grenadier	1865-1894	711	Lost in collision in North Sea 1 August 1894
Iona (tug)	1866-1892	67	Given as part exchange to Schlesinger Davis & Co for new tug *WDS*
C M Palmer	1870-1878	817	Lengthened 1872; lost in collision with the steamer *Ludworth* on 17 February 1878 off Bawdrey Shoal on passage from Newcastle to London
Earl Percy	1870-1888	715	Built as *Earl Percy* in 1865 for Tyne General Ferry Co; sold 1870 to Tyne Steam Shipping Co; lengthened 1872; lost off Whitby in collision with steamer *Wear* on 15 September 1888 on passage Newcastle to Rotterdam
John Ormston	1873-1903	970	To Tyne-Tees Steam Shipping Co
Royal Dane	1875-1903	1,282	To Tyne-Tees Steam Shipping Co
Zingari	1875-1883	406	Built 1854 for R W Jackson, Hartlepool; sold 1862 to Long and Curtiss, West Hartlepool; sold 1864 to W S Curtiss, West Hartlepool; sold 1867 to C A Baker, West Hartlepool; sold 1868 to Justinian Barrell Clarke, Norwich; sold to Yarmouth Line and acquired by Tyne Steam Shipping Co; sold; scrapped 1897

Miaca	1875-1886	412	Built 1866 for Thomas Steele, Ayr; sold to Yarmouth Line and acquired by Tyne Steam Shipping Co; sold to Norwegian owner; wrecked off Iceland 1888
Warkworth	1882-1903	697	Built 1880 as *Warkworth Harbour* for H Andrews; to Tyne-Tees Steam Shipping Co
Busy Bee	1883-1896	961	Built 1865 for W D Stephens; sunk in collision off the Belgian Wielingen Light 9 February 1896
Tynesider	1888-1903	1,290	To Tyne-Tees Steam Shipping Co
Juno	1888-1903	1,311	Built 1882 for Thomas Wilson, Sons & Co; to Tyne-Tees Steam Shipping Co
Minx (steam wherry)	1889-1903	51	To Tyne-Tees Steam Shipping Co
Londoner	1891-1893	1,513	Sunk on passage London to Newcastle in collision with Manchester, Sheffield & Lincolnshire Railway steamer *Sheffield* 14 May 1893 off North Haisborough
WDS (tug)	1892-1903	103	To Tyne-Tees Steam Shipping Co
New Londoner	1894-1903	1,456	To Tyne-Tees Steam Shipping Co
Grenadier	1895-1903	1,004	To Tyne-Tees Steam Shipping Co
Faraday	1896-1903	892	Built 1873 as *Faraday* for G Reid & Co, Newcastle; to Tyne-Tees Steam Shipping Co

Tyne-Tees Steam Shipping Company

Name	T-TSSgC service	Gross tons	Comments
Admiral	1903-1905	625	Built 1864 for Tyne Steam Shipping Co; acquired by Tyne-Tees Steam Shipping Co; scrapped 1905
Faraday	1903-1906	892	Built 1873 as *Faraday* for G Reid & Co; sold 1896 to Tyne Steam Shipping Co; acquired by Tyne-Tees Steam Shipping Co; sold to Furness Withy & Company, no change of name; scrapped 1909
Royal Dane	1903-1907	1,282	Built 1875 for Tyne Steam Shipping Co; acquired by Tyne-Tees Steam Shipping Co; sold to Cie Oranaise de Nav, Oran, no change of name; later renamed *Eugene Etienne*; several subsequent owners; scrapped 1913
Dione	1903-1908	849	Built 1868; ex-London & Middlesbrough Steamship Co; ex-Tees Union Shipping Co; acquired by Tyne-Tees Steam Shipping Co; sold to Spanish owners and renamed *Parayas*; sold 1909 to Cia Nav Vapour Aurora of Bilbao and renamed *Aurora*; scrapped 1964
Tynesider	1903-1908	1,378	Built 1888 for Tyne Steam Shipping Company; acquired by Tyne-Tees Steam Shipping Co; sold to Cie Hellénique de Navigation à Vapeur de Syra, Greece (A A Capparis) renamed *Neilos*; sold to Arab Steamers, Bombay 1912 and renamed *Faris*; scrapped 1914
Minx (steam wherry)	1903-1909	51	Built 1889 for Tyne Steam Shipping Co; acquired by Tyne-Tees Steam Shipping Co; sold 1909 sold on again October 1910 to River Wear Commissioners, Sunderland; scrapped 1929
John Ormston	1903-1910	970	Built 1873 for Tyne Steam Shipping Co; acquired by Tyne-Tees Steam Shipping Co; sold to A Kumpanyasi and renamed *Heybeliada*; destroyed by Russian gunfire 7 March 1915 at Karadeniz-Eregli
New Londoner	1903-1911	1,456	Built 1894 for Tyne Steam Shipping Company; acquired by Tyne-Tees Steam Shipping Co; sold to Societa Naviera e Industria, Barcelona, and renamed *Atlante*; scrapped 1940
Warkworth	1903-1913	697	Built 1880 as *Warkworth Harbour* for H Andrews; sold to Tyne Steam Shipping Co 1882 and renamed *Warkworth*; acquired by Tyne-Tees Steam Shipping Co; sold to G Germano (Italy) and renamed *Mariannina*; sold to S Biraderler (Turkey) 1924 and renamed *Arslan* and in 1926 *Arslan I*; wrecked near Bandirma 28 February 1930
Juno	1903-1915	1,311	Built 1882 as *Juno* for Thomas Wilson Sons & Co; sold to Tyne Steam Shipping Co 1888; acquired by Tyne-Tees Steam Shipping Co; detained at Hamburg August 1914 and abandoned to insurers January 1915; returned to British Government December 1918 and sold by London brokers Abraham Lazurus to Portuguese owners and renamed *Afra*; several subsequent owners; scrapped 1935
New Oporto	1903-1915	502	Built 1903 for Furness Withy & Co; acquired by Tyne-Tees Steam Shipping Co; lengthened 1909; wrecked Haisborough Sands on 8 January 1915 on passage Middlesbrough to London
Claudia	1903-1916	1,144	Built 1897 for Tees Union Shipping Co; acquired by Tyne-Tees Steam Shipping Co; mined and sunk off Lowestoft, 30 July 1916
Grenadier	1903-1917	1,004	Built 1895 for Tyne Steam Shipping Co; acquired by Tyne-Tees Steam Shipping Co; stranded Frisian coast July 1908, salvaged; torpedoed and sunk near Shipwash Light Vessel, 23 February 1917

WDS (tug)	1903-1919	103	Built 1892 for Tyne Steam Shipping Co; acquired by Tyne-Tees Steam Shipping Co; sold to J Batey & Son, Newcastle; several subsequent owners; scrapped 1949
Buccaneer	1903-1925	925	Built 1890 for Tatham Bromage, to Furness Withy & Co 1902; acquired by Tyne-Tees Steam Shipping Co; sold to P Bauman and renamed **Agathe** and again renamed **Herman**; several subsequent owners; scrapped 1936
Sir William Stephenson	1906-1915	1,540	Mined near Cockle Light Vessel and towed to Yarmouth Roads and sank 29 August 1915
Richard Welford / Hethpool	1908-1925	1,410	Capsized at Newcastle February 1924, refurbished as **Hethpool**; sold to Canadian owners and renamed **Farnorth**; several subsequent owners; scrapped 1957
Teessider	1909-1929	1,134	Sold to Soc Algérienne de Navigation pour l'Afrique du Nord (Charles Schiaffino & Cie), Algiers and renamed **Finistère** ; scrapped 1955
Poodle (steam wherry)	1909-1919	130	Sold and renamed **Kinsol**; wrecked on Clyde coast 28 September 1939
Stephen Furness	1910-1917	1,712	Converted to armed boarding vessel 1916; torpedoed and sunk 15 miles NW of Peel, Isle of Man, 13 December 1917 on passage from Lerwick to Liverpool
New Londoner	1912-1936	1,342	Sold to J Billmeir & Co, London, renamed **Kenwood**; several subsequent owners; scrapped 1960
General Havelock	1913-1923	733	Built 1884 as **Leona** for Goole Steam Shipping Co; sold to G B Wadsworth & Co, Goole, 1895; sold to Havelock Line 1904 and renamed **General Havelock**; sold to Soc Algérienne de Navigation pour l'Afrique du Nord (Charles Schiaffino & Cie), Algiers, and renamed **Finistère**; sold to Scotto Mazzella & Co 1930 and renamed **Sidi-Belyout**; sank 1932; scrapped 1936
Howden	1913-1925	1,020	Built as **Howden** 1909 for Furness Withy & Co; sold to Tyne-Tees Steam Shipping Co, no change of name; sold to D/S A/S Aslaug of Haugesund, Norway and renamed **Aslaug**; wrecked Bayona 25 December 1929
Novocastrian	1915	1,151	Mined and sunk off Lowestoft, 5 October 1915 on passage London to Newcastle
Wendy	1915-1936	958	Built 1913 for George V Turnbull & Co, Leith (50% owned by Furness Withy from 1909, wholly owned by Furness Withy from 1914); sold to Tyne-Tees Steam Shipping Co, no change of name; sold to Anglo Iberian Steamship Co, London, and renamed **Briardale**; several subsequent owners; sunk in collision off Robin Hood's Bay 15 February 1941
Dunstanburgh	1921-1935	1,400	Built 1912 as **Greif** for Dampfs-Ges 'Argo', Bremen; renamed **Sirena** by Russian military 1915; returned to Dampfs-Ges 'Argo' 1918 and renamed **Greif**; taken by British Government 1921; sold to Tyne-Tees Steam Shipping Co and renamed **Dunstanburgh**; sold to Stanhope Steamship Co and renamed **Stanburgh**; destroyed by fire when loading cased petrol at Sète 4 November 1938
Bamburgh	1922-1938	648	Built 1914 as **Arkleside** for Wear Steam Shipping Co/Thomas Rose & Partners, Sunderland; sold to Tyne-Tees Steam Shipping Co and renamed **Bamburgh**; sold to Matthew Taylor, Methil, and renamed **Methilhill**; scrapped 1954
Bernicia	1923-1934	1,839	Laid up 1932; sold to Hellenic Coast Lines, Piraeus, and renamed **Ionia**; taken by Germany and later wrecked near Skiathos 14 December 1944
Hadrian	1923-1934	1,738	Laid up 1932; sold to Khedivial Mail Steamship & Graving Dock Co, London and renamed **Fouadieh**; transferred to Khedivial Mail Line SAE, Alexandria,1939 and renamed **Isis** 1956; sold to United Arab Maritime Co, Alexandria 1961, no change of name; scrapped 1966
Middlesbro'	1924-1939	989	Sank after striking submerged object off Flamborough Head 9 December 1939
Cragside / Crag	1925-1935	458	Built 1903 as **Helmsman** for C Rowbotham, London; sold to Tyne-Tees Steam Shipping Co and renamed **Cragside**; renamed **Crag** 1935; scrapped 1935
Lindisfarne	1925-1942	968	Sunk by German E-Boat off Lowestoft 12 December 1942
Newminster / Dorian Coast	1925-1947	967	Renamed **Dorian Coast** 1946; sold to Eastern Navigation Co (S Hassum & Co), Bombay, 1947 and renamed **Azadi**; scrapped 1951
Marden	1926-1929	715	Built as **Main** 1904 for Main Colliery Co, Cardiff; torpedoed and sunk October 1917, later raised, refitted and put back into service in 1922 by Ford Shipping Co, Glasgow, no change of name; sold to Tyne-Tees Steam Shipping Co renamed **Marden**; sunk in collision off Cromer Knoll 27 May 1929 on voyage London to Newcastle
Ayresome	1927-1935	835	Built 1916 as **Boekelo** for NV Stoomvaart Mij Nordzee, Amsterdam; sold to Tyne-Tees Steam Shipping Co and renamed **Ayresome**; sold to Brook Shipping Co (Comben Longstaff & Co), Middlesbrough, and renamed **Surreybrook**; several further owners; sunk by torpedo 26 September 1940 on passage Clyde to Lisbon

Ship	Years	Tonnage	Details
Lowick	1927-1936	562	Built 1907 as *Steersman* for C Rowbotham, London; sold to Continental Lines, London and renamed *Continental Trader* 1925; sold to Tyne-Tees Steam Shipping Co and renamed *Lowick*; sold to Buchan & Hogg, Grangemouth, and renamed *Dunmoir*; scrapped 1954
Gateshead	1928-1932	731	Built as *Gowzee* 1917 for NV ss Gowzee, Rotterdam; sold 1919 to NV Algemeene Nederlandsche Scheepvaart Mij, Rotterdam, and renamed *Wilhelminapolder*; sold to Tyne-Tees Steam Shipping Co and renamed *Gateshead*; sunk in collision off Seaham Harbour 21 December 1932
Wooler	1928-1934	559	Built 1919 as *Marsdiep* for NV Hollandsche Vrachtvaart Mij, Rotterdam; sold 1919 to Walford Lines, London, and renamed *Jolly Kate*; sold to Tyne-Tees Steam Shipping Co and renamed *Wooler*; sold to Stanhope Steamship Co, London, and renamed *Stanmore*; sold 1938 to John S Monks, Liverpool and renamed *Stanville*; scrapped 1951
Belford	1928-1936	366	Built 1920 as *War Arun*, completed as *Mickleham* for John Harrison, London; sold to Walford Lines, London, 1920 and renamed *Jolly Laura*; sold to Tyne-Tees Steam Shipping Co and renamed *Belford*; sold to J M Piggins, Montrose, renamed *Glen Foam* 1948, several subsequent owners; scrapped 1963
Sandhill	1928-1934	538	Built 1920 as *Pekelderdiep* for Gebr Boot, Leiderdorp; sold to E Noronha Barros, Lisbon 1920 and renamed *Estoril*; sold to James W Cook & Co, London, 1923 and renamed *London Trader*; sold to Bulk Oil Steamship Co, London, 1925, no change of name; sold to Tyne-Tees Steam Shipping Co and renamed *Sandhill*; sold to Stanhope Steamship Co, London, and renamed *Stanhope*; several further owners; scrapped 1957
Alnwick	1929-1935	1,383	Sold to A S Ganger Rolf (Fred. Olsen), Oslo, and renamed *Bali*; sold to Burmese Government 1952 and renamed *Pyidawtha*; wrecked off Burma 6 May 1955
Bilton	1929-1946	746	Built 1920 as *Bilton* for Coombes, Marshall & Co, Middlesbrough; bought by Tyne-Tees Steam Shipping Co, no change of name; sold to J Kelly, Belfast, and renamed *Coleraine*; renamed *Ballyhalbert* 1951; ashore at Ardrossan January 1958; scrapped 1959
Akeld	1933-1940	633	Built as *Mayfield* for Cargo Steamships Co, Dublin, 1922; sold to J Hay & Sons, Glasgow, and renamed *The Earl* 1922; sold to Tyne-Tees Steam Shipping Co and renamed *Akeld*; sunk by torpedo on passage Rotterdam to Newcastle 9 March 1940
Gateshead / *Persian Coast*	1933-1951	754	Built 1919 as *War Colne* and completed as *Catherine Annie* for J Leete Co, London; sold to J Hay & Sons, Glasgow, 1922 and renamed *The President*; bought by Tyne-Tees Steam Shipping Co and renamed *Gateshead*; renamed *Persian Coast* 1946; sold to Mersey Ports Stevedoring Co, Liverpool, and renamed *Celia Mary*; sold to Glynwood Navigation Co, Hull, 1955 and renamed *Cupholder*; scrapped 1956
Glen / *Belgian Coast*	1935-1947	471	Renamed *Belgian Coast* 1946; to Burns & Laird Lines, Glasgow, and renamed *Lairdsrock*; several subsequent owners; wrecked off Karpathos Island, Greece, 10 December 1980
Craster / *Caspian Coast*	1935-1947	733	Renamed *Caspian Coast* 1946; sold to London Scottish Lines 1947 and renamed *London Merchant*; sold to owners in the Maldives 1959 and renamed *Maldive Crescent*; wrecked off the Burmese coast 28 June 1967 and abandoned the following day
Cragside / *Elysian Coast*	1935-1952	495	Renamed *Elysian Coast* 1946; to Zillah Shipping Co Liverpool and renamed *Westfield*; scrapped 1956
Thornaby / *Northumbrian Coast*	1935-1963	1,171	Renamed *Northumbrian Coast* 1946; scrapped 1963
Beal/Sylvian Coast	1936-1959	504	Renamed *Sylvian Coast* 1946; to Burns & Laird Lines, Glasgow, and renamed *Lairdsburn*; several subsequent owners; sank 5 March 1979 at Augusta, Sicily, on passage to Barcelona
Alnwick / Cyprian Coast	1936-1968	508	Renamed *Cyprian Coast* 1946; scrapped 1968
Wooler / Novian Coast	1936-1968	507	Renamed *Novian Coast* 1946; to Coast Lines, no change of name; scrapped 1968
Lowick / Frisian Coast	1937-1967	586	Renamed *Frisian Coast* 1946; sold to D Varverikis and others, Piraeus 1967 and renamed *Agia Eleni*; wrecked near Rhodes 26 November 1977
Sandhill / Valerian Coast *Hebridean Coast* *Durham Coast*	1938-1948 1951-1953 1956-1960	586	Renamed *Valerian Coast* 1946; to Coast Lines as *Hebridean Coast*; to Aberdeen Steam Navigation Co 1948; time charter to Tyne-Tees Steam Shipping Co 1949; to Tyne-Tees Steam Shipping Co 1951, no change of name; to Belfast Steamship Company and renamed *Ulster Chieftain* in 1953; back to Tyne-Tees Steam Shipping Co in 1956 and renamed *Durham Coast*; to British & Irish Steam Packet Co 1960 and renamed *Wicklow*; sold to G A Callitsis Sccrs, Nicosia 1970 and renamed *Sinergasia*; several subsequent owners; scrapped in 1980

The versatility of the motor ships was demonstrated by the **Sandhill** (1938) which bore many names in the Coast Lines group fleet post-war and served as the **Wicklow** for the British & Irish Steam Packet Company between 1960 and 1970.

(Pat Sweeney)

Hadrian Coast	1946-1948	692	Built 1941 as **Empire Atoll** for Ministry of War Transport (ordered by Coast Lines) and managed by Coast Lines for Ministry of War Transport 1941-1945; to Tyne-Tees Steam Shipping Co and renamed **Hadrian Coast**; September 1948 to Aberdeen Steam Navigation Co; transferred to Coast Lines 1964 (still named **Hadrian Coast**); sold to Daviou Agoudimos & Klissiaunis, Piraeus and renamed **Elda**; wrecked off Morocco 10 January 1970
Olivian Coast	1946-1968	749	Scrapped 1968
Maurice Rose	1947	1,600	Built 1930 for Richard Hughes & Co (Liverpool); sold to Tyne-Tees Steam Shipping Co, no change of name; to A Cocker & Co, Liverpool, and renamed **Baltic King** (never sailed on Tyne-Tees business); 1949 to Queenship Navigation Co and renamed **Richmond Queen**; scrapped 1957
Virginian Coast	1947-1953	1,600	Built 1930 as **Dennis Rose** for Richard Hughes & Co (Liverpool); sold to Tyne-Tees Steam Shipping Co and renamed **Virginian Coast**; sold to Urain & Zatica and renamed **Julian Presa**; scrapped 1958
Belgian Coast	1947-1957	1,600	Built 1929 as **Dorothy Rose** for Richard Hughes & Co (Liverpool); sold to Tyne-Tees Steam Shipping Co and renamed **Belgian Coast**; scrapped 1957

The **Belgian Coast** (1929) on the Thames, December 1952, with New Zealand Line's **Hinakura** (1949) at anchor.

(Richard Danielson collection)

Grampian Coast	1947-1963	481	Built as *Welsh Coast* for Coast Lines, completed as *Emerald Queen* 1937 for Plymouth, Channel Islands & Brittany Steamship Co; to Tyne-Tees Steam Shipping Co and renamed *Grampian Coast*; sold to S Lucchi, Italy, and renamed *Gilda*; became static restaurant in Italy 1975
Iberian Coast	1950-1966	1,188	Launched as *Sandringham Queen* for Queenship Navigation Co, but completed as *Iberian Coast* for Tyne-Tees Steam Shipping Co; sold to Spiridioni Locchi, Venice, and renamed *Pupi*; sold to Annivas Maritime Hellas, Piraeus, 1976 and renamed *Agios Nicolaos*; destroyed by fire on passage to Beira 26 August 1978
Hebridean Coast	1951-1953	586	See *Sandhill* (1938)
Suffolk Coast	1951-1963	541	Built 1938 as *Marili* for M Porn, Holland; bought by Coast Lines 1939 and renamed *Suffolk Coast*; re-engined April 1948; to Tyne-Tees Steam Shipping Co, no change of name; sold to Meloni L G, Italy and renamed *Melania*; foundered 9 February 1970 off Leghorn
Hampshire Coast	1952-1959	1,224	Built 1940 as *Stuart Queen* for British Channel Islands Shipping Co; to Coast Lines 1946 and renamed *Hampshire Coast*; to Tyne-Tees Steam Shipping Co, no change of name; scrapped 1959
Netherlands Coast	1953-1968	867	Sold to Bat Harim Mediterranean Lines, Ashdod and Haifa, and renamed *Bat Harim*; several subsequent owners, still in service 1974, fate unknown
Durham Coast	1956-1960	586	See *Sandhill* (1938)
Yorkshire Coast	1959-1972	785	Sold to J & A Gardner, Glasgow, and renamed *St Enoch*; several subsequent owners; sunk in collision on passage Beirut to Limassol 13 March 1986
Stormont	1966-1976	906	Built 1954 for Coast Lines as *Fife Coast*; to William Sloan & Co 1958 and renamed *Fruin*; to Belfast Steamship Co. 1963 and renamed *Stormont*; transferred to Coast Lines 1965 and to Tyne-Tees Steam Shipping Co, no change of name; management to P&O Short Sea Shipping 1971 and to P&O Ferries 1975; ownership transferred to P&O Ferries (General European) Liverpool 1976; sold to Lebanese owners and renamed *Rabunion VII* 1976; resold and renamed *Baraaz* 1992; scrapped 1994
Grangefield	1968-1969	504	Built 1954 as *Statensingel* for Invoer- en Transportonderneming 'Invotra', Rotterdam; sold 1955 to Zillah Shipping Co, Liverpool, and renamed *Grangefield*; to W A Savage, Liverpool 1964, no change of name; to Tyne-Tees Steam Shipping Co, no change of name; sold to Trans Sea Shipping Corporation, Panama, and in 1973 renamed *Sea Goblin*; several subsequent owners; deleted from register 1998
Norbank	1972-1976	1,343	Built 1962 as *Bison* for Coast Lines; renamed *Norbank* on charter to North Sea Ferries 1971; transferred to Tyne-Tees Steam Shipping Co, no change of name; transferred to P&O (General European); sold to National Suriname Shipping 1978 and later renamed *Flamingo*; laid up 1979, scrapped 1990
Norbrae / *Roe Deer*	1972-1976	1,482	Built 1962 for Coast Lines as *Buffalo*; renamed *Norbrae* on charter to North Sea Ferries 1972; transferred to Tyne-Tees Steam Shipping Co and in 1974 renamed *Roe Deer*; ownership transferred to P&O Ferries (General European) 1976; sold 1977 and renamed *Newfoundland Container*; last known trading as *Container Express* since 1992 for International Shipping Corporation, Belize; scuttled at sea 1999

The *Suffolk Coast* (1938), at Jersey, on 20 April 1959.　　　　　　　*(Dave Hocquard)*

FLEET LISTS: GLOBAL TRAMP SHIP SERVICES

Secondhand ships show the previous names and ownership, and ships sold for further service show the name of the purchaser, if known, but not of any subsequent owners.

R M Hudson and R M Hudson & Sons

Name	Hudson service	Gross tons	Comments
Claremont	1871-1873	1,129	Built 1871 for R M Hudson; sold to William Wilson of Newcastle, no change of name; sold 1880 to Fisher Renwick, no change of name; wrecked off Isle of Wight 1881
Mecca	1871-1872	1,567	Sold to Lloyd Italiano, no change of name; sold 1876 to R Rubattino and renamed ***Bengala***; several subsequent owners; wrecked on passage Trieste to Genoa 10 April 1889
Mecca	1872-1879	1,067	Built for R M Hudson & Partners; wrecked Torres Strait 24 December 1979
Silbury	1875-1877	958	Built 1872 for Charles J Fox, London, as ***Silbury***; sold to John Chapman, London, no change of name; bought by R M Hudson Junior, no change of name; sold to John Chapman, London; sold 1883 to Mersey Steamship Co, Liverpool, and renamed ***Mogador***; wrecked on Hats and Barrels Rocks, Pembrokeshire, 25 July 1895
Consort	1876-1882	1,074	Built 1871 as ***Consort*** for W Swainston and others, Sunderland; sold 1871 to Det Nordenfjeldske D/S, Trondheim and renamed ***Olaf Trygvesen***; bought by R M Hudson and renamed ***Consort***; sold to Soc Rouennaise de Transports Maritimes à Vapeur of Rouen and renamed ***Denis Papin***; foundered 5 October 1884 in Bay of Biscay
Meath	1879-1902	2,047	Built for R M Hudson; sold to N Dubuisson and renamed ***Rene***; foundered Bay of Biscay 25 September 1903
Westmeath	1882-1892	3,343	Built for R M Hudson; sold to S I Telephones and renamed ***Francois Arago***; sold 1916 to Francais Commerce and renamed ***Peronne***; sunk by torpedo 1 September 1917 off Berry Head
Wexford	1883-1897	2,043	Built for R M Hudson & Sons; sold to N Dubuisson and renamed ***Elise***; foundered Lake Huron 9 November 1913
Kildare	1884-1888	3,463	Built for R M Hudson & Sons; foundered Indian Ocean 4 October 1888
Wicklow	1889-1893	2,967	Built 1882 as ***Selembria*** for Crow Rudolf & Co; bought by R M Hudson and renamed ***Wicklow***; wrecked off Calais 7 January 1893
Connemara	1889-1895	3,379	Built 1881 for Bordelaise as ***Chateau Leoville***; bought by R M Hudson & Sons and renamed ***Connemara***; sold to G B Hunter and renamed ***Belgian King***; foundered off Cape Kureli 20 September 1914
Westmeath	1893-1894	6,238	Built for R M Hudson & Sons; sold to Shaw, Savill & Albion Co and renamed ***Tokomaru***; sunk by torpedo off Le Havre 30 January 1915
Westmeath	1895-1898	6,851	Built for R M Hudson & Sons; foundered North Atlantic 6 November 1898
Leitrim	1896-1913	4,284	Built for R M Hudson & Sons; wrecked off Corfu 5 May 1913
Melbourne	1898-1913	3,819	Built 1890 for William Kish, Sunderland as ***Melbourne***; bought by R M Hudson & Sons; wrecked Philippines 6 October 2013
Queensland	1898-1927	3,892	Built 1890 for William Kish, Sunderland as ***Queensland***; bought by R M Hudson & Sons; sold to F Graduslatvia of Riga and renamed ***Everita***; scrapped 1935

Several other vessels were part-owned and registered under other owners' names, e.g. during the early 1890s: **Cascapedia**, **Mascotte** *and* **Victoria**.

B J Sutherland & Company / A M Sutherland / Sutherland Steam Ship Company / Munro Shipping Company / Dunrobin Shipping Company

Name	S Service	Gross tons	Comments
Sutherland	1898-1900	2,279	Sold to Portillo & Ibanez and renamed ***Carranza***; foundered off Armen Rocks, 11 September 1908
*Caithness**	1898-1917	3,503	Sunk by torpedo off Corunna 19 April 1917
*Inverness**	1899-1901	3,314	Built 1899 as ***Beechmore*** for W Johnston & Co; to A M Sutherland and

Ship	Years	Tonnage	Details
			renamed *Inverness*; to Barrakur Coal Co and renamed *Flamingo*; sold to A Parodi 1912 and renamed *Trento*; sunk by mine 150 miles from Ushant 7 August 1917
Cromarty	1899-1919	2,742	Built 1892 as *Abendana* for J Graham & Co; to B J Sutherland & Co and renamed *Cromarty*; sold to S M Belge and renamed *General Michel*; scrapped 1922
*Sutherland**	1901-1916	3,542	Sunk by gunfire NW of Madeira 17 January 1916
*Argyll**	1901-1917	3,547	Sunk by torpedo on voyage Port Kelah to Middlesbrough 13 April 1917
*Inverness / Ross**	1902-1920	3,734	Renamed *Ross* 1902; sold to Anglo-Celtic Shipping Co and renamed *Inverness*; sold 1929 to Stepho G Farkouh, Piraeus, and renamed *Morias*; scrapped 1933
*Dunrobin / Harefield**	1903-1906 1909-1911	3,617	Built 1903 as *Dunrobin* for Dunrobin Shipping Co; renamed *Harefield* 1903; sold to Sutherland Steam Ship Co and renamed *Dunrobin* 1909; sold to Sunderland Steam Ship Co 1911, no change of name; sunk by torpedo Western Approaches 24 November 1917
*Elgin / Gwynmead**	1906-1920 1921-1929	3,835	Sold to Western Counties Shipping Co 1920 and renamed *Gwynmead* but repossessed, no change of name; sold to Rederi A/B Iris, Stockholm and renamed *Virgo*; scrapped 1936
*Fife**	1907-1917	3,918	Built as *Fife* for Dunrobin Shipping Co 1907; later to Sutherland Steam Ship Co, no change of name; sunk in collision 200 miles NW of Cape Wrath 15 February 1917
Kinross	1911-1917	4,120	Sunk by torpedo Western Approaches 7 May 1917
Peebles	1911-1917	4,284	Sunk by torpedo 14 nautical miles SE of Flamborough Head 12 October 1917
*Claveresk / Renfrew**	1911-1920	3,829	Built 1907 as *Claveresk* for Claverhill Shipping Co; sold to J Sunley & Co and renamed *Billiter Buildings* 1907; sold to Sandhill Shipping Co and renamed *Claveresk* 1908; sold to Sutherland Steam Ship Co, no change of name; renamed *Renfrew* 1919; sold to Western Counties Shipping Co and renamed *Ulversmead*; several subsequent owners; sunk as block ship *Neuchatel* at Scapa Flow October 1939; raised and scrapped 1948
*Roxburgh**	1912-1918	4,630	Built 1906 as *Drumeldrie* for Astral Shipping Co; sold to Munro Shipping Co and renamed *Roxburgh*; sunk by torpedo off Crete 5 March 1918
*Dumfries**	1915	4,121	Built 1905 as *Carthusian* for J Mathias & Sons; sold to Cambrian Steam Navigation Co 1909, no change of name; sold to Sutherland Steam Ship Co and renamed *Dumfries*; sunk by torpedo off Trevose Head 19 May 1915
*Renfrew**	1915	3,488	Built 1898 as *Meridian* for G Horsley & Son; sold to A M Sutherland and renamed *Renfrew*; sunk by gunfire 85 nautical miles SSW of the Wolf Rock 3 July 1915
*Forfar**	1915-1917	3,827	Built 1907 as *Braziliana* for British Maritime Trust/Furness Withy & Co; sold to J Sunley & Co and renamed *Billiter Avenue* 1907; sold to Sutherland Steam Ship Co and renamed *Forfar*; sunk by torpedo 115 nautical miles off the Lizard 4 December 1917
*Kincardine**	1916-1917	4,108	Built 1906 as *Countess Warwick* for Countess Warwick Steamship Co; sold to Sutherland Steam Ship Co and renamed *Kincardine*; sunk by torpedo off south-west Ireland 3 March 1917
Priestfield	1917-1919	4,033	Built 1901 as *Priestfield* for Priestfield Steamship Co: sold 1907 to Peareth Steamship Co, no change of name; sold to Sutherland Steam Ship Co, no change of name; sold to Cia de Commercio SA, Bilbao, and renamed *Donata*; two subsequent owners; scrapped 1934
Etolia / Dunrobin	1917-1920	3,733	Built 1911 as *Etolia* for International Steamship Co; sold to Sutherland Steam Ship Co, no change of name; renamed *Dunrobin* 1919; sold to Western Counties Shipping Co and renamed *Nethermead*; several subsequent owners; wrecked off Providence Key West 17 April 1934
Ramsay / Caithness	1917-1920	4,318	Built 1902 as *Ramsay* for Bolton Steam Shipping Co; sold to Sutherland Steam Ship Co, no change of name; renamed *Caithness* 1919; sold to Anglo Celtic Shipping Co, no change of name; sold to Achille Lauro, Naples 1926 and renamed *Edera*; wrecked off Dutch coast 11 September 1930
Corinthia / Dumfries	1917-1921	3,625	Built as *Corinthia* 1901 for International Line Steam Ship Co; sold to Sutherland Steam Ship Co, no change of name; renamed *Dumfries* 1919; sold to Anglo-Celtic Shipping Co, no change of name; scrapped 1933
Sutherland	1917-1923	6,563	Built 1917 as *Clan Macmaster* for Clan Line; sold to B J Sutherland & Co and renamed *Sutherland*; wrecked off Calf of Man 30 September 1923
Archbank	1918	3,767	Built 1905 as *Archbank* for Peareth Steamship Co; sold to Sutherland Steam Ship Co, no change of name; sunk by torpedo in Eastern Mediterranean 5 June 1918
Florentia	1918	3,688	Built as *Florentia* for International Line Steamship Co; sold to Sutherland Steam Ship Co, no change of name; sunk by torpedo off Robin Hood's Bay 29 June 1918

Clivegrove / Fife	1918-1920	3,546	Built 1906 as **Clivegrove** for Grove Steamship Co; sold to Sutherland Steam Ship Co, no change of name; renamed **Fife** 1919; sold to Western Counties Shipping Co and renamed **Yorkmead**; sold to E K Vlassopoulos and renamed **Makis** 1921; mined in the Sicilian Channel 11 June 1940
Cressington Court / Roxburgh	1918-1920	4,396	Built 1908 as **Cressington Court** for Cressington Steamship Co; sold to Sutherland Steam Ship Co, no change of name; renamed **Roxburgh** 1919; sold to Western Counties Shipping Co. no change of name; several subsequent owners; scrapped 1935
Thessalia / Forfar	1918-1921	3,691	Built 1912 as **Thessalia** for International Line Steamship Co; sold to Sutherland Steamship Co, no change of name; renamed **Forfar** 1920; sold to Western Counties Shipping Co, no change of name; sold to Boyazides Brother & Co 1921 and renamed **Thrasyvoulos**; sunk by torpedo off south coast of Ireland 30 October 1939
Dumfries	1918-1924	6,608	Built 1918 as **Clan Macmillan** for Clan Line; sold to B J Sutherland & Co; wrecked Bay of Bengal 20 June 1924
Sutherland / Caithness	1918 1929-1935	5,277	Renamed **War Aspen** 1918 for Ministry of Transport; sold to Western Counties Shipping Co 1920 and renamed **Southmead**; sold 1921 to McIlwraith & McEacharn & Co and renamed **Koolonga**; sold to B J Sutherland & Co and renamed **Caithness**; sold to Jubilee Steam Navigation Co and renamed **David Dawson**; sold to Avon Steamship Co 1936 and renamed **Avon River**; wrecked Hudson Bay on passage to Churchill 16 September 1936
Cromarty	1919	5,263	Built 1918 as **War Jasmine** for Ministry of Transport; sold to B J Sutherland & Co and renamed **Cromarty**; sold to Western Counties Shipping Co and renamed **Highmead**; several subsequent owners; wrecked Takoradi Breakwater 22 December 1950
Stroma	1923-1929	3,748	Built 1910 as **Leucadia** for International Line Steamship Co; sold to Isles Steamship Co 1917, no change of name; renamed **Stroma** 1919; sold to Sutherland Steam Ship Co, no change of name; sold to G A Georgilis and renamed **Papalemos**; sunk by torpedo off West African coast 28 May 1941
Rassay*	1923-1932	4,147	Built 1905 as **Hatumet** for Hathor Steamship Co; sold 1915 to Isles Steamship Co, no change of name; renamed **Rassay** 1919; sold to Sutherland Steam Ship Co, no change of name; scrapped 1932
Peebles	1923-1933	5,260	Built 1918 as **Peebles** for Isles Steam Shipping Co; renamed **War Petunia** for Ministry of Transport 1918; sold to Sutherland Steam Ship Co and renamed **Peebles**; sold to D J Dambassis and renamed **Heleni D**; several subsequent owners; scrapped 1959
Taransay	1923-1933	5,241	Built 1918 as **Taransay** for Isles Steam Shipping Co; renamed **War Teasel** for Ministry of Transport 1918; sold to Sutherland Steam Ship Co and renamed **Taransay**; sold to Petros M Nomikos and renamed **Marietta Nomikos**; two subsequent owners; scuttled Skagerrak 17 October 1945
Sutherland	1926-1934	5,175	Built 1919 as **Gasconier** for Lloyd Royal Belge (UK); renamed **War Ruler** for Ministry of Transport 1919; to Royal Lloyd Belge and renamed **Gasconier** 1923; sold to Sutherland Steam Ship Co and renamed **Sutherland**; sold to E M Tricoglu and renamed **Nikos T**; several subsequent owners; scrapped 1959
Kinross	1927-1934	5,242	Built 1918 as **War Spartan** for Ministry of Transport; sold to Lloyd Royal Belge 1919 and renamed **Taxandrier** (UK flag until 1923 then re-registered at Antwerp); sold to Sutherland Steam Ship Co and renamed **Kinross**; sold to Carras Brothers/Constantine; sunk by torpedo North Atlantic 19 March 1943
Nairn	1932-1934	4,971	Built 1929 as **Lammer Law** for Thomas Law & Co; sold to B J Sutherland & Co and renamed **Nairn**; sold to Garibaldi group and renamed **XXVII Octobre**; scuttled at Phuket 8 December 1941

The **Nairn** 1929 at Duncan Dock, Cape Town. Completed as the **Lammer Law** for Thomas Law & Company of Glasgow in December 1929, she was bought for a low price by B J Sutherland & Company in 1932 and resold in 1934 for an inflated value as the recession lifted.

Fife	1932-1936	4,251	Built 1929 as **Pen-y-bryn** for Lundegaard & Sons; sold to B J Sutherland & Co and renamed **Fife**; sold to Rethymnis Kulukundis and renamed **Leith Hill**; two subsequent owners; scrapped 1959
Easterner	1933	618	Built as patrol frigate **Kilham** 1918 for Admiralty; sold to Brown Shipping Co 1920 converted to cargo ship and renamed **Easterner**; sold to B J Sutherland & Co; scrapped 1933
Southerner	1933	627	Built as patrol frigate **Kildimo** 1918 for Admiralty; sold to Brown Shipping Company 1920 converted to cargo ship and renamed **Southerner**; sold to B J Sutherland & Co; scrapped 1933
Bombardier	1933-1934	611	Built as patrol frigate **Kilchenan** 1918 for Admiralty; sold to Brown Shipping Co 1920 converted to cargo ship and renamed **Bombardier**; to B J Sutherland & Co; sold to Marino Queri and renamed **Collodi**; several subsequent owners; sunk by torpedo off Portuguese coast 6 August 1941
Curler	1933-1934	628	Built 1918 as patrol frigate **Killowen** 1918 for Admiralty; sold to Brown Shipping Co 1918 converted to cargo ship and renamed **Curler**; sold to B J Sutherland & Co, no change of name; sold to Abdul Salam el Chaffei and renamed **Salam**; several subsequent owners; wrecked at Cyprus 29 March 1944
Cromarty	1933-1936	5,073	Built 1930 as **Petersfield** for Woods Tylor Brown; sold to B J Sutherland & Co and renamed **Cromarty**; sold to Hudig & Veder and renamed **Arundo**; sunk by torpedo North Atlantic 28 April 1942
Peebles	1933-1936	4,318	Built 1930 as **Gracechurch** for James, Muers & Co; sold to B J Sutherland & Co and renamed **Peebles**; sold Rethymnis Kulukundis and renamed **Mill Hill**; sunk by torpedo north of Isle of Lewis 30 August 1940
Stirling	1935-1936	4,995	Sold to A F Klaveness & Co and renamed **Stirlingville**; sold to L G Matsas and renamed **Georgios M II** 1959; destroyed by fire off North African coast 20 November 1968
Sutherland	1935-1936	4,979	Sold to Furness Withy and renamed **British Prince**; sunk by bomb off Yorkshire coast 26 September 1941
Roxburgh	1935-1937	4,241	Sold to Rethymnis Kulukundis and renamed **Tower Field**; to Ministry of War Transport 1942 and renamed **Empire Tower**; sunk by torpedo off Portugal 5 March 1943
Kinross	1935-1941	4,956	Sunk by torpedo North Atlantic 24 June 1941
Dumfries	1935-1944	5,149	Sunk by torpedo English Channel 23 December 1944
Caithness	1935-1951	4,970	Sold to Westralian Farmers and renamed **Swan Valley**; two subsequent owners; foundered North Pacific 17 January 1967
Ross	1936-1942	4,978	Sunk by torpedo South Atlantic 29 October 1942
Peebles	1936-1951	4,982	Sold to Westralian Farmers and renamed **Swanstream;** two subsequent owners; scrapped 1967
Sutherland	1938-1939	5,083	Sold to G Nisbet & Co and renamed **Blairclova**; sold to T Y Chao 1961 and renamed **Ocean Venture**; wrecked Hong Kong harbour 1 September 1962
Cromarty	1938-1954	4,974	Built 1936 as **Skipsea** for Brown Atkinson & Co; sold to B J Sutherland & Co and renamed **Cromarty**; sold to J Larsson and renamed **Ostbris**; several subsequent owners; scrapped 1972
Argyll	1939-1940 1943-1954	4,897	To Vichy French Government and renamed **Saint Henri**; returned to B J Sutherland & Co and renamed **Argyll** 1943; sold to Savolax Shipping Co, no change of name; two subsequent owners, scrapped 1961
Inverness	1940-1941	4,897	Sunk by torpedo North Atlantic 9 July 1941
Sutherland	1940-1953	5,172	Sold to Carlton Steamship Co and renamed **Grainton**; several subsequent owners; wrecked Indian Ocean 11 November 1967
Inverness	1946-1953	7,131	Built 1945 as **Empire Freetown** for Ministry of War Transport; sold to B J Sutherland & Co and renamed **Inverness**; sold to Turnbull Scott Shipping Co and renamed **Redgate**; two subsequent owners; scrapped 1968
Dumfries	1947-1954	7,307	Built 1945 as **Empire Rabaul** for Ministry of War Transport; sold to B J Sutherland & Co and renamed **Dumfries**; sold to Chine Shipping Co and renamed **Charles Dickens**; sold to Splosna Plovba and renamed **Pohorje** 1956; scrapped 1967

* *Turret ship*

INDEX OF SHIP NAMES

The date in brackets is the year each vessel was built.